Oversight Hearing on the A–12 Navy Aircraft

Oversight Hearing on the A–12 Navy Aircraft

Hearings
before the
Legislation and National Security Subcommittee
of the
Committee on Government Operations House of Representatives

One Hundred Second Congress
First Session

April 11 and July 24, 1991

GOVERNMENT REPRINTS PRESS
Washington, D.C.

© Ross & Perry, Inc. 2001 All rights reserved.

No claim to U.S. government work contained throughout this book.

Protected under the Berne Convention. Published 2001

Printed in The United States of America
Ross & Perry, Inc. Publishers
717 Second St., N.E., Suite 200
Washington, D.C. 20002
Telephone (202) 675-8300
Facsimile (202) 675-8400
info@RossPerry.com

SAN 253-8555

Government Reprints Press Edition 2001

Government Reprints Press is an Imprint of Ross & Perry, Inc.

Library of Congress Control Number:2001093412
http://www.GPOreprints.com

ISBN 1-931641-31-5

♾ The paper used in this publication meets the requirements for permanence established by the American National Standard for Information Sciences "Permanence of Paper for Printed Library Materials" (ANSI Z39.48-1984).

All rights reserved. No copyrighted part of this publication may be reproduced, stored in a retrieval system, or transmitted, in any form or by any means, electronic, photocopying, recording, or otherwise, without the prior written permission of the publisher.

COMMITTEE ON GOVERNMENT OPERATIONS

JOHN CONYERS, JR., Michigan, *Chairman*

CARDISS COLLINS, Illinois
GLENN ENGLISH, Oklahoma
HENRY A. WAXMAN, California
TED WEISS, New York
MIKE SYNAR, Oklahoma
STEPHEN L. NEAL, North Carolina
DOUG BARNARD, JR., Georgia
TOM LANTOS, California
ROBERT E. WISE, JR., West Virginia
BARBARA BOXER, California
MAJOR R. OWENS, New York
EDOLPHUS TOWNS, New York
BEN ERDREICH, Alabama
GERALD D. KLECZKA, Wisconsin
ALBERT G. BUSTAMANTE, Texas
MATTHEW G. MARTINEZ, California
DONALD M. PAYNE, New Jersey
GARY A. CONDIT, California
PATSY T. MINK, Hawaii
RAY THORNTON, Arkansas
COLLIN C. PETERSON, Minnesota
ROSA L. DeLAURO, Connecticut
CHARLES J. LUKEN, Ohio
JOHN W. COX, JR., Illinois

FRANK HORTON, New York
WILLIAM F. CLINGER, JR., Pennsylvania
AL McCANDLESS, California
J. DENNIS HASTERT, Illinois
JON L. KYL, Arizona
CHRISTOPHER SHAYS, Connecticut
STEVEN SCHIFF, New Mexico
C. CHRISTOPHER COX, California
CRAIG THOMAS, Wyoming
ILEANA ROS-LEHTINEN, Florida
RONALD K. MACHTLEY, Rhode Island
DICK ZIMMER, New Jersey
WILLIAM H. ZELIFF, JR., New Hampshire
DAVID L. HOBSON, Ohio
SCOTT L. KLUG, Wisconsin

—

BERNARD SANDERS, Vermont
(Independent)

JULIAN EPSTEIN, *Staff Director*
DONALD W. UPSON, *Minority Staff Director*

LEGISLATION AND NATIONAL SECURITY SUBCOMMITTEE

JOHN CONYERS, JR., Michigan, *Chairman*

GLENN ENGLISH, Oklahoma
STEPHEN L. NEAL, North Carolina
GERALD D. KLECZKA, Wisconsin
CARDISS COLLINS, Illinois
RAY THORNTON, Arkansas
COLLIN C. PETERSON, Minnesota

FRANK HORTON, New York
JON L. KYL, Arizona
CHRISTOPHER SHAYS, Connecticut
STEVEN SCHIFF, New Mexico

ROBERT J. KURZ, *Deputy Staff Director*
JAMES C. TURNER, *Associate Counsel*
MIRANDA G. KATSOYANNIS, *Professional Staff Member*
CHERYL A. PHELPS, *Professional Staff Member*
ERIC M. THORSON, *Professional Staff Member*
JOSEPH CIRINCIONE, *Professional Staff Member*
BENNIE B. WILLIAMS, *Clerk*
CHERYL G. MATCHO, *Clerk*
ROSALIND BURKE-ALEXANDER, *Staff Assistant*
JAMES L. GEORGE, *Minority Professional Staff*

CONTENTS

	Page
Hearing held on:	
April 11, 1991	1
July 24, 1991	145

Statement of:
- Conahan, Frank C., Assistant Comptroller General, U.S. General Accounting Office, accompanied by Paul F. Math, Director of Research, Development, Acquisition and Procurement Issues.................................. 150
- Conyers, Hon. John, Jr., a Representative in Congress from the State of Michigan, and chairman, Legislation and National Security Subcommittee: Opening statement 1
- Lanese, Herbert J., senior vice president, finance, McDonnell Douglas Corp 107
- Math, Paul F., Director, Research, Development, Acquisition, and Procurement Issues, U.S. General Accounting Office, accompanied by Brad Hathaway, Associate Director, Navy Issues, and William Woods, assistant general counsel 12
- Morris, Rear Adm. William R., Assistant Commander for Contracts, Naval Air Systems Command 60
- Putnam, Donald W., corporate director, contracts and technical analysis, General Dynamics Corp 114
- Spector, Eleanor R., Director of Defense Procurement, Department of Defense, accompanied by Dennis Trosch, assistant general counsel, Office of the Secretary of Defense.. 48
- Yockey, Donald J., Under Secretary of Defense (Acquisition), accompanied by Dennis Trosch, assistant general counsel (Logistics); Robert C. McCormack, Assistant Secretary of the Navy (Financial Management); and Eleanor R. Spector, Director of Defense Procurement, Department of Defense 198

Letters, statements, etc., submitted for the record by:
- Conahan, Frank C., Assistant Comptroller General, U.S. General Accounting Office:
  - Financial status of McDonnell Douglas and General Dynamics............ 196
  - Information regarding A-12 deferment decision.. 191
  - Prepared statement... 153
- Conyers, Hon. John, Jr., a Representative in Congress from the State of Michigan, and chairman, Legislation and National Security Subcommittee: Prepared statement... 4
- Horton, Hon. Frank, a Representative in Congress from the State of New York: Documents relative to the hearing.. 41
- Lanese, Herbert J., senior vice president, finance, McDonnell Douglas Corp.:
  - Excerpt from annual report concerning dispute on A-12 contract 130
  - Prepared statement... 108
- Math, Paul F., Director, Research, Development, Acquisition, and Procurement Issues, U.S. General Accounting Office: Prepared statement... 16
- Putnam, Donald W., corporate director, contracts and technical analysis, General Dynamics Corp.: Prepared statement 115
- Spector, Eleanor R., Director of Defense Procurement, Department of Defense:
  - Information regarding analysis of deferment agreement........................ 213
  - Prepared statement... 51
  - Submissions to additional questions of Chairman Conyers.................... 94
- Yockey, Donald J., Under Secretary of Defense (Acquisition): Prepared statement 200

APPENDIX

Material submitted for the hearing record 235

(III)

OVERSIGHT HEARING ON THE A-12 NAVY AIRCRAFT

THURSDAY, APRIL 11, 1991

House of Representatives,
Legislation and National Security Subcommittee
of the Committee on Government Operations,
Washington, DC.

The subcommittee met, pursuant to notice, at 10 a.m., in room 2154, Rayburn House Office Building, Hon. John Conyers, Jr. (chairman of the subcommittee) presiding.

Members present: Representatives John Conyers, Jr., Glenn English, Collin C. Peterson, Frank Horton, Christopher Shays, and Steven Schiff.

Also present: Representative Andy Ireland.

Subcommittee staff present: Robert J. Kurz, deputy staff director; Eric M. Thorson, professional staff member; Cheryl G. Matcho, clerk; and James L. George, minority professional staff.

Full committee staff present: Julian Epstein, staff director; and Donald W. Upson, minority staff director.

OPENING STATEMENT OF CHAIRMAN CONYERS

Mr. CONYERS. The Committee on Government Operations' Subcommittee on Legislation and National Security will come to order.

We are here today to have an oversight hearing on the A-12 Navy aircraft. I am joined by the gentleman from New York, Mr. Frank Horton; Mr. Steve Schiff from New Mexico; and from the Armed Services Committee and former member of Government Operations, Mr. Andy Ireland of Florida.

I would like to make brief opening remarks, and then I would yield to the gentleman from New York. Then we will have our first witnesses, who will be the General Accounting Office representatives.

Today we are looking into something very extraordinary, the inner workings of the Pentagon, the process by which the Department of Defense granted a team of the two largest defense contractors the use of nearly $1.5 billion of taxpayer moneys. What is disturbing is that, according to the Department of Defense, they are not entitled to this money.

The exact amount is $1,352,459,644. This represents that amount of overpayment held by the contractors when the A-12 aircraft program was terminated for default. In a default termination, the Government only pays for those items delivered. All remaining funds paid to the contractors should come back to the Government.

Instead of getting the money back, as would be expected, the Department of Defense deferred the amount due until all issues are resolved, and this will take years. This committee is going to ask some disturbing questions, and it is determined to get the answers.

What we want to know is: What was the basis for the deferral? What was the legislative authority? What procedures were followed? What financial records were requested and when? Who made the decision, and what role did the contractors play in the approval of it?

The subcommittee wants to know what was done to protect the taxpayer in this arrangement, because, in this circumstance, these citizens in the United States are involuntary lenders. The taxpayers do not want to pay taxes to loan over $1 billion to the two largest defense contractors in the United States. This is especially true in a program that was canceled because of the allegation of poor performance by the contractors.

The plane that was supposed to fly in June of last year has never even been built. So we question the authority for such a loan. It is an extraordinary concession to the top two defense contractors and simply constitutes a form of bailout. Let me remind you that the amount gives this the potential to be the largest bailout ever.

Now, while we applaud Secretary Cheney's decision to cancel the A-12 program, we don't believe that his job description should include loan officer, nor should the taxpayer be obligated to act as a credit union for the defense industry. The Pentagon told the companies that they would not have to pay the money back right away because it would put them in difficult positions.

As we approach April 15 in the United States, tax day for all Americans, how many would like to give a similar excuse for not paying the money they owe the Government? This kind of preferential treatment to corporations must be made known to the American people.

Our investigation shows that the original letter demanding the return of these funds included a line suggesting a deferment could be requested if immediate payment is not practical. How nice. Of course, the contractors responded immediately, and then the open-ended deferment agreement was created, tied only to a full and complete settlement.

And more curious than anything else is that all three of these documents are executed on the very same day. What is also disturbing is that on this Tuesday the Department of Defense has asserted that Congress is not entitled to the information that the contractors supplied it because it is proprietary and sensitive. I have told the Department of Defense that this is unacceptable.

It seems to me this entire situation sets a terrible precedent. Already Lockheed Corporation has claimed discrimination and is requesting a deferment in the termination of another airplane program, because their request for deferment was denied. I think that we will see this as a new trend if this matter is allowed to continue.

In the course of our investigation, we found that one of these same contractors, McDonnell Douglas, has an additional deferment for income taxes. In that matter, the Internal Revenue Service secured their interest with a block of stock, but the Department of Defense has not even asked for any collateral whatsoever.

The bottom line is, no principal reductions, no interest payments, no collateral, no firm due date. We want to know what is going on in this matter. We find the use of this part of the Federal Acquisition Regulations for this deferment highly irregular. We believe the intent was for the application of disadvantaged businesses.

When reviewing all the deferments of 1990 that were granted, and there were seven others reported to us, the amounts deferred for the most part ranged from $20,000 to $½ million. This particular deferment that we are examining today was 378 times greater than the average of all seven other deferments.

Our investigation found another interesting fact, that on August 15 of last year, the Defense Contract Audit Agency asked the treasurer of McDonnell Douglas if they had sufficient funds to absorb any reductions or demands for payment related to the A-12 program, and the treasurer indicated that sufficient financing existed.

We think that this is an unusual procedure used by the Department of Defense, and we plan to make a full inquiry of it this morning.

[The prepared statement of Mr. Conyers follows:]

OPENING STATEMENT

BY

CHAIRMAN JOHN CONYERS, JR.

COMMITTEE ON GOVERNMENT OPERATIONS
SUBCOMMITTEE ON LEGISLATION AND NATIONAL SECURITY

AN OVERSIGHT HEARING

ON

THE A-12 NAVY AIRCRAFT

THURSDAY APRIL 11, 1991

THE SUBCOMMITTEE ON LEGISLATION AND NATIONAL SECURITY WILL COME TO ORDER.

TODAY WE ARE GOING TO LOOK INTO SOMETHING VERY EXTRAORDINARY -- THE INNER WORKINGS OF THE PENTAGON -- THE PROCESS BY WHICH THE DEPARTMENT OF DEFENSE GRANTED A TEAM OF THE TWO LARGEST DEFENSE CONTRACTORS THE USE OF NEARLY $1.5 BILLION OF THE TAXPAYERS MONEY. WHAT IS DISTURBING IS THAT ACCORDING TO DOD, THEY ARE NOT ENTITLED TO THIS MONEY. TO BE EXACT THAT NUMBER IS $1,352,459,644.00. (ONE BILLION, THREE HUNDRED FIFTY-TWO MILLION, FOUR HUNDRED FIFTY-NINE THOUSAND, SIX HUNDRED FORTY-FOUR DOLLARS AND ZERO CENTS.)

THIS REPRESENTS THE AMOUNT OF OVERPAYMENT HELD BY THE CONTRACTORS WHEN THE A-12 AIRCRAFT PROGRAM WAS TERMINATED FOR DEFAULT. IN A DEFAULT TERMINATION THE GOVERNMENT ONLY PAYS FOR THOSE ITEMS DELIVERED. ALL REMAINING FUNDS PAID TO THE CONTRACTOR SHOULD COME BACK TO THE GOVERNMENT. INSTEAD OF GETTING THE MONEY BACK, AS WOULD BE EXPECTED, THE DEPARTMENT OF DEFENSE DEFERRED THE AMOUNT DUE UNTIL ALL ISSUES ARE RESOLVED.

THIS WILL TAKE SEVERAL YEARS.

THIS COMMITTEE IS GOING TO ASK DISTURBING QUESTIONS AND IS DETERMINED TO GET THE ANSWERS. HERE IS WHAT WE WANT TO KNOW: WHAT WAS THE BASIS FOR THE DEFERRAL? WHAT IS THE LEGISLATIVE AUTHORITY? WHAT PROCEDURES WERE FOLLOWED? WHAT FINANCIAL RECORDS WERE REQUESTED AND WHEN? WHO MADE THE DECISION? AND WHAT ROLE DID THE CONTRACTORS PLAY IN THE APPROVAL OF IT?

THIS SUBCOMMITTEE WANTS TO KNOW WHAT WAS DONE TO PROTECT THE TAXPAYER IN THIS ARRANGEMENT. THE TAXPAYER IS AN INVOLUNTARY LENDER! THE TAXPAYER DOES NOT WANT TO PAY TAXES TO LOAN OVER $1 BILLION TO THE LARGEST 2 DEFENSE CONTRACTORS IN THE WORLD! THIS IS ESPECIALLY TRUE IN A PROGRAM THAT WAS CANCELLED BECAUSE OF AN ALLEGATION OF POOR PERFORMANCE BY THE CONTRACTORS. THE PLANE THAT WAS SUPPOSED TO FLY IN JUNE OF 1990 WAS NEVER EVEN BUILT.

FIRST WE QUESTION THE AUTHORITY FOR SUCH A LOAN. THIS IS AN EXTRAORDINARY CONCESSION TO THE TOP TWO

DEFENSE CONTRACTORS IN THE WORLD. IT SIMPLY CONSTITUTES A FORM OF BAILOUT. WHILE THE DEPARTMENT OF DEFENSE DISPUTES THE TERM, LET ME REMIND YOU THAT THE AMOUNT GIVES THIS THE POTENTIAL TO BE THE LARGEST BAILOUT IN HISTORY. WHILE WE RESPECT SECRETARY CHENEY'S DECISION TO CANCEL THE A-12 PROGRAM, WE DON'T BELIEVE HIS JOB DESCRIPTION SHOULD INCLUDE "LOAN OFFICER." NOR SHOULD THE TAXPAYER BE OBLIGATED TO ACT AS A CREDIT UNION FOR THE DEFENSE INDUSTRY.

AND DOD TOLD THE COMPANIES THAT THEY WOULD NOT HAVE TO PAY THE MONEY BACK RIGHT AWAY BECAUSE IT WOULD PUT THEM IN "DIFFICULT POSITIONS." AS WE APPROACH APRIL 15TH -- TAX DAY -- ALL AMERICANS WOULD LIKE TO GET SIMILAR EXCUSES FOR NOT PAYING THE MONEY THEY OWE THE GOVERNMENT. THIS KIND OF PREFERENTIAL TREATMENT TO CORPORATIONS MUST BE MADE KNOWN TO THE AMERICAN PEOPLE.

OUR INVESTIGATION SHOWS THAT THE ORIGINAL LETTER DEMANDING THE RETURN OF THESE FUNDS INCLUDED A LINE SUGGESTING A DEFERMENT COULD BE REQUESTED IF "IMMEDIATE

PAYMENT IS NOT PRACTICAL." OF COURSE THE CONTRACTORS RESPONDED IMMEDIATELY. THEN THE OPEN ENDED DEFERMENT AGREEMENT WAS CREATED, TIED ONLY TO A FULL AND COMPLETE SETTLEMENT. WHAT MAKES THIS CURIOUS IS THAT ALL THREE OF THESE DOCUMENTS ARE DATED THE SAME DAY, FEBRUARY 5, 1991.

WHAT IS ALSO UPSETTING IS THAT ON TUESDAY THE DEPARTMENT ASSERTED THAT THE CONGRESS IS NOT ENTITLED TO THE INFORMATION THE CONTRACTORS SUPPLIED BECAUSE IT IS "PROPRIETARY" AND "SENSITIVE." YESTERDAY I TOLD THE DEPARTMENT OF DEFENSE THAT THIS WAS UNACCEPTABLE.

IT SEEMS TO ME THAT THIS ENTIRE SITUATION SETS A TERRIBLE PRECEDENT. ALREADY THE LOCKHEED CORPORATION HAS FILED A SUIT IN FEDERAL COURT CLAIMING DISCRIMINATION, SINCE THEIR REQUEST FOR DEFERMENT IN THE TERMINATED P-7 AIRPLANE PROGRAM WAS DENIED. I'M SURE WE WILL SEE MANY OTHERS FOLLOW THE SAME COURSE.

IN OUR INVESTIGATION, WE FOUND THAT ONE OF THESE

SAME CONTRACTORS, MCDONNELL DOUGLAS, HAS AN ADDITIONAL DEFERMENT FOR INCOME TAXES. THE IRS, HOWEVER, SECURED THEIR INTEREST WITH A BLOCK OF STOCK. WE WILL FIND OUT TODAY THAT THE DEPARTMENT OF DEFENSE DID NOT ASK FOR, NOR DID THEY RECEIVE ANY COLLATERAL WHATSOEVER. THE BOTTOM LINE IS NO PRINCIPAL REDUCTIONS, NO INTEREST PAYMENTS, NO COLLATERAL, NO FIRM DUE DATE. JUST WHAT HAPPENED HERE?

WE FIND THE USE OF THIS PART OF THE FEDERAL ACQUISITION REGULATIONS HIGHLY SUSPICIOUS. WE BELIEVE THE INTENT WAS FOR APPLICATION TO SMALL AND DISADVANTAGED BUSINESSES. WHEN REVIEWING ALL THE DEFERMENTS FOR 1990, OF WHICH THERE WERE SEVEN OTHERS REPORTED TO US, WE FOUND THAT THE AMOUNTS WERE MOSTLY IN THE $20,000 TO HALF MILLION DOLLAR RANGE. THIS PARTICULAR DEFERMENT WAS 378 TIMES GREATER THAN THE AVERAGE OF ALL SEVEN OTHER DEFERMENTS.

OUR INVESTIGATION FOUND ANOTHER INTERESTING FACT. ON AUGUST 15, 1990, LESS THAN SIX MONTHS EARLIER, THE DEFENSE CONTRACT AUDIT AGENCY ASKED THE TREASURER OF

MCDONNELL DOUGLAS IF THEY HAD SUFFICIENT FUNDS TO ABSORB ANY REDUCTIONS, SUSPENSIONS, OR DEMANDS FOR REPAYMENT RELATED TO THE A-12 PROGRAM. THE TREASURER INDICATED THAT SUFFICIENT FINANCING EXISTED.

    WHAT WE DO WANT IS TO LOOK OUT FOR THE TAXPAYERS WHO PUT UP THIS MONEY AND TO FOCUS ON THE PROCEDURES USED BY THE DEPARTMENT OF DEFENSE IN MAKING SUCH AN EXTRAORDINARY CONCESSION.

Mr. CONYERS. I would like to now yield to the gentleman from New York, the distinguished ranking member of Government Operations, Mr. Frank Horton.

Mr. HORTON. Thank you, Mr. Chairman. At the outset, I want to congratulate you on calling this hearing. I think this is a very important matter.

There are really two major questions: First of all is the matter that you have emphasized, and that is the deferral of the $1.3 billion. And then the second, of course, is the overall analysis of the A-12 contract and the performance by the two contractors.

Mr. Chairman, on January 7 of this year, the Navy terminated for default the A-12 attack plane program which they had consistently called their top priority. This was the largest cancellation in the history of the Pentagon. Nine months earlier, after reviewing the results of a major aircraft review, the Secretary of Defense had told the Congress that the A-12 program was healthy.

Just 34 days after that testimony, however, the contractors reported a major cost overrun and schedule problems, and asked for a bailout, which the Secretary refused. Instead, the Navy terminated the contract and demanded that the contractors reimburse the Government for $1.3 billion in progress payments which they had received for work that never was done.

Mr. Chairman, today we have what amounts to a national security crisis. The Navy desperately needs modern planes, but because of the failure of the A-12 program, it may have to wait at least 15 years before getting them.

Although the focus of the hearing today is on the Government's deferment of the $1.3 billion debt owed by the contractors, I hope that we will not overlook some of the broader issues, such as the Navy's continuing need for a new attack aircraft, the failure of oversight procedures, and, perhaps more importantly, the issue of accountability.

I almost feel like this is deja vu. I remember hearings we held in this very committee room on the C-5A. It was very similar to this, where there were cost overruns, where the performance was not on schedule. We didn't have the same problems that we have here, however, where the plane was not being built, but it was just a case of being over schedule, overruns, terrible expenses that had not been expected, and ultimately it resulted in the establishment of the Procurement Commission, on which I serve.

Mr. Chairman, I must confess that after all the work this committee has done on procurement and contract reform, I find a certain frustration reading the results of the two Department of Defense reports on the problem surrounding the A-12. As the Beach report concluded, "Existing control mechanisms, properly operated, would have been sufficient to identify the nature and extent of the problems, but they were not operated."

The report is full of examples of officials who did not perform their duty, from a contractor officer not physically seeing if work was being accomplished, and a program manager giving unwarranted good news briefs to his superiors, to a lack of oversight by high-level Navy officers.

The military services and the Department of Defense are always quick to criticize Congress for micromanaging programs. Every time I meet with a general or an admiral, they invariably raise the question of micromanagement. Over the years, I have had great sympathy for their complaints. However, if the program managers and other officials simply ignore regulations and negative information, maybe we need to do more micromanaging.

Of course, the big loser in this is the air needs of the Navy. The current A-6, whose original design can be traced to the late 1950's and was last upgraded in the early 1970's, desperately needs replacement. Now, with the cancellation of the A-12, the Navy has announced a new program, the A-X, with reports it will take another 15 years and cost approximately $11 billion.

Finally, I am concerned with the Department of Defense's deferment of the $1.3 billion debt without asking the contractors to post any bond or collateral whatsoever. So I agree with you completely that this is a very serious problem that we face.

Mr. Chairman, I hope that the main benefit of this hearing is a notice to the military and our defense contractors that business as usual will no longer be tolerated. From newspaper accounts, private conversations, and personal observation, it appears that although some official oversight procedures might have been ignored, the unofficial practices in the A-12 program might not have been any worse than that of any other major defense acquisition. In an era of tight fiscal budget restraints, inefficiency, unfounded optimism, and lack of proper oversight can no longer be tolerated.

Mr. CONYERS. Thank you for an excellent opening statement.

Our first witnesses from the General Accounting Office will be the Director of Research, Development, Acquisition, and Procurement for the Accounting Office, Mr. Paul Math. With him is Associate Director of Navy Issues, Mr. Brad Hathaway. And the assistant general counsel of the Office of the General Counsel of GAO, Mr. William Woods.

Gentlemen, would you stand and raise your right hand and prepare to take the witness oath.

[Witnesses sworn.]

Mr. CONYERS. Thank you very much. Please be seated.

Of course, we have your opening statement, and it, like all other prepared statements, will be included in the record in their entirety, without objection. We would appreciate a summary, Mr. Math, of the testimony that you bring to this subject matter.

STATEMENT OF PAUL F. MATH, DIRECTOR, RESEARCH, DEVELOPMENT, ACQUISITION, AND PROCUREMENT ISSUES, U.S. GENERAL ACCOUNTING OFFICE, ACCOMPANIED BY BRAD HATHAWAY, ASSOCIATE DIRECTOR, NAVY ISSUES, AND WILLIAM WOODS, ASSISTANT GENERAL COUNSEL

Mr. MATH. Thank you, Mr. Chairman. First of all, we are pleased to appear before your committee to present information on the termination of the Navy's A-12 contract. I will summarize our prepared statement.

As you are aware, the A-12 was being developed to provide a stealthy replacement for the Navy's aging fleet of A-6 medium attack aircraft, which are no longer in production. Full-scale development of the A-12 by the contractor team of General Dynamics and McDonnell Douglas had been underway since 1988, when the team was awarded a fixed price incentive contract with a target price of $4.4 billion and a ceiling price of $4.8 billion.

On January 7, 1991, the Government terminated the A-12 contract for default, because the team was unable to complete the design, development, fabrication, assembly, and test of the A-12 aircraft within contract schedule and deliver an aircraft that would meet the contract requirements.

At the request of the chairman of the House Armed Services Committee, we have reviewed and reported on the Navy's total cost of the A-12 program and the aircraft requirements. Our current work is focusing on the alternatives to the A-12 aircraft and the financial implications of the termination, including Government liability and the deferral agreement.

On the issue of the deferral agreement, we stated in our prepared statement that we were continuing our efforts to obtain detailed information from DOD on its rationale and analysis performed in support of the decision to defer repayment. We added that, at the time of the prepared statement, we had not been provided the access that we believed was necessary to perform our analysis.

We continued by stating that DOD had recently provided restricted access to the information, and we were working toward an agreement that would allow us to perform the work requested by this and other committees. I can report now that DOD agreed yesterday afternoon to provide us the access that we believe is necessary to perform our analysis.

In terms of the A-12 program, the total appropriations, including research conducted before full-scale development phase, as well as production funding, totaled just over $6.7 billion. The Navy has spent about $3 billion on the total program. The development contract progress payments to the team totaled about $2.6 billion, as of the termination date, and another about $100 million spent on lot one and lot two production options, for a total of about $2.7 billion.

The Navy received six design and management reviews, which it priced at $1.34 billion. On February 5, 1991, the Navy issued a demand letter to the team requesting repayment of the $1.35 billion for which no completed items had been accepted by the Government. However, at the team's request, the Navy agreed to defer the repayment until litigation over termination is resolved in court or a negotiated settlement is reached.

Initially, the amount of repayment was reported as $1.9 billion. According to the Navy's explanation, this was a computational error. The DOD stated, in their formal response to us, that the $1.9 billion figure was a rough, order-of-magnitude estimate made at the time of termination. Both the Navy and the DOD now state that the correct amount is $1.35 billion.

Regarding Government liability in terminations, the financial liability of the U.S. Government, over and above goods and services delivered, is generally limited under termination for default. According to the Navy contracting officer, this financial liability on the A-12 default termination is limited to the contract line items that have been delivered; that is, the $1.34 billion.

There also may be additional costs for protection and preservation of property in which the Government has an interest. According to Navy officials, while the exact cost is not known, they believe that these costs could be significant, given the need to safeguard the program's special access items.

Federal regulations provide that if, after termination, the U.S. Claims Court or the Armed Services Board of Contract Appeals determines that the team was not in default or that the default was excusable, then the rights and obligations of the parties will be the same as if the termination had been issued for convenience of the Government.

Government liability would increase substantially if the termination is for convenience. In that case, the Government's liability would include costs for work done and preparations made for the terminated portions of the contract, adjusted by the application of an appropriate loss ratio.

In terms of the deferment agreement, according to Federal regulations, the Government can defer the collection of debts owed the Government. Deferments pending disposition of appeal may be granted to small business concerns and financially weak contractors, with reasonable balance of the need for Government security against loss and undue hardship on the contractor.

The Navy advised the team, in its February 5, 1991, demand letter, that the team could submit a request for deferment of collection if immediate payment is not practical or if the amount is disputed. On the same day, the team requested deferral of payment, and the parties signed the deferral agreement.

The deferral agreement provides that the Government will take no action except as otherwise provided to enforce collection pending: One, a decision by the Armed Forces Board of Contract Appeals or the Claims Court on the team's appeal; or, two, a negotiated settlement between the Government and the team.

The deferment agreement also provides for the payment of interest to the Government at a rate established by the Secretary of the Treasury, as provided in section 12 of the Contract Disputes Act. That rate is currently 8⅜ percent and will be reviewed every 6 months. The agreement will remain in full force and effect until it is reviewed on December 1, 1992, and annually thereafter.

According to the Navy contracting officer, the team advised the Government that the issuance of a demand letter and the resulting reaction of the credit markets would cause financial hardship; therefore, coordinated action was taken so that the demand letter, the request for deferment, and the deferment agreement were all executed on the same day.

The apparent purpose of the deferment provisions of the Federal Acquisition Regulation [FAR] is to provide relief to contractors who are not in a position to effect payment of contract debts. According to DOD, it granted the deferment to the team to avoid placing the contractors in a financial condition that would endanger essential defense programs.

As mentioned earlier, DOD agreed yesterday to provide us the access we believe is necessary to perform our analysis. We have begun our indepth review of the information DOD contends substantiates the assertion that the immediate repayment by the team was impractical. We will report on the results of our work as soon as possible.

Another issue is, what does the Government own under the A-12 contract? As stated earlier, the Government has accepted and paid for six design and management reviews priced at $1.34 billion. In addition, under the progress payment clause, the Government obtains title to work in process, materials, tools, and similar items.

In other words, the Government currently has title to the aforementioned items included in the unliquidated progress payment amount of $1.35 billion. Once the team repays the unliquidated progress payments, title to all material not accepted by the Government shall vest in the team. If the Government wants to acquire other items related to the A-12 from the team, a price must be negotiated between the Government and the team.

According to Navy program officials, the Navy is conducting a review of undelivered technical information and material developed under the A-12 contract that may be purchased by the U.S. Government.

And, finally, on December 31, 1990, the team filed a claim of $1.4 billion for equitable price adjustment. As the basis for the claim, the team cited: One, the Navy's failure to disclose what they called its superior knowledge of facts vital to the team's performance; two, delays and disruptions, which the team claims resulted from the Navy's conduct; three, the Navy's flawed acquisition strategy; and, four, commercial impossibility of performance.

On February 22, 1991, the Navy notified the team that the claim would be considered when properly certified.

Mr. Chairman, that concludes my prepared statement. We will be happy to answer any questions.

[The prepared statement of Mr. Math follows:]

GAO

United States General Accounting Office

Testimony

For Release
on Delivery
Expected at
10:00 a.m. EDT,
Thursday,
April 11, 1991

Information on the A-12
Default Termination

Joint Statement of
Paul F. Math, Director, Research, Development,
  Acquisition, and Procurement Issues
Brad Hathaway, Associate Director, Navy Issues
National Security and International
  Affairs Division

Before the
House Committee on Government Operations
Subcommittee on Legislation and National
  Security

GAO/T-NSIAD-91-15

Mr. Chairman, we are pleased to appear before the House Committee on Government Operations, Subcommittee on Legislation and National Security to present information on the termination of the Navy's A-12 aircraft program.

As you are aware, the A-12 was being developed to provide a stealthy replacement for the Navy's aging fleet of A-6 medium attack aircraft, which are no longer in production. Full-scale development of the A-12 by the contractor team of General Dynamics and McDonnell Douglas (the Team) had been underway since January 1988 when the Team was awarded a fixed-price incentive contract with a target price of $4.4 billion and a ceiling price of $4.8 billion.

The details of what transpired in the 3-year period since the contract was awarded are far beyond what we are prepared to discuss today. Many of those details have been presented in the Navy's report which is frequently called the "Beach Report" and various reports by the Department of Defense (DOD) Office of the Inspector General and the Defense Contract Audit Agency.

At the request of the Chairman, House Armed Services Committee, we have reviewed and reported[1] on the Navy's total cost of the A-12 program and aircraft requirements. Our current work is focusing on alternatives to the A-12 aircraft, and the financial implications of the termination including government liability and the deferral agreement.

On the issue of the deferral agreement, we are continuing our efforts to obtain detailed information from DOD on its rationale and analysis performed in support of the decision to defer repayment. At the time this statement was prepared we had not been provided the access that we believe is necessary to perform our analysis. DOD recently provided restricted access to the

---

[1] NAVY A-12: Cost and Requirements, (GAO/NSIAD-91-98) Dec. 31, 1990

information, and we are working towards an agreement that will allow us to perform the work required by this and other committees.

As requested, we will discuss the information we have gathered on the A-12 program and the possible impact of the termination on the government. Specifically, we will talk about the potential government liability arising from the termination and consequences of the termination on Navy efforts to address their medium attack aircraft needs subsequent to the termination.

In summary, total appropriations for the A-12 program, including research conducted before the full-scale development phase as well as production funding, totaled just over $6.7 billion. At termination, just under $3 billion had been spent on the program. Research and development and miscellaneous support costs accounted for about $300 million of the amount spent. Of the remaining $2.6 billion paid to the Team for the full-scale development effort and $0.1 billion for the first two production options, the Navy demanded that $1.35 billion be returned. This amount represented progress payments the Navy made for work it had not yet accepted as of the date of the termination.

On January 7, 1991, the government terminated the A-12 contract for default because the Team was unable to complete the design, development, fabrication, assembly and test of the A-12 aircraft within contract schedule, and deliver an aircraft that would meet the contract requirements.

The contractors have stated their intent to file legal action to contest the default termination and assert their rights to convert the termination to one for the convenience of the government. In addition, the Team submitted claims against the government stating that it is entitled to price adjustments that have yet to be resolved.

19

The government's liability would increase substantially if the termination is converted to one for the convenience of the government. In that case, the government's liability could include most costs incurred by the Team on the contract. Regardless of whether the termination of the A-12 contract is for default or convenience, the Navy will have to take action to meet its need for attack aircraft.

Before I elaborate on these points, let me present some background on the A-12 program.

BACKGROUND

The Navy's A-12 medium attack aircraft was being developed to replace its A-6E aircraft. The first version of the A-6, the A-6A, was introduced into the fleet in 1963 as the Navy's only day/night, all-weather, medium attack aircraft. The A-6 is also used to refuel other carrier-based aircraft. The latest version of the A-6, the A-6E, was introduced into the fleet in 1972. However, in the early 1980s wing cracks caused many of the A-6Es to be restricted to less demanding flight maneuvers or to be removed from flight status until appropriate repairs could be made. In fiscal year 1988, the Navy awarded a contract for the last A-6E production lot of eight aircraft to be delivered in 1991. The Navy has no plans to buy additional A-6Es. In 1988, the Navy awarded the Team a $4.4 billion fixed-price incentive contract for full-scale development of the A-12. The Navy expected the A-12 to be significantly more capable and survivable against increasingly sophisticated integrated air defense systems being deployed by the Soviets and third world countries.

In December 1989, the Secretary of Defense directed a Major Aircraft Review of four aircraft programs, including the A-12. During his April 26, 1990, testimony on the Major Aircraft Review, the Secretary of Defense projected that the first flight of the A-12 would take place by early 1991 and that the full-scale development program would be completed within the current fixed-price incentive contract ceiling. On June 1, 1990, the Team advised the Navy that a significant slip occurred in the schedule for the first flight, the full-scale development effort would overrun the contract ceiling by an amount that the Team could not absorb, and certain performance specifications of the contract could not be met. On July 9, 1990, the Secretary of the Navy ordered an inquiry to determine the facts and circumstances surrounding the variance between the current status of the A-12 program and representations made to the Secretary of Defense on behalf of the Navy regarding the program during the course of the Major Aircraft Review.

The investigation determined that the Navy and the Office of the Secretary of Defense had information that should have been considered during the Major Aircraft Review but was not. The investigation resulted in the censure and reassignment of two high-level Navy officers involved with the A-12 program. A third officer was forced to retire. Shortly thereafter, the Under Secretary of Defense for Acquisition resigned, and the Secretary of Defense gave the Navy until January 4, 1991, to show why the A-12 program should not be cancelled.

On January 7, 1991, the Navy terminated the A-12 contract for default because of difficulties the Team had in performing the contract and because the Secretary of Defense decided against restructuring the contract.

In our recent report[2] to Representative Andy Ireland on A-12 funding we reported that the A-12 program received total appropriations of $6.74 billion through fiscal year 1991. These appropriations provided funds for research, development, test and evaluation, concept exploration, demonstration and validation, miscellaneous support, and other costs associated with the full-scale engineering development contract. The appropriations also provided funds for procurement of aircraft under production options which were part of the A-12 development contract.

As of February 25, 1991, the Navy had spent about $2.97 billion on the total program. The development contract progress payments to the Team totaled $2.58 billion, as of the termination date, and another $104 million more was spent on Lot I and Lot II production options, for a total of $2.69 billion. The Navy received six design and management reviews[3] which it priced at $1.34 billion. On February 5, 1991, the Navy issued a demand letter to the Team requesting repayment of the $1.35 billion for which no completed items had been accepted by the government. However, at the Team's request, the Navy has agreed to defer the repayment until litigation over termination is resolved in court or a negotiated settlement is reached.

Initially, the amount of repayment was reported as $1.9 billion. Based on an explanation by the Navy's contracting officer the $1.9 billion appears to have been a computational error. The DOD stated that the $1.9 billion figure was a "rough order of magnitude estimate" made at the time of termination. Both the Navy and DOD now state that the correct amount is $1.35 billion.

---

[2]NAVAL AVIATION: Navy A-12 Aircraft Funding Status (GAO/NSIAD-91-171) Mar. 22, 1991

[3]These items are initial, preliminary, and critical design reviews, a program management review, and phase IA test.

TERMINATION FOR DEFAULT VERSUS TERMINATION FOR CONVENIENCE
DEFINITION

According to Federal Acquisition Regulation (FAR), termination for default is generally the exercise of the government's contractual right to completely or partially terminate a contract because of a contractor's actual or anticipated failure to perform its contractual obligations. On the other hand, termination for convenience is the exercise of the government's contractual right to terminate a contract without regard to a contractor's failure to perform.

The Navy's termination letter described two procedures available to the Team to appeal the default termination. First, the Team may appeal to the Armed Services Board of Contract Appeals within 90 days of the receipt of the termination letter. Second, the Team may instead bring an action directly in the U.S. Claims Court within 12 months from the date the termination letter was received.

GOVERNMENT LIABILITY

The financial liability of the U.S. Government, over and above goods and services delivered, is generally limited under a termination for default. According to the Navy contracting officer, this financial liability on the A-12 default termination is limited to the contract line items that have been delivered, that is, $1.34 billion. There also may be additional costs for protection and preservation of property in which the government has an interest. According to Navy officials, while the exact cost is not known, they believe that these costs could be significant given the need to safeguard the program's special access items.

The FAR provides that if, after termination, the U.S. Claims
Court or the Armed Services Board of Contract Appeals determine
that the Team was not in default or that the default was
excusable, then the rights and obligations of the parties will be
the same as if the termination had been issued for the
convenience of the government. Government liability would
increase substantially if the termination is for convenience. In
that case, the government's liability would include costs for the
work done and preparations made for the terminated portions of
the contract, adjusted by the application of an appropriate loss
ratio.

DEFERMENT AGREEMENT

According to FAR 32.613, the government can defer the collection
of debts owed the government. Deferments pending disposition of
appeal may be granted to small business concerns and financially
weak contractors, with reasonable balance of the need for
government security against loss and undue hardship on the
contractor.

The Navy advised the Team, in its February 5, 1991 demand letter,
that the Team could submit a request for deferment of collection
if immediate payment is not practical or if the amount is
disputed. On the same day, February 5, 1991, the Team requested
deferral of payment and the parties signed the deferral
agreement.

The deferral agreement provides that the government will take no
action, except as otherwise provided, to enforce collection
pending (1) a decision by the Armed Forces Board of Contract
Appeals (ASBCA) or the Claims Court on the Team's appeal, or (2)
a negotiated settlement between the government and the Team.

The deferment agreement also provides for the payment of interest to the government at the rate established by the Secretary of the Treasury as provided in section 12 of the Contract Disputes Act. That rate is currently 8 3/8 percent, and will be reviewed every 6 months. The agreement will remain in full force and effect until it is reviewed on December 1, 1992, and annually thereafter.

According to the Navy contracting officer, the Team advised the government that the issuance of a demand letter and the resulting reaction of the credit markets would cause financial hardship. Therefore, coordinated action was taken so that the demand letter, the request for deferment and the deferment agreement were all executed on the same day, February 5, 1991.

The apparent purpose of the deferment provisions of the FAR is to provide relief to contractors who are not in a position to effect immediate payment of contract debts. According to DOD, it granted a deferment to the Team to avoid placing the contractors in a financial condition that would endanger essential defense programs.

As indicated earlier, DOD has not provided us with sufficient access to the information it contends substantiated the assertion that immediate repayment was impracticable. DOD also has not provided us with its analysis of this information. We would expect that the DOD's review and analysis would have included comprehensive written financial analysis of operations and cash flows, so that a rational assessment of the Team's financial situation could be made. We are continuing to work towards an agreement that will provide the necessary access.

GOVERNMENT PROPERTY

What does the government own under the A-12 contract? As stated earlier, the government has accepted and paid for six design and management reviews priced at $1.34 billion. In addition, under the progress payment clause, the government obtains title to work-in-process, materials, tools, and similar items. In other words, the government currently has title to the aforementioned items included in the unliquidated progress payment amount of $1.35 billion.

Once the Team repays the unliquidated progress payments, title to all material not accepted by the government shall vest in the Team. If the government wants to acquire other items related to the A-12 from the Team, a price must be negotiated between the government and the Team. According to Navy program office officials, the Navy is conducting a review of undelivered technical information and material developed under the A-12 contract that may be purchased by the U.S. Government.

CONTRACTOR CLAIMS

On December 31, 1990, the Team filed a claim of $1.4 billion for equitable price adjustment. As the basis for the claim, the Team cited (1) the Navy's failure to disclose what they called its superior knowledge of facts vital to the Team's performance, (2) delays and disruptions, which the Team claims resulted from the Navy's conduct, (3) the Navy's flawed acquisition strategy, and (4) commercial impossibility of performance. On February 22, 1991, the Navy notified the Team that the claim would be considered when properly certified.

SUBCONTRACTOR CLAIMS

The FAR provides that subcontractors have no contractual rights against the government upon the termination of a prime contract. A subcontractor may have rights against the prime contractor or intermediate subcontractors with whom they have contracted. The termination clauses in the prime contract and each of the subcontracts will determine the rights and liabilities of the respective parties.

OTHER CONSEQUENCES OF TERMINATION

Regardless of whether the termination of the A-12 contract is for default or convenience, the Navy will have to take action to meet its need for attack aircraft. Since the early 1980s, the A-6 fleet has experienced wing cracks which have led to flight restrictions and groundings for a large portion of the A-6E inventory. To counter the resulting drop in the A-6E inventory, the Navy contracted with the Boeing Corporation to produce composite wings for retrofit on the A-6E fleet. The Navy originally planned to procure 174 sets of composite wings to maintain A-6E inventory levels until the A-12 entered the fleet in sufficient numbers. However, now the A-6E must continue to fulfill the Navy's medium attack requirements longer than planned. According to Navy officials, this situation requires the Navy to purchase at least 120 additional sets of composite wings at an estimated cost of $2 billion. Approximately one half of this is because of the A-12 termination.

Further, in the wake of the termination, the Secretary of the Navy directed that alternative plans be developed to modernize Navy tactical aircraft. Specifically, he wanted the Navy to develop a short term alternative to supplement the declining A-6E fleet. Alternatives being considered are the F-14 or the F/A-18 and we have been told that the Office of the Secretary of Defense favors the F/A-18 alternative because it is less expensive than the F-14. Improvements to both these aircraft were already planned before the A-12 termination. In either case the aircraft's attack capabilities would be less than the A-6E.

As of December 31, 1990, the Navy had an inventory of 637 F/A-18 aircraft, of which 260 were F/18C and D models. In the near term the Navy plans to purchase more F/18 C and D models--it has proposed that the fiscal year 1992 supplemental request include 228 additional aircraft over 6 years, but the Office of the Secretary of Defense has not yet approved it. In the longer term the Navy plans to procure an upgraded version of the F/A-18 that will be designated the F/A-18E and F. The F/A-18E and F will include a three-foot long plug in the fuselage and larger wings, which will provide for approximately 3,000 pounds of additional fuel capacity and a payload capacity of approximately 18,000 pounds. The larger wings will also accommodate 2 additional external weapons stations for a total of 11. The aircraft will also be given a more powerful engine. Night attack and under-the-weather capabilities have already been incorporated into the F/A-18 C and D. The F/A-18F is a two-seat version of the F/A-18E.

The Navy has an inventory of approximately 489 F-14 aircraft of all models. The model of the F-14 which would assume the attack role is the F-14D, of which the Navy has 43. There are several upgrades which make the F-14D unique from other versions of the aircraft. It contains digital avionics, a Hughes AN/APG-71 radar, and an infra-red search and tracking system. A F-14D upgrade called "Quickstrike" would provide night-time and under-the-weather capabilities and other attack enhancements. However, plans by the Navy to increase their F-14D inventory by remanufacturing F-14As were not approved by the Secretary of Defense.

Limitations to the F-14 and F/A-18 attack capabilities have forced the Navy to continue with their long term plan to replace the A-6E with a new start stealth aircraft now designated the AX. The Navy established a program office, prepared planing briefings for staff of the Office of the Secretary of Defense, and intends to submit a formal proposal to the Secretary of Defense in June 1991. Currently the Navy anticipates that it will take at least 15 years for the AX aircraft to reach the fleet with a research and development cost of $11 billion. A total estimated program cost has not been made. It is not clear how much of the technology developed for the A-12 can be applied to the AX. Navy officials told us they are not sure to what extent they will be able to use A-12 design studies to reduce the cost of developing another stealth aircraft because the studies were very A-12 design specific, and may not be applicable to another aircraft.

Mr. Chairman, that concludes our prepared remarks. We will be happy to answer any questions.

(396937)

Mr. CONYERS. Well, let's try to figure out what you said. Now, first of all, you didn't get the information that was necessary to make the kind of analysis; is that right?

Mr. MATH. Initially; that's right, Mr. Chairman.

Mr. CONYERS. You didn't get it until yesterday?

Mr. MATH. We did not get unrestricted access to the information that we believed was necessary until yesterday; that's true.

Mr. CONYERS. And you are going to need some more time to make a complete analysis, now that you have the information?

Mr. MATH. Yes, sir, Mr. Chairman.

Mr. CONYERS. OK. May I ask you what time yesterday you received this information?

Mr. MATH. It was yesterday afternoon when we discussed access with the Department of Defense and they agreed that we would have the required access to information. I don't recall the exact time. It was about 4 o'clock, as I recall.

Mr. CONYERS. About 4 o'clock. And you had been trying to get this for, I guess, a number of weeks?

Mr. MATH. That is correct.

Mr. CONYERS. OK. Now, just what did the Government get under the A-12 contract for which it has already given the two cocontractors about $1.3 billion? What have we got now that this contract is terminated and a deferral granted?

Mr. MATH. Basically, as I mentioned in the statement, they got design and management review information. That would include some drawings. That would include some information based on discussions, reviews, et cetera.

Mr. CONYERS. So we got a stack of papers, blueprints, and descriptions about what was going to happen, in terms of getting a new airplane?

Mr. MATH. That's correct, Mr. Chairman. We received information, which would include design drawings, et cetera.

Mr. CONYERS. Now, are there any restrictions or limits on your access to the documents relating to A-12? I hope not.

Mr. MATH. No, Mr. Chairman. We're happy to report there will be no restrictions. We will have unrestricted access to the documents we believe are necessary to perform the audit.

Mr. CONYERS. OK. Now, let me come to the heart of this matter. Was this deferral to these contractors in the best interest of the United States of America?

Mr. MATH. That's what we plan to determine as part of this analysis. When we look at the information, our objective is to determine whether the information was sufficient, whether the analysis were sufficient, and methodology when they received the information, and we will determine whether that analysis was sufficient to enter that agreement. And we will report that as soon as we can to the chairman.

Mr. CONYERS. Well, I appreciate that. Has anyone from the Department of Defense or either of the contractors suggested in any way that this issue should not be given complete scrutiny?

Mr. MATH. To us?

Mr. CONYERS. Yes.

Mr. MATH. Not to my knowledge.

Mr. CONYERS. All right. In a termination for default, there is usually a reprocurement clause. What does that clause provide, and was there one in this case?

Mr. MATH. According to the FAR, there is the clause on reprocurement, and basically that means that, if a contractor terminates for default, and the Government has to go out and buy that particular item to those specifications and they incur an additional cost, then the previous contractor could be held responsible for that additional cost.

And it would have to be the same item. In other words, if we ordered a particular piece of equipment and they didn't deliver on that piece of equipment, as I understand it, you would have to go out and buy that particular equipment. You couldn't redesign, redevelop another piece of equipment and then hold those contractors responsible.

Mr. CONYERS. So there is a reprocurement clause, and it will not be enforced?

Mr. MATH. It is in the agreement, and we don't know whether it will be enforced or not. That remains to be seen.

Mr. CONYERS. OK. Thank you very much.

I would like to recognize for 5 minutes the gentleman from New York, Mr. Horton.

Mr. HORTON. Thank you, Mr. Chairman.

In other words, you don't have all the information that you need to present to the committee at the present time because of the lack of access until yesterday afternoon; is that correct?

Mr. MATH. Yes. We cannot report the results of our review because we didn't have the DOD's agreement on complete access until yesterday afternoon.

Mr. HORTON. How long had the request been made for this material?

Mr. MATH. We began the request in March, and the DOD provided us some information when we asked them specific questions that were of interest to this committee. And when we asked those questions, they provided us a response on April 4. Part of that response indicated that there was significant data furnished by the contractors that was used by the Department of Defense to make their decision.

We received that on April 4. We went back to them the next day and said, we need that information to perform our analysis. And we had discussions through our liaisons in the IG office. We also had discussions with the Navy, and we had the discussions at the OSD level.

Last Monday, we received a call from the OSD level, which basically said that you can come over and look at the information. We told them at that time that looking at the information was not satisfactory, in terms of our performing an analysis; we needed complete access to that information, to include taking notes, making copies, et cetera.

But we did send a team over Tuesday morning, and, basically, we decided to send a team over because there was——

Mr. HORTON. Tuesday? Is that of this week?

Mr. MATH. That's correct. We were preparing not only for this hearing but also for a hearing on Tuesday.

There was some speculation that there wasn't any data or the data that was submitted was insufficient, and there was also speculation that there wasn't an indepth analysis prepared. So we sent the team over there with the primary objective, at that time, to determine if that speculation was correct.

We again, on that date, informed the Department of Defense that, again, this was not the access that we believed was necessary to perform our analysis and report to you.

Mr. HORTON. So then you got some information yesterday?

Mr. MATH. We got DOD's agreement that we would have the access that we believe is necessary yesterday. We have not gone over as yet and made the analysis and made the copies that we believe is necessary.

Mr. HORTON. Do you have any reason to believe that you will not be able to get this additional information?

Mr. MATH. We don't have any reason at this time, and you will be the first to know if we have any problem.

Mr. HORTON. All right. I want to ask you about the deferment. Is that unusual?

Mr. MATH. Is it unusual?

Mr. HORTON. Yes.

Mr. MATH. It's unusual in contracts of this magnitude. There have been deferments in the past, but, as the chairman mentioned, the examples that have been provided have been for lesser dollar values.

Mr. HORTON. Much smaller?

Mr. MATH. Smaller dollar values, yes.

Mr. HORTON. The $1.3-plus billion, is that money that has been actually advanced by the Federal Government to these contractors.

Mr. MATH. That's correct.

Mr. HORTON. You mean to say that they have money which the DOD advanced to them, which they have to pay back, and they're not going to have to do anything until December 1991?

Mr. MATH. Mr. Horton, I wouldn't term it "in advance." The money that was furnished to the contractors——

Mr. HORTON. $1.3 billion.

Mr. MATH. $1.35 billion are unliquidated progress payments. They are payments for actual costs incurred. When the contractor incurs a cost, they, on a monthly or quarterly basis, whatever the contract provides for, submit to the Government a listing of those costs incurred. Those costs incurred are evaluated by the Government, and they receive 80 percent progress payments for those costs.

So it's costs incurred; it's not an advance; it's not a loan. They actually incurred those costs. The contractor has incurred those costs.

Mr. HORTON. But is there a likelihood that we will get the $1.3 billion back, I mean the Federal Government when I say "we"?

Mr. MATH. That will depend on two things: First of all, does the termination for default stick? If it does, then the Government will require the contractors to pay that money back. And the Government should get the money back if, again, the contractors have the money to pay.

Mr. HORTON. Is there a legitimate reason for this deferral to December 1992?

Mr. MATH. Is there a reason?

Mr. HORTON. A legitimate reason for the deferral until December 1992.

Mr. MATH. The FAR provides for that provision. Whether it was reasonable or not is what we're going to determine as part of our evaluation.

The one thing I might add on those progress payments is that within that $1.35 billion, there are materials, work in process, there's tooling, dies, jigs, whatever, again, items that the contractor listed as costs incurred. Now, as long as the contractors, or the team, has not repaid the Government for these items the Government has title, under the FAR provisions for progress payments.

So we have title to whatever has been costed out in terms of progress payments.

Mr. HORTON. Why didn't the DOD require the contractor to post a good and sufficient bond or other collateral?

Mr. WOODS. The FAR does provide for provision of collateral if——

Mr. HORTON. It does or doesn't?

Mr. WOODS. It does. It does provide for——

Mr. HORTON. Well, what is the collateral that is required?

Mr. WOODS. It provides for either a bond or sufficient collateral.

Mr. HORTON. Has that been presented?

Mr. WOODS. The provision in the FAR that discusses that talks in terms of the contractor providing either a bond or collateral within 30 days after filing its appeal under the disputes clause.

Mr. HORTON. Has it been demanded, to your knowledge?

Mr. WOODS. A bond or collateral?

Mr. HORTON. Yes.

Mr. WOODS. No, sir.

Mr. HORTON. Is there any reason to believe that it will or will not?

Mr. WOODS. We don't have any reason to know either way. We would note, however, that there are provisions in the deferment agreement for the contractors to maintain a certain level of financial stability.

Mr. HORTON. Do you have any explanation as to why the Navy's demand letter to the contractors and the request for deferral and the deferment agreement were all dated February 5, 1991?

Mr. MATH. According to the Department of Defense, and I think the next witness can amplify that further, we were told, that when the termination on January 7 was made, that the contractors, or the team, in anticipation of the demand for repayment, came in with what they called extensive information and requested that there be simultaneous demand and deferral agreement, and they said that it was based on their contention that, if the demand came first and there wasn't a deferral, that would have an adverse impact on their lines of credit.

Mr. HORTON. Well, the fact that this was all done on one day, wouldn't that indicate that there had been some arrangements made beforehand?

Mr. MATH. Well, I think it did transpire in 1 day. It did transpire in 1 day.

Mr. HORTON. It's like you go out and buy a home, and have a closing all on one day. I mean, you do a lot of things that build up to the closing. Then on that day, you sign the deed, start the mortgage, and do all the other things. So they must have had all kinds of discussions prior to that particular day.

The fact of the matter is, all of those things were executed on the same day, those three items; right?

Mr. MATH. That is a matter of fact, Mr. Horton.

Mr. HORTON. What conclusion do you draw from that?

Mr. MATH. Well, again, until we look at that information, when that information was furnished, when the analysis was made——

Mr. HORTON. In other words, you don't know at this point.

Mr. MATH. We don't know at this time. But all we know is that we were told that, you know, prior to that date——

Mr. HORTON. I may be out of time, but I do want to get into it, the contract. I'm concerned about the fact that the contractors were not accomplishing what the contract called for.

Just briefly, when did these two contractors enter into a contract to build this A-12? In other words, how long had the contract been in existence?

Mr. HATHAWAY. It was January 1988, sir.

Mr. HORTON. And what had been accomplished, do you know that?

Mr. MATH. What had been accomplished?

Mr. HORTON. Yes. What had been accomplished?

Mr. MATH. According to the Government, in terms of the termination, the deliverables were those design and management reviews. Now, there were other things accomplished——

Mr. HORTON. Do you have any information that you can furnish the committee as to the cost overruns and other problems with regard to the plane?

Mr. MATH. What we can provide is the estimate at completion that was a part of the decision that this was in an overrun position. They were behind, significantly, on schedule. And we can provide that information.

Mr. HORTON. Do you have the specifics on those: Behind schedule, the amount of overrun, any other problems with it? Had they produced anything that was close to what they were——

Mr. MATH. They produced——

Mr. HORTON. There was some question about whether or not they even had the skills to produce the plane.

Mr. MATH. They have produced certain items. I don't know that we have a complete list of everything that was produced, like cockpits, wings, structures, et cetera.

Mr. HORTON. All right. Mr. Chairman, I will get back to that later.

Mr. CONYERS. Thank you very much.

The gentleman from Minnesota, Mr. Peterson.

The gentleman from New Mexico, Mr. Schiff.

Mr. SCHIFF. Thank you, Mr. Chairman. May I begin by complimenting you for having this hearing.

Mr. CONYERS. Thank you.

Mr. SCHIFF. I think it's an important subject, not only based on the contract, but on the overall situation with the A-12 and the major impact that this cancellation has had on our defense situation.

Mr. Math, I have one area that I would like to ask you about, regarding the situation of the A-12 and the deferral, which is the central part of this hearing.

It is my understanding that the Department of Defense has made a claim for repayment of approximately $1.3 billion or $1.4 billion but has stated that the money does not have to be paid at the present time by the contractors from whom it is claimed, until the matter is litigated or negotiated. Is that the basis of what happened here? Do I have that right?

Mr. MATH. That's the basis of the $1.35 billion deferral; yes, sir.

Mr. SCHIFF. $1.35 billion. But do I understand what happened; have I correctly stated it?

Mr. MATH. Yes.

Mr. SCHIFF. That they made the claim and then requesting the deferral at the same time.

Mr. MATH. Yes, that's correct. They made the demand for repayment and the deferral at the same time.

Mr. SCHIFF. And, of course, that raises the issue here before us of the wisdom of the deferral. What I would like to ask is, what would normally happen differently if the Government had made this claim and not used the deferral?

In other words, it is my understanding, at least under normal contract law, although, of course, the Department of Defense may operate differently, that if one makes a claim, the other side does not fork over the money because a claim is made upon them. Nothing is paid until a matter is litigated in court or negotiated anyway.

So can you explain what would have been different here had the Department of Defense not offered the deferral from what exists with the deferral?

Mr. MATH. The difference would have been that the team would have had to repay the $1.35 billion.

Mr. SCHIFF. What if they didn't?

Mr. MATH. What if they didn't?

Mr. SCHIFF. Right.

Mr. MATH. Then the Government has several options. They have other contracts with these contractors, and if they are not repaying their debts, then they can withhold progress payments on the other contracts, or use other alternatives.

Mr. SCHIFF. All right. So if the Government were not holding other money, the Government would have to sue anyway; isn't that right?

Mr. MATH. That's correct.

Mr. SCHIFF. Right back to where we are right now?

Mr. MATH. Yes, sir.

Mr. SCHIFF. So this means that the Government is not going to withhold progress money that it owes the team on other contracts, because they have offered the deferral. Is that something they normally do?

Mr. MATH. The deferral, or that they withhold progress payments on other contracts?

Mr. SCHIFF. Well, I'm trying to get at the actual impact on the U.S. Government of the deferral versus where we are when there is any other kind of dispute. When there is any other kind of dispute, normally, those holding funds continue to hold funds until the matter is litigated in court. And I'm hearing here that there is a special problem with the Government agreeing to that, when I thought that was the situation normally.

Mr. MATH. But under termination for default, the Government states that we are only going to pay you, because you defaulted on your contract, we're only going to pay you for those items that have been actually delivered. Now, for those items that haven't been delivered but we've given you progress payments, we want that money back.

Mr. SCHIFF. You owe us the money back, yes.

Mr. MATH. Because it was a termination for default, not a termination for convenience.

Mr. SCHIFF. But the deferral states that the Government is not insisting upon immediate repayment until litigation or negotiated resolution.

Mr. MATH. Correct.

Mr. SCHIFF. I am bringing up the point that that is normally the case anyway, when there is a dispute between contracting parties. And you stated, well, but in this case the Government could withhold progress payments from other contracts to keep the money, which it isn't doing; right?

Mr. MATH. Well, if——

Mr. HORTON. Will the gentleman yield?

Mr. SCHIFF. Yes.

Mr. HORTON. I think to clarify you ought to emphasize the type of cancellation. This was by default.

Mr. MATH. That's correct.

Mr. HORTON. And not for convenience.

Mr. MATH. That's absolutely right.

Mr. HORTON. And different events flow as a result of that; is that correct?

Mr. MATH. That's correct.

Mr. HORTON. In other words, what the gentleman is asking now would be a cancellation at the convenience of the Government.

Mr. MATH. That's correct. And there is a difference between the Government contracting and other contracting.

Mr. WOODS. The distinction that you pointed out, Mr. Horton, is an important one.

Another distinction, however, between the normal process and the process here is that, normally, if the Government had a claim that it wished to assert against a contractor, even if it were in dispute, there is a setoff procedure. It's not that they would withhold progress payments under other contracts but other amounts that were due contractors; they would be able to set off those amounts otherwise due the contractor against the amount of the claim.

Mr. SCHIFF. Do they normally do that in these kinds of situations? Do we expect the Government to withhold progress payments on a contract for which it has no dispute because it has a dispute on another contract?

Mr. WOODS. Again, Mr. Congressman, it's not a withholding of progress payments but of payments to which the contractors on these other contracts would otherwise be entitled.

And, in answer to your first question, that right of setoff is used quite frequently by the Government to collect debts owed to it.

Mr. SCHIFF. So the right of setoff is used frequently, but it has been effectively given up through the deferral process; is that what we have going on here?

Mr. WOODS. That's essentially what—they have said that they would forego whatever rights of collection they might have until this particular dispute is resolved.

Mr. SCHIFF. And the basis of your position, as an agency, is that the deferral is inconsistent with a cancellation on a basis of default; is that right?

Mr. WOODS. No, I don't think that's what we're saying.

Mr. SCHIFF. Then the problem with the deferral is what?

Mr. WOODS. Well, I'm not sure that we've yet identified a problem with the deferral. Again, as Mr. Math pointed out, the Government's position, quite simply, is that the contractors owe this $1.3 billion. The contractors dispute that. And the parties have agreed to defer collection pending resolution of the underlying dispute.

Mr. SCHIFF. Well, maybe I can just rephrase the question. Is it unusual for the parties to defer payment until the resolution of the dispute?

Mr. WOODS. No, sir, that is not an unusual procedure. As Mr. Math pointed out earlier, it's unusual in this particular case, because we usually don't have claims of this magnitude. We have not experienced default terminations of this magnitude in the past. So, to that extent, we're in somewhat uncharted waters.

Mr. SCHIFF. But then the procedure of allowing deferring collection until the resolution of dispute, as a procedure, is not unusual.

Mr. WOODS. That's correct.

Mr. SCHIFF. Thank you, Mr. Chairman. I have no further questions.

Mr. CONYERS. The Chair recognizes the gentleman from Florida, Mr. Ireland, a member of the Armed Services Committee, if he seeks recognition.

Mr. IRELAND. Thank you, Mr. Chairman. I appreciate that recognition.

Mr. CONYERS. We also welcome him again to our subcommittee proceedings.

Mr. IRELAND. Thank you. I appreciate it.

Mr. Math, I think that we kind of danced around this, but this deferment was made because somewhere along the line the rationale used was that one or both of these contractors is in financial difficulty. And two things would happen if you don't defer, first, it's not in the best interest of the Government, and second, we run out of good defense contractors that are capable—it's almost a blackmail routine.

If that is true, and it has almost become a buzzword among the contractors and among the Navy and the DOD, that, oh, my goodness, terrible things would happen if we asked for this and somebody had to file bankruptcy, chapter 11, chapter 7, or anything else.

It would seem to me that if that kind of major decision was made at any level, be it in the Navy or in the Department of Defense at a high level, that somebody must have committed something to paper that said, we analyzed these companies' financial statements, and we hereby declare, and here are our reasons, and here is what backs it up, a summary paper saying what would happen to our national defense if this happened. And that goes beyond just the financial statements of the company.

Are you privy to that, or do you think something of that nature exists? Or, was that kind of a decision made and then people at Defense and the Navy hoped that if they used this kind of rhetoric, "Oh, my goodness, in general, we'll be in a terrible way," that they could get away with the deferment without substantiating it?

Mr. MATH. At this point in time, we know that information was furnished; we know it was analyzed. We don't know the depth of any report, briefings, et cetera—we know that there were briefings. I have not seen a report as yet, but I'm not saying that one doesn't exist.

Mr. IRELAND. I would think this Congress would want to know about that report. I would think that you would want to see it, because, if they didn't commit it to writing and put it down, it makes a wonderful way to avoid responsibility throughout this whole thing by just saying, well, we all got together and talked about it, and there's nothing there.

And it would seem that if they don't have something like that, they had better be putting one together pretty quick, I would think.

Mr. MATH. I would agree, Mr. Ireland, and that is part of our charge in this analysis.

Mr. CONYERS. Would the gentleman yield?

Mr. IRELAND. Yes, indeed, Mr. Chairman.

Mr. CONYERS. It would be a pretty sorry situation if they were putting one together after the fact.

Mr. IRELAND. Well, I would think so too. And I wonder whether if that is what they concluded looks very much, as we have all looked into this, that perhaps there isn't one and that there's just miscellaneous information out there. When you send up a report like that, somebody has to sign off on it, and I'm sure we would all like to know who signed off on it, because then we can pinpoint a little responsibility. Taking responsibility is in short supply here.

I had two other questions along this line. The law, as I understand it, the Government has the right to terminate if the litigation is not being diligently pursued or there is a substantial change in the contractor's financial condition; is that correct?

Mr. WOODS. That's essentially correct.

Mr. IRELAND. All right. Those two things: If the litigation is slow, and litigation is always slow, that ought to be able to fulfill that condition and we can terminate the agreement because of that. And then "the financial condition should change," I wondered about this monitoring of the financial condition, if you could help us get an idea of what kind of a person you think could be of the skill that could monitor the financial condition.

Certainly, we know that the major investment banking establishments in this country maintain securities analysis departments that analyze multibillion dollar corporations of this kind. Could you describe the kinds of skills that would be necessary to analyze, to be able to fulfill this thing that says "if the financial condition changes"?

Mr. MATH. I guess at the top of my list would be the type of financial analyst that you just spoke about.

I think you obviously need financial analyzers that can take a look at cash-flows, look at revenues, projected revenues, projected expenditures, look at those on a recurring basis or a monthly basis, and determine whether the team can in fact pay their bills, and whether there are lines of credit available, so that if they're not getting reimbursement through progress payments, or wherever the revenues are coming from, that they can borrow the money to pay their requirements and their bills.

Mr. IRELAND. Is there any indication to you that there are those kinds of people at DOD or the Navy that prepared the analysis, No. 1, initially, to recommend a deferral; or, No. 2, are in place to monitor the condition? Are those skills available? I mean, you see those people, and you've seen what they produce.

Mr. MATH. I think, within the Department of Defense, the skills are available. Now, whether those skills were utilized in the upfront determination or are being used in terms of monitoring, this is something we will report back to you at the completion of our analysis.

Mr. IRELAND. If I may, one final thing along that line, I think we are all aware that one of these two companies has a bonus system that is about to trigger in as we speak here that gives its 25 most senior employees a substantial bonus of some $7 million or $8 million as the stock goes up, with an opportunity for them to even double that up to $15 million or $16 million in bonuses.

Is there any indication that the fact that this kind of cash-flow is going out was part of the analysis? Because, you know, that money could be paid on interest on the deferred—or paid and not deferred. Has that kind of thing been analyzed by the Department of Defense?

Mr. MATH. Again, I apologize, we haven't had the time to look at that. But, again, we'll certainly look at that issue and other issues as part of our evaluation.

Mr. IRELAND. Thank you, Mr. Chairman.

Mr. CONYERS. We thank the gentleman.

The gentleman from Connecticut, Mr. Chris Shays.

Mr. SHAYS. Thank you, Mr. Chairman. Thank you, Mr. Math.

Mr. Math, the A-6 was designed in the late 1950's, first put into production, I guess, around 1963, and then later upgraded, 10 years later, in 1973. There is no doubt in my mind that we need a more updated version. We need the A-12. You know, it strikes me that we're almost like starting over again.

I would like to follow up on two lines of questioning but then really develop that with the witnesses who will follow you. It strikes me that, clearly, McDonnell Douglas and General Dynamics underbid to the tune of $1 billion and then proceeded to come up to their nearest competitor, who had bid $1 billion more. But they got the bid, unfortunately for our country, and we proceeded to spend almost $2.6 billion. You're looking to get back $1.3 billion. I am just puzzled by the value of items received, the amount that we're not seeking to get back. What do we ultimately have now from this contract? We don't have a plane that can fly. We don't even have parts. How much of the technology that they had worked on will be transferable to someone else, and do we have the right to take all of that development and transfer it to whomever may get the contract?

Mr. MATH. As we said earlier, we have those designs, and the program reviews, and that information. The amount that will be transferable is an unknown right now. We've been told by the Navy that they are in the process of determining what is transferable to the next aircraft.

Do we have a right to that technology? We have a right to that technology if we paid for it. To whatever extent that technology was developed and we paid for it, we have the right to it.

Mr. SHAYS. Do you have any argument from McDonnell Douglas or General Dynamics that we have that right? I mean, there are two issues: They have to agree to repay us the $1.3 billion. And I don't think there is much doubt in my mind and the minds of others on this committee that that has to be repaid and the concern that there is even the deferment.

The other question, though, is of the amount spent we are not asking for repayment, is McDonnell Douglas accepting, without argument, the fact we have the right to all of the findings?

Mr. MATH. To my knowledge, they are not objecting to the $1.3 billion for which there were deliverables. Now, when we get into the overpayment of progress payments——

Mr. SHAYS. Well, I know they are not objecting to the fact that they received the money for it. What I'm asking is, are they objecting to the fact we have the right to all the information that was developed?

Mr. MATH. To my knowledge, they are not.

Mr. SHAYS. OK. Would you care to put a value on the amount? We know what we spent for it. Does it have much value?

Mr. MATH. I think, if you ask the Navy, in terms of, if you go out and look at what was obtained for that $1.3 billion, I think they would agree that it doesn't look like it's worth that. You're talking about paper; you're talking about notes; of meetings, et cetera.

But there's one caveat I would add to it, is that there were costs incurred, like engineering costs, design engineer costs, support engineer costs, and those salary costs go into the design and development of systems.

So the costs were reimbursed, and whatever comes out of the——

Mr. SHAYS. I think I have the answer to my question.

One last question, and that is, do you feel there is complicity on the part of the Navy that will give McDonnell Douglas and General Dynamics a strong argument not to even repay the $1.3 billion?

Mr. MATH. I can't comment on that, Mr. Shays. We haven't done the analysis, and that is part of the dispute. And that will be determined by the courts, eventually.

Mr. SHAYS. Well, it will be determined by the courts, but let me say to you that I really buy Mr. Ireland's argument that there is more than one party here, and the Navy is right in the center of it. And to the extent that they have screwed up, they have to be held accountable. And I certainly, as a member of this committee, want to know to what extent they are involved and to what extent their involvement would affect the return of any of this money.

Thank you, Mr. Chairman.

Mr. MATH. I think the extent of involvement was outlined in the Beach report and the IG reports. The impact of that will be determined by the courts.

Mr. CONYERS. Thank you very much, Mr. Shays.

We will be looking for a return, because you have testified, I think very ably, Mr. Math, under very limited circumstances; namely, you've only been told as of yesterday at 4 o'clock that you could get the information that really would be required to answer many of these questions that you have had to postpone.

We appreciate very much your appearance here with Mr. Hathaway and Mr. Woods.

Mr. HORTON. Mr. Chairman, I have a couple of other questions I'd like to ask of Mr. Math.

Mr. CONYERS. All right.

Mr. HORTON. I would like to ask unanimous consent that we include in the record these three documents: One is the document from the Navy, signed by W.R. Morris, Rear Admiral, that's dated February 5; and this is the demand letter that is addressed to the two contractors, and, in essence, it says, on 7 January 1991, the Government terminated the contract due to the contractors' default.

"The progress payments clause of the contract provides the contractors shall, on demand, repay the Government the amount of unliquidated progress payments." And then it says in the next paragraph, "The amount payable on account is" a certain amount, $1.3-plus billion, and then "Any portion of this payment not paid within 30 days after the date of the letter shall be subject to interest at a rate of," and so forth.

Then it says, "The contractors have the right to inspect and copy agency records pertaining to the debt to obtain review," and so forth. And then it says, "The contractors may also submit a request for deferment of the collection, if immediate payment is not practical or if the amount is disputed."

And then there is a letter dated February 5, signed by the two companies, addressed to Admiral Morris, dated the same day, "This will acknowledge your demand for repayment," and in this they ask for deferred payment.

And then I would like to include the so-called deferment agreement, which says, "This agreement entered into as of 5 February between the government and General Dynamics and McDonnell," and so forth, that sets the deferment and the default, and so forth.

Mr. CONYERS. Without objection, all three documents will be entered into the record.

[The material follows:]

DEPARTMENT OF THE NAVY
NAVAL AIR SYSTEMS COMMAND
NAVAL AIR SYSTEMS COMMAND HEADQUARTERS
WASHINGTON, DC 20361

IN REPLY REFER TO

6 FEB 1991

Mr. George Kostohrys
Vice President, Contracts
General Dynamics Corporation
Fort Worth Division
P.O. Box 748
Fort Worth, Texas 76101

Mr. Roger Witte
Vice President, Contracts and Pricing
McDonnell Douglas Corporation
McDonnell Aircraft Company
P.O. Box 516
St. Louis, Missouri 63166

Dear Gentlemen:

On 7 January 1991, the Government terminated Contract N00019-88-C-0050 due to the Contractors' default. The progress payments clause of the contract provides that the Contractors shall, on demand, repay the Government the amount of unliquidated progress payments. Subpart 32.6 of the Federal Acquisition Regulation requires the Contracting Officer to take prompt action to collect contract debts such as this. This letter constitutes the Government's demand for payment of unliquidated progress payments under the contract.

The amount payable to the Government on account of unliquidated progress payments is $1,352,459,644.00. Payment is to be made by check made payable to the "Department of the Navy" and forwarded to the following address:

Comptroller of the Navy
Room 4E768, The Pentagon
Washington, DC 20350

Any portion of this amount not paid within 30 days from the date of this letter shall be subject to interest at a rate established by the Secretary of the Treasury, for the period affected, under 50 U.S.C. App. 1215(b)(2). If, in the future, additional amounts are determined to be due the Government by reason of the default, we will make demand for payment of those amounts at that time.

The Contractors have the right to inspect and copy agency records pertaining to the debt, to obtain review within the agency of the determination of this indebtedness, and an opportunity to make a written agreement with the head of the agency to repay

this debt. The Contractors may also submit a request for deferment of the collection if immediate payment is not practical or if the amount is disputed. Any such requests should be forwarded to Rear Admiral W. R. Morris, SC, USN, Assistant Commander for Contracts, Naval Air Systems Command, who has been designated the responsible official for determining the amount of this debt and for its collection.

Sincerely,

W. R. Morris
Rear Admiral, SC, USN
Assistant Commander for
Contracts

MCDONNELL DOUGLAS CORPORATION
ST. LOUIS, MISSOURI

GENERAL DYNAMICS CORPORATION
ST. LOUIS, MISSOURI

February 5, 1991

W. R. Morris
Rear Admiral, SC, U.S. Navy
Contracting Officer
Department of the Navy
Naval Air Systems Command
Naval Air Systems Command Headquarters
Washington, D.C. 20361

Re: Contract N00019-88-C-0050 - A-12 Program Request for Deferred Payment Agreement

Dear Admiral Morris:

This will acknowledge your demand for repayment of unliquidated progress payments in accordance with subpart 32.6 of the Federal Acquisition Regulation.

In accordance with FAR 32.613, this will constitute a request by the Contractor Team for deferment of repayment. The basis for this request is:

(a) immediate payment of the amount demanded is not practical; and
(b) the amount is disputed.

While the Team has not yet filed a notice of appeal from or complaint in respect to the A-12 Program termination for default, such a filing is intended.

We believe that the Team members, as well as prior audits performed by the Department of Defense, have established that repayment at this time is not practical; that such repayment would impair their continuing operations, and more particularly those operations under national defense contracts. In support of these representations, each Team member has provided financial data for its respective company.

This will serve as our request for a deferred payment agreement in accordance with the terms of FAR 32.613. We are prepared to execute such an agreement at your earliest convenience.

Sincerely yours,

MCDONNELL DOUGLAS CORPORATION
James M. Gardner
Staff Vice President
Contracts & Pricing

GENERAL DYNAMICS CORPORATION
D. Elaine Scheideman
Corporate Vice President
Contracts, Pricing and
International Offset

DEFERMENT AGREEMENT

This Agreement entered into as of 5 February 1991, between the United States of America (hereinafter called the "Government") and General Dynamics Corporation and McDonnell Douglas Corporation, McDonnell Aircraft Company (hereinafter called the "Contractors") having principal places of business at Fort Worth Division, P.O. Box 748, Fort Worth, Texas 76101 and P.O. Box 516, St. Louis, Missouri 63166, respectively.

WHEREAS, the Contracting Officer, Naval Air Systems Command, Arlington, Virginia, by Certified Letter dated 5 February 1991, demanded payment of $1,352,459,644.00 arising out of the default of the Contractors under contract N00019-88-C-0050;

WHEREAS, the Contractors represent that they will appeal to the Armed Services Board of Contract Appeals or file suit in the Claims Court on the Contracting Officer's final decision within the time limits set forth therein;

WHEREAS, the Contractors, by a letter dated 5 February 1991, requested that government collection action regarding the amount demanded by the Contracting Officer be deferred pending the outcome of the Contractors' appeal or suit;

WHEREAS, the Contractors have made a showing to the Department of Defense that, absent deferment, one or both Contractors may be placed in a financial condition that would endanger essential defense programs;

WHEREAS, the Contractors are jointly and severally liable under the contract and the Department of Defense has determined that it is not in the best interest of the Government to have either of the Contractors in a financial condition that endangers essential defense programs;

NOW THEREFORE, the parties agree that collection of the Government's claim will be deferred subject to the following terms and conditions:

(1) **Indebtedness.** The Contractors acknowledge that the principal sum of $1,352,459,644.00 represents the amount demanded by the Government under Contract N00019-88-C-0050. The Contractors disagree that any amount is due to the Government.

(2) **Deferment**. The Government will take no action, except as otherwise hereinafter provided, to enforce collection of the amount demanded pending (a) a decision by the Armed Services Board of Contract Appeals or the Claims Court on the Contractors' appeal, or (b) a negotiated settlement by and between the Government and the Contractors without such decision. The statute of limitations for collection of this debt will be suspended while awaiting a decision or dismissal from the Board or the Claims Court.

(3) **Interest**. The Contractors shall pay interest to the Government at the rate established by the Secretary of the Treasury as provided in Section 12 of the Contract Disputes Act of 1978 (Public Law 95-563). The rate is adjusted each January and July by the Secretary of the Treasury and shall apply to the amount determined due upon (a) decision by the Board or the Claims Court (less any prepayments made under paragraph (4) below); (b) a negotiated settlement; or (c) a default under paragraph (5) below. Such interest shall accrue and be payable from 5 February 1991 until the date of receipt of such payment.

(4) **Prepayment**. The Contractors may at their option, at any time before the Board or the Claims Court renders its decision, notwithstanding the deferment of collection by this Agreement, pay to the Government all or any of the amount determined to be due by the Contracting Officer's decision. Any prepayments hereunder shall be without prejudice to the Contractors' rights under their appeal before the Board or the Claims Court. Prepayments and related interest will be adjusted if the amount of the prepayment is at variance with the decision of the Board or the Claims Court or if settlement is agreed to at some different principal amount without decision of the Board or the Claims Court.

(5) **Default**. The Government shall have the right to require immediate payment of the principal sum of $1,352,459,644.00, plus accrued interest in accordance with paragraph (3) above, should any of the following events of default occur: (a) failure to appeal to the Armed Services Board of Contract Appeals or file suit in the Claims Court on the Contracting Officer's final decision within the time limits set forth therein, (b) failure by the Contractors diligently to pursue resolution of their appeal to the Armed Services Board of Contract Appeals or their suit in the Claims Court, or (c) appointment of a trustee, receiver or liquidator for all or a substantial part of either Contractor's property, or institution

of bankruptcy, reorganization, arrangement of liquidation proceedings by or against either Contractor. In the event the Government does not exercise its right to require immediate payment, such a forebearance shall not be construed as a waiver of the Government's right to do so, or as an approval of the act, or a failure to act, that constituted the default.

(6) <u>Access to Records</u>. The Contractors agree to submit any financial information requested by the Government, and for reasonable access to the Contractors' records and property by Government representatives. These requirements apply equally to the Contractors' commercial business as well as government business.

(7) <u>Financial Responsibility</u>. The Contractors and their respective successors-in-interest agree to maintain sufficient assets or available credit to pay the Government the full amount of the debt. Upon request, the Contractors or their successors-in-interest agree to provide the Government documentation that evidences, to the satisfaction of the Government, compliance with this requirement.

(8) <u>Waiver</u>. Nothing in this Agreement shall be construed as a limitation, or waiver of any right, remedy or defense which the Contractors or the Government could otherwise advance in any legal action.

(9) <u>Payment</u>. Within thirty (30) days after the date of the decision by the Board or the Claims Court, or upon settlement of this matter by and between the Contractors and the Government prior to such decision, payment of the principal amount and interest determined to be due the Government will be made by the Contractors. All payments shall be made by check drawn payable to the "Department of the Navy" and forwarded to the following address:

        Comptroller of the Navy
        Room 4E768, the Pentagon
        Washington, D.C. 20350

(10) <u>Applicability</u>. The terms of this Agreement apply to the Contractors and their successors-in-interest jointly and severably.

(11) **Term of Agreement.** This Agreement shall remain in full force and effect as set forth herein, subject to review on 1 December 1992 and annually thereafter. Notwithstanding any other provision of this Agreement, this Agreement may be terminated after such review if the Government determines (within its sole discretion) that (a) either of the Contractors has failed diligently to pursue resolution of their appeal to the Armed Services Board of Contract Appeals or their suit in the Claims Court, or (b) there is a substantial change in either Contractors' financial condition such that deferment is no longer in the best interest of the Government. Such termination shall be effective 30 days after written notice is provided.

IN WITNESS THEREOF, the parties hereto have executed this Agreement as of the day and year first above written.

THE UNITED STATES OF AMERICA

By _Robert C. McCormack_
Assistant Secretary of the Navy

GENERAL DYNAMICS CORPORATION

By _[signature]_

Name _Donna J. McClure_   Name and _Peirce W. Putnam_
My Commission Expires July 29, 1994   Title _Executive Program Manager_
ATTEST:

MCDONNELL DOUGLAS CORPORATION

By _[signature]_

Name _Donna J. McClure_   Name and _J.M. Gardner_
My Commission Expires July 29, 1994   Title _Sr. V.P. Contracts & Pricing_
ATTEST:

Mr. HORTON. And then I think it would be important for you to give us, at some point later on, perhaps, in writing, some of the background information with regard to the cost overruns, the fact that it was not on time, and the bloating of this contract, and then perhaps tell us in writing what, in essence, the Government has as of this date.

In other words, what do we have that's tangible, that we can put our hands on? We don't have an airplane. We've got some things, and I think it would be helpful for the record if we had that information.

Thank you, Mr. Chairman.

Mr. MATH. Be happy to, Mr. Horton.

Mr. CONYERS. Thank you very much, gentlemen.

Mr. MATH. And thank you, Mr. Chairman.

Mr. CONYERS. We would like now to call a panel consisting of Rear Adm. William Morris, Mrs. Eleanor Spector, and Mr. Dennis Trosch. We would like to welcome you all. You have agreed to be sworn witnesses. If you would, please, stand and raise your right hand.

[Witnesses sworn.]

Mr. CONYERS. Thank you very much. Please be seated. We welcome you to the committee.

Rear Admiral Morris is the Assistant Commander for Contracts. Mrs. Spector is Director of Defense Procurement at DOD. And Mr. Trosch is the assistant general counsel, Logistics Office of the Secretary of Defense.

We welcome you all for your important testimony here today. We would like to begin with comments of Rear Admiral Morris.

We note also that there is no prepared testimony from either witness.

Mrs. SPECTOR. I believe we did have a prepared statement that we submitted to the committee.

Mr. CONYERS. You have a prepared statement?

Mrs. SPECTOR. Yes, sir.

Mr. CONYERS. All right. Excuse me, Mrs. Spector. Your statement will be included in the record.

Let's have Admiral Morris start this off.

Admiral MORRIS. Mr. Chairman, I do not have a statement. Mrs. Spector had a statement; she inserted it for the record.

Mr. CONYERS. I see. Then, Mrs. Spector, we will welcome you to proceed.

STATEMENT OF ELEANOR R. SPECTOR, DIRECTOR OF DEFENSE PROCUREMENT, DEPARTMENT OF DEFENSE, ACCOMPANIED BY DENNIS TROSCH, ASSISTANT GENERAL COUNSEL, OFFICE OF THE SECRETARY OF DEFENSE

Mrs. SPECTOR. Good morning, Mr. Chairman and members of the subcommittee. I am pleased to appear before you today to address your concerns regarding the Navy's recent decision to defer repayment of unliquidated progress payments on the A-12 program.

As you know, the A-12 contract was terminated on January 7, 1991, because it was behind schedule and over cost. Secretary

Cheney decided not to pursue any extraordinary relief for the A-12 contractors.

On February 5, 1991, the Navy issued a demand letter to the A-12 contractors, McDonnell Douglas and General Dynamics, for repayment of $1.35 billion in unliquidated progress payments. This amount reflects partial payments previously made by the Government to the contractors for work not delivered as of the date of the contract termination.

A demand for repayment of this nature is a normal and expected consequence of a termination for default. The contractors immediately advised of their intention to contest the default termination either before the Armed Services Board of Contract Appeals or in the Claims Court. They stated that they will seek to convert the termination for default into a termination for the convenience of the Government.

The contractors indicated they do not agree with the amount of the demanded repayment. They have also submitted $1.4 billion in a variety of claims against the Government under the now terminated contract. I understand that the claims have since been rejected by the Navy for improper certification.

The contractors requested and received deferment of repayment. The formal determination to grant a deferment was made, in this instance, by the Assistant Secretary of the Navy for Financial Management. In deciding to grant that request, the Department followed the policy regarding the deferment of collection, which is set forth in Part 32 of the Federal Acquisition Regulations.

Deferment requests are evaluated on a case-by-case basis against the criteria established in the Acquisition Regulations.

Mr. CONYERS. Mrs. Spector, excuse me, please.

Mrs. SPECTOR. Yes.

Mr. CONYERS. I hoped that you would summarize, and it looks like you may be planning to read the entire statement into the record.

Mrs. SPECTOR. I will try to summarize it, then.

Mr. CONYERS. It is going to be incorporated in its entirety.

Mrs. SPECTOR. Fine. It's not very long, but I will summarize it.

The contractors seeking deferments are required to provide financial data establishing their need for deferment, and that was certainly done in this case. There was ample evidence provided to us. I would say also, at this point, that we welcome GAO's analysis of that data.

Once we established financial need, we were assured that any deferment protected our interests. The deferment decision was made in accordance with the criteria and the fact that both contractors in this case were critical to the defense industrial base. We were involved in a war at the time, and their criticality was even more pronounced, if you will, at that point.

We are fully satisfied they've demonstrated financial need. We were concerned that immediate demand for repayment could have resulted in their lending institutions withdrawing sources of credit, and that was a major reason for the deferment. We believed that if either of the contractors went into bankruptcy that many of our programs could be put at risk at the time.

The detail of the data itself that was provided, much of it is proprietary, and if released could damage the contractors' position in world markets. Some of it is commercial data that is not normally shared with us at all; it was entrusted to us. We were also concerned that if we were to press demands on one contractor, that contractor could sue the other for half of the amount that we demanded.

We are convinced that the deferment agreement fully protects us. In addition to other protective measures, we are collecting interest, and we review the agreement annually. If there is a substantial change in the financial condition so that deferment is no longer in our best interest, we can terminate the agreement.

The agreement requires contractors to maintain sufficient assets to repay us. The assets of the contractors are jointly worth $5 billion. There is no question that they have assets to repay us, though those are not liquid assets at this point.

The deferment agreement is not precedent-setting. It does not have any broader implications as to the way we conduct our business, and each individual request is considered on its own merits.

I will conclude by saying that we welcome GAO's analysis. I first became aware of their difficulty in getting the data this Monday, and by Tuesday they had access to all the data. Three of their people came over and looked at everything that we had available. And we will continue to provide whatever access GAO needs to do its analysis.

Were I to do it all over again, I think we would do exactly the same thing. I know we would. The data is adequate, and we've done a very thorough analysis.

I welcome any questions you might have.

[The prepared statement of Mrs. Spector follows:]

STATEMENT

of

ELEANOR R. SPECTOR

DIRECTOR OF DEFENSE PROCUREMENT

On

DEFERMENT OF REPAYMENT OF A-12 DEBT

Before The

SUBCOMMITTEE ON LEGISLATION AND NATIONAL SECURITY

of The

COMMITTEE ON GOVERNMENT OPERATIONS

U.S. HOUSE OF REPRESENTATIVES

APRIL 11, 1991

For Official Use Only Until Released By The Subcommittee

GOOD MORNING, MR. CHAIRMAN AND MEMBERS OF THE SUBCOMMITTEE. I AM PLEASED TO APPEAR BEFORE YOU TODAY TO ADDRESS YOUR CONCERNS REGARDING THE NAVY'S RECENT DECISION TO DEFER REPAYMENT OF UNLIQUIDATED PROGRESS PAYMENTS ON THE A-12 PROGRAM.

AS YOU KNOW, THE A-12 CONTRACT WAS TERMINATED ON JANUARY 7, 1991, BECAUSE IT WAS BEHIND SCHEDULE AND OVER COST. SECRETARY CHENEY DECIDED NOT TO PURSUE ANY EXTRAORDINARY RELIEF FOR THE A-12 CONTRACTORS.

ON FEBRUARY 5, 1991, THE NAVY ISSUED A DEMAND LETTER TO THE A-12 CONTRACTORS, MCDONNELL DOUGLAS AND GENERAL DYNAMICS, FOR REPAYMENT OF $1.35 BILLION IN UNLIQUIDATED PROGRESS PAYMENTS. THIS AMOUNT REFLECTS PARTIAL PAYMENTS PREVIOUSLY MADE BY THE GOVERNMENT TO THE CONTRACTORS FOR WORK NOT DELIVERED AS OF THE DATE OF CONTRACT TERMINATION. A

DEMAND FOR REPAYMENT OF THIS NATURE IS A NORMAL AND EXPECTED CONSEQUENCE OF A TERMINATION FOR DEFAULT.

THE CONTRACTORS IMMEDIATELY ADVISED OF THEIR INTENTION TO CONTEST THE DEFAULT TERMINATION, EITHER BEFORE THE ARMED SERVICES BOARD OF CONTRACT APPEALS OR IN CLAIMS COURT. THEY STATED THAT THEY WILL SEEK TO CONVERT THE TERMINATION FOR DEFAULT INTO A TERMINATION FOR THE CONVENIENCE OF THE GOVERNMENT. THE CONTRACTORS INDICATED THEY DO NOT AGREE WITH THE AMOUNT OF THE DEMANDED REPAYMENT. THEY ARE ALSO SUBMITTING $1.4 BILLION IN VARIOUS CLAIMS AGAINST THE GOVERNMENT UNDER THE NOW-TERMINATED CONTRACT.

THE CONTRACTORS REQUESTED, AND RECEIVED, DEFERMENT OF REPAYMENT. THE FORMAL DETERMINATION TO GRANT A DEFERMENT WAS MADE IN THIS INSTANCE BY THE ASSISTANT SECRETARY OF THE NAVY FOR FINANCIAL MANAGEMENT. IN DECIDING TO GRANT THAT REQUEST, THE DEPARTMENT FOLLOWED THE POLICY REGARDING DEFERMENT OF COLLECTION WHICH IS SET FORTH IN PART 32 OF THE FEDERAL ACQUISITION REGULATION.

DEFERMENT REQUESTS ARE EVALUATED ON A CASE-BY-CASE BASIS AGAINST THE CRITERIA ESTABLISHED IN THE ACQUISITION REGULATIONS. THE CRITERIA ARE RELATIVELY STRAIGHTFORWARD. DEFERMENTS PENDING DISPOSITION OF APPEAL OF THE DEBT MAY BE GRANTED TO FINANCIALLY WEAK CONTRACTORS. A FURTHER CONSIDERATION IS THE EXTENT TO WHICH THE CONTRACTOR'S OPERATIONS UNDER NATIONAL DEFENSE CONTRACTS WOULD BE SERIOUSLY IMPAIRED IF A DEFERMENT WERE NOT GRANTED.

CONTRACTORS SEEKING DEFERMENTS ARE REQUIRED TO PROVIDE FINANCIAL DATA ESTABLISHING THEIR NEED FOR THE DEFERMENT. ONCE FINANCIAL NEED IS ESTABLISHED, THE GOVERNMENT MUST ENSURE THAT ANY AGREEMENT TO DEFER CONTAINS PROVISIONS NECESSARY TO PROTECT THE GOVERNMENT'S INTERESTS.

THE A-12 DEFERMENT DECISION WAS MADE IN ACCORDANCE WITH THESE CRITERIA. THE LIST OF MAJOR DEFENSE PROGRAMS PRODUCED BY MCDONNELL DOUGLAS AND GENERAL DYNAMICS IS AN EXTENSIVE ONE. NO ONE

QUESTIONS THEIR CRITICALITY TO THE DEFENSE INDUSTRIAL BASE. MOREOVER, WE ARE FULLY SATISFIED THAT FINANCIAL NEED HAS BEEN DEMONSTRATED. WE WERE CONCERNED THAT DEMAND FOR IMMEDIATE REPAYMENT COULD RESULT IN LENDING INSTITUTIONS WITHDRAWING CURRENT SOURCES OF CREDIT FOR THE CONTRACTORS, THUS EXACERBATING EXISTING FINANCIAL PROBLEMS. IF EITHER CONTRACTOR SUBSEQUENTLY FILED FOR BANKRUPTCY UNDER CHAPTER 11, CRITICAL DOD PROGRAMS WOULD BE PUT AT RISK, AND THE DEPARTMENT WOULD BE FAR LESS LIKELY TO COLLECT ON ITS A-12 CLAIM.

I KNOW YOU WILL UNDERSTAND THAT I CANNOT DISCUSS IN DETAIL THE FINANCIAL DATA PROVIDED BY THE CONTRACTORS PURSUANT TO DEMONSTRATING THEIR FINANCIAL NEED. IT IS EXTREMELY SENSITIVE AND PROPRIETARY IN NATURE, AND WAS ENTRUSTED TO THE DEPARTMENT ON THAT BASIS. I SHOULD ALSO MENTION THAT, SINCE THE A-12 CONTRACTORS WERE JOINTLY AND SEVERALLY LIABLE FOR THE CONTRACT IN QUESTION, THEY ARE JOINTLY LIABLE FOR THE DEMANDED REPAYMENT. WE CONCLUDED THAT IF WE WERE TO MAKE THE CLAIM AGAINST ONLY ONE

CONTRACTOR, THAT CONTRACTOR COULD PURSUE THE OTHER CONTRACTOR FOR COLLECTION OF ITS SHARE.

THE DEFERMENT AGREEMENT FULLY PROTECTS THE GOVERNMENT. INTEREST WILL BE ADDED TO THE DEFERRED AMOUNT AT THE RATE CALCULATED BY THE SECRETARY OF THE TREASURY IN ACCORDANCE WITH PUBLIC LAW 92-41. FOR THE PERIOD COMMENCING JANUARY 1, 1991, THAT RATE IS 8-3/8 PERCENT, AND THE RATE IS ADJUSTED EVERY SIX MONTHS.

IN ADDITION TO OTHER PROTECTIVE FEATURES, THE AGREEMENT PROVIDES FOR AN ANNUAL REVIEW BEGINNING DECEMBER 1, 1992. AFTER THIS REVIEW THE GOVERNMENT MAY TERMINATE THE AGREEMENT IF THE CONTRACTORS DO NOT DILIGENTLY PURSUE THEIR APPEAL, OR IF THERE IS A SUBSTANTIAL CHANGE IN THE CONTRACTORS' FINANCIAL CONDITION SO THAT DEFERMENT IS NO LONGER IN THE BEST INTERESTS OF THE GOVERNMENT. THE AGREEMENT REQUIRES THE CONTRACTORS TO SUBMIT FINANCIAL INFORMATION AND PROVIDE REASONABLE ACCESS TO THEIR FINANCIAL RECORDS, FOR THEIR COMMERCIAL AS WELL AS THEIR GOVERNMENT

BUSINESS. THEY ARE REQUIRED TO DILIGENTLY PURSUE THEIR LEGAL ACTION BEFORE THE ARMED SERVICES BOARD OF CONTRACT APPEALS OR THE CLAIMS COURT.

THE AGREEMENT ALSO REQUIRES THE CONTRACTORS TO MAINTAIN SUFFICIENT ASSETS OR AVAILABLE CREDIT TO PAY THE FULL AMOUNT OF THE DEBT. THE CONTRACTORS WILL BE REQUIRED TO REPAY THE FULL AMOUNT, PLUS INTEREST, 30 DAYS AFTER ANY DECISION IN THE GOVERNMENT'S FAVOR BY THE ARMED SERVICES BOARD OF CONTRACT APPEALS OR THE CLAIMS COURT. THE AGREEMENT DOES NOT COVER ANY SUBSEQUENT APPEAL. OF COURSE, THE CONTRACTORS MAY PREPAY ANY OR ALL OF THE DEBT AT ANY TIME WITHOUT PREJUDICING THEIR CASE. A SETTLEMENT OF THE OUTSTANDING ISSUES WOULD ALSO RESULT IN TERMINATION OF THE AGREEMENT.

THIS DEFERMENT DECISION IS NOT PRECEDENT SETTING. NOR DOES IT HAVE ANY BROADER IMPLICATIONS FOR THE WAY THE DEPARTMENT CONDUCTS ITS BUSINESS WITH THE DEFENSE INDUSTRY. I CAN ONLY REITERATE THAT EACH INDIVIDUAL REQUEST FOR DEFERMENT OF COLLECTION IS

EVALUATED ON THE SPECIFIC CIRCUMSTANCES THAT PERTAIN TO THAT REQUEST. WHILE THE AMOUNT DEFERRED ON THE A-12 MAY BE UNPRECEDENTED, I CAN ASSURE YOU THAT THE GRANTING OF DEFERMENTS IS NOT. THE DEPARTMENT DOES NOT MAINTAIN A STANDING DATA BASE REGARDING THE FREQUENCY AND BASIS FOR PAST DEFERMENTS. HOWEVER, I AM PROVIDING THE COMMITTEE WITH A VARIETY OF RECENT EXAMPLES OF SUCH DEFERMENTS, WHICH HAVE BEEN MADE TO BOTH LARGE, SMALL, AND SMALL DISADVANTAGED BUSINESSES.

I HOPE THAT I HAVE ADDRESSED YOUR CONCERNS REGARDING THIS MATTER. THIS CONCLUDES MY REMARKS AND I WILL BE PLEASED TO RESPOND TO ANY QUESTIONS THAT YOU OR OTHER MEMBERS MAY HAVE AT THIS TIME.

EXAMPLES OF DEFERRALS RESULTING FROM TERMINATIONS FOR DEFAULT

FXC Corp. (SB)	T for D	$ 42,000	Appeal to ASBCA	April 89
Kammerer Construction (SB)	T for D	$235,000	Appeal to ASBCA	May 90
Cincinnati Electronics	T for D	$11 million	Appeal to Claims Court	Feb 91
Thabco Inc. (SDB)	T for D	$ 28,284	Appeal to ASBCA	1990
Pauluhn Electric (SB)	T for D	$ 21,622	Appeal to ASBCA	1990

EXAMPLES OF OTHER DEFERRALS

Sundstrand Turbomach   T for C $20 million   Appeal to ASBCA   1990
Reason: Unliquidated progress payments owed

Monroe Wire & Cable (SDB) $356,582   Appeal to ASBCA   1990
Reason: Alleged nonconformance to contract specs--multiple contracts

Delco Electronics $1.7 million   Appeal to ASBCA   1990
Reason: Alleged defective pricing

ATAC (SDB) $208,177   Appeal to ASBCA   1990
Reason: Amounts owed for disallowed costs

Lockheed Aeronautical $2.4 million   Appeal to ASBCA   1990
Reason: Alleged defective pricing

SB = Small Business
SDB = Small Disadvantaged Business

Mr. CONYERS. Thank you very much.

Well, they must have been dialing the wrong phone number all the time before they got you, the day before yesterday, because they had said that they couldn't get anything up until then, as I heard their testimony.

Mrs. SPECTOR. What I believe happened is, they sent us a list of questions, initially. I believe Mr. Math said those responses were provided as of April 4. We sent responses to all of their questions.

At that point, which is about a week ago, I understand they started trying to get the data. And, by Monday, I spoke to Mr. Math, when I understood they were having some difficulty getting it, and said that I would surely see that those difficulties were eliminated. It wasn't a matter of weeks; it was just a couple of days.

There was some sensitivity to giving out the data because it is proprietary. It has information on commercial customers, commercial bank loans that could have damaged——

Mr. CONYERS. That has—I don't know. We're going to get into that question in just a while. You have already said that proprietary information doesn't need to be provided to the Congress. I am glad you have your counsel here, because we will be talking about it.

But, before I do, let's get Admiral Morris into this equation here, because you signed the deferment agreement, the demand letter. What I need to know about this demand letter was a description, on your part, as to the events that led up to you sending the demand letter.

STATEMENT OF REAR ADM. WILLIAM R. MORRIS, ASSISTANT COMMANDER FOR CONTRACTS, NAVAL AIR SYSTEMS COMMAND

Admiral MORRIS. Yes, sir. Mr. Chairman, upon taking action to terminate a contract for default, the Government will then normally reconcile what the value of the unliquidated progress payments are; that is, what has the contractor spent, what have we paid him, in terms of progress payments, but for which we have received no material or no end items. That value was $1.35 billion.

Normally, the Government, consistent with law and regulation, would demand repayment of that amount. But, prior to doing that, the contractors in this particular case, given the size of the demand and anticipating that it would be forthcoming, requested that the demand letter and their ability to request deferment, which is also provided for in the regulations, be coordinated so that there did not exist a separate demand letter on the street where the financial markets would not know what action the Government would take upon the contractors' request for deferment.

So the date of 5 February on the demand letter, the request for deferment, and, ultimately, the deferment agreement were coordinated, at the contractors' request, so that we did not have a demand for such an amount of money that would seriously, or potentially seriously, impact one or both companies in the marketplace.

Mr. CONYERS. So what did you do, though, before we got to the agreement. We all know they were all signed the same day. Who were you talking with? Who made the investigations? The corporations made an allegation that this would be inconvenient, that this would be difficult to do. But what I want to know is, who were you discussing this matter with, and what was the nature of the meetings that went on leading up to this statement?

Admiral MORRIS. In anticipation of the demand, the corporations came in, indicating they would request deferral of the expected demand, and they provided extensive financial data that supported their request for deferral. This information was provided to both the Navy and DOD. Our evaluation of the data they provided supported the deferral, given the conditions that we were establishing——

Mr. CONYERS. When did you get this information and from whom in the corporation did you get it?

Mrs. SPECTOR. If I may address that question, a lot of this was going on at the OSD level. I am in the Office of the Secretary of Defense—we began getting data indicating that the contractors were having liquidity problems, cash-flow problems, as early as last summer.

We received heads-up information from the Defense Contract Audit Agency and the corporate administrative contracting officers on both contractors. The indications then were that there were some liquidity problems. We were getting data all through the fall on this, months prior to the decision to terminate the A-12. This information was coming into OSD, and we were sharing it with the services, but it was coming to the Office of the Secretary.

The data then was primarily coming in from our own people, our field offices, Air Force analyses that were ongoing. There was extensive information being submitted all during the fall.

Now, prior to this deferment, we received extensive information from the CEO's and treasurers of the two companies which had been terminated for default. So there were several months of analysis of data ongoing that indicated cash-flow and liquidity problems.

Mr. HORTON. Would you yield?

Mr. CONYERS. Yes, I yield to the gentleman from New York.

Mr. HORTON. Were negotiations going on all this time?

Mrs. SPECTOR. No, sir. Mr. Horton, the——

Mr. HORTON. Well, let me ask another question, and then maybe you can answer. You say there were no negotiations going on. Did there come a time in this process, before the letter was written——

Mrs. SPECTOR. Yes, indeed.

Mr. HORTON [continuing]. That they were told, the contractors were told, that they owed a certain amount, $1.3-plus billion, and then did they—or were they told that they had to pay it as of the time of the demand letter, and then were they told that they would perhaps have an opportunity for a deferment? How did that come up?

Mrs. SPECTOR. Here's the chronology of what occurred. The termination for default, as I recall, occurred at the beginning of January, around the 7th. Within days after that, or a day or so after that, the Department was asked how much the contractors owe. And that's when the error was made. Based on a rough estimate, the answer was given, $1.9 billion.

Shortly after that answer was given, the contractors came in to say that the report of an outstanding demand for $1.9 billion that was in the newspapers was causing some of their banks to question whether to possibly continue loans, since that was considered a material adverse financial condition. They came in and said they did not believe they owed the money, that they could show us that they didn't have that amount of money on hand, and that it would damage their performance of Government contracts were we to insist on its immediate repayment.

It was before any demand letter went out that the contractors became aware of the possible amount—that proved to be erroneous—and that there would be a demand. So, yes, from about the early part of January until February 5, when all three of these documents were signed in a coordinated manner, we were in discussions with the contractors on the implications and why a deferment was the prudent thing to do at that point.

So, indeed, that was ongoing for about a month.

Mr. CONYERS. Well, I'm disturbed, as the gentleman from New York is, in connection with the implications of this comment that there apparently had been conversations for a long time about their condition.

Admiral Morris, we have the so-called Beach report from the Navy that says that, "With respect to the A-12 contract, contractor requests for progress payments were not properly reviewed to assess their validity, and required analyses supporting critical estimates used to determine contract physical progress were not performed.

"Special procedures established to expedite progress payments to the contractor team defused Government personnel responsibilities for review and approval of contractor requests. The government may be due substantial credits to liquidate excess progress payments associated with contractually-accepted work."

So here we have, on one hand, Mrs. Spector discussing the problems, the financial difficulties, months ahead of time, before this thing all collapsed, and we have a Navy report saying that there was not proper Navy supervision of the advance payments being made, in effect.

Now, can you help us out here?

Admiral MORRIS. Mr. Chairman, as I understand the so-called Beach report, it was evaluating, in conjunction with those comments, an observation that the estimates at completion being established by the administrative contracting officer were understated.

Perhaps, if I may in my own words, the Beach report indicated that the estimates at completion should have been higher, and we should have been aware of that sooner, which in turn would have reduced the amount of progress payments that the contractor was being provided at a point in time.

I think that's a very separate issue from the issue of the termination and the demand for repayment and the subsequent deferral of that demand.

Mr. CONYERS. Well, you're not reviewing the contracts as the requests are being made, and the Pentagon is at the same time talking with them about their difficulties. They're getting money up front at the same time they're saying that they're in a sensitive financial condition.

I mean, it seems to me, this Beach report is very material to the question that brings us all here. "Contractor requests for progress payments were not properly reviewed to assess their validity," and that "physical progress contracts were not performed."

This suggests to me, within the Navy, that this memorandum for the Secretary of Defense showed that you weren't on the job as far as making the advance payments are concerned. At the same time, we were talking about them folding up considerably in front of the time that the Secretary suspended the entire operation.

So I find this very disturbing, and I'm now asking Mrs. Spector, what documents did you receive from the contractors to indicate what their financial condition was?

Mrs. SPECTOR. Sir, maybe if I may start to give the discrimination between those two items. The Beach report is saying that, because progress was not matching the estimate at completion, we were perhaps paying too quickly because their progress was slower.

Mr. HORTON. Not only too quickly——

Mr. CONYERS. It wasn't being reviewed.

Mrs. SPECTOR. There were no advance payments made at all. It's a question of whether progress payments should have been reduced below 80 percent of what they were actually incurring. That's the question raised by the Beach report. Should we have reduced progress payments because there was a loss on the contract?

Mr. HORTON. Will the gentleman yield?

That point that you're talking about occurred before the date that——

Mrs. SPECTOR. Yes, it did, sir, way before.

Mr. HORTON. Excuse me.

Mrs. SPECTOR. Yes.

Mr. HORTON. That occurred before the date that the Secretary canceled the contract in January.

Mrs. SPECTOR. Way before; yes, sir.

Mr. HORTON. In other words, what you're saying is, or what that report says, in essence, is that the Government was not giving the proper oversight with regard to making those progress payments and that they shouldn't have been paying as much as they had been paying.

Now, in my judgment, when the time came for the deferment, the Government should have been looking at that with a very hard nose, because the contractors had been getting a lot more than what they were entitled to get.

Mrs. SPECTOR. Bear in mind there was a tremendous loss being incurred on this contract. It's the amount of that loss that the Beach report is discussing. Should the contractors have continued to get whatever percent of incurred costs they were getting, or should they get less. It's that very loss that drove problems on liquidity.

The contractors, at this point——

Mr. HORTON. Well, that's their problem.

Mrs. SPECTOR. Sir, it's very much connected.

Mr. HORTON. But the Federal Government—I mean, you played very soft with them. In other words, you kind of put your arm around them and said, "Sure you've got a problem, fellows, and we'll be glad to help you out. We won't really make our demand. We'll give you until December 1992 before you're really going to have to do anything. In the meantime, go to it, if you can reduce it."

It seems to me that with the report that you had before, you should have been playing a lot more hardnose with these people at that particular point rather than to say, "Okay. We're going to give you a deferment. We're going to let you go."

Mr. CONYERS. Well, I want to tell you that if you suggest to us here today that the progress payments are irrelevant, as pointed out in the Beach report, to the fact that we're questioning the deferral, I would suggest to you that all of this is part of the same pattern. If you want to compartmentalize this, I don't think it's going to work in this subcommittee.

Now, my question to you was, what documents did you receive from the contractors to indicate what their financial position was?

Mrs. SPECTOR. We received cash-flow analyses on—this is from one of the contractors. We received cash-flow analyses on all of their programs, and we felt that was the most indicative of their ability to repay. We also received information that we don't normally get on commercial sales and on commercial pricing—or cash-flow—and on available bank credit.

Essentially, that's the information that we received.

Mr. HORTON. Would you yield on that?

You know, if I have a problem with the IRS, and April 15 is coming up, and I have a cash-flow problem, they don't worry about that. If I don't pay it, I have to pay interest, and they're going to hit me with that interest payment.

So here's a case where they had those similar kinds of problems, but why shouldn't the Federal Government at that point have said, "You've got to pay it now"?

Mrs. SPECTOR. The reason is, we were concerned, because neither company had that much money. We knew that. And we were concerned——

Mr. HORTON. OK. Well, maybe you could have made a deal and you could have let them pay some? Are they paying interest on this now?

Mrs. SPECTOR. Yes, they are. We are charging interest. The interest will be collected at the time the debt is collected. So, yes, indeed, they're paying interest on it.

Mr. CONYERS. Is it compounded interest?

Mrs. SPECTOR. It's simple interest.

Mr. CONYERS. It's simple interest?

Mrs. SPECTOR. Yes. It's the Treasury rate that is prescribed for debts owed the Government.

Mr. CONYERS. It is not compounded interest?

Mrs. SPECTOR. No, sir.

Mr. CONYERS. Is there any particular reason why they are not paying on the total?

Mrs. SPECTOR. That's what the regulations stipulate we charge in these circumstances.

Mr. CONYERS. Well, let's turn to counsel here for my final question here. This committee has been denied the receipt of important documents that you have just talked about, and I am trying to find, for the life of me, why proprietary information is not available to this committee? After being on it for more than a dozen years, I can assure you we have not only received proprietary information routinely, but we have received classified information. So for me to be explained to very patiently that this was sensitive, proprietary information about the condition of the corporation is not exactly the point here.

We receive that all the time. There is very little of that kind of information that we don't get, because it's necessary to our oversight responsibilities. I want to tell you that if proprietary information was not available to this committee, we would be out of business. So because they are large contractors doesn't make it any different, as far as I'm concerned.

So can you suggest some reason in law that we should not issue a subpoena to get this information?

Mr. TROSCH. Mr. Chairman, I don't believe we have ever discussed, in any great detail with the committee, what the committee needs to evaluate. We have received the information from the contractors and this is information that we don't normally get, certainly not in the form that we received it with expressions of very grave concern on the part of the contractors, what the impact of disclosure of that information would be to the contractors' worldwide competitive position.

We received it in a fashion that is quite clear requires us to protect the data under, for example, 18 U.S.C. 1905, which would provide some criminal penalties on us for disclosing the data. Notwithstanding that, Mr. Chairman, I don't think that there is an issue between the committee and the Department over our satisfying the committee that we've looked at the data, that the data supports the analyses that we've made, that the conclusions we've arrived at based on the data are justified.

I think what we are trying to do is given the extremely sensitive nature of the data and the extreme harm that could come to the contractors in their competition in world markets, that we're trying to focus on a way to limit the number of copies made of this data that have a way of——

Mr. CONYERS. You cannot make that determination for the legislative committee and the Congress; that is not a decision for you to make.

Mr. TROSCH. Mr Chairman, I'm not trying to make that determination.

Mr. CONYERS. Well, you have, in effect, made it for us, and I want to tell you that proprietary documents coming in and out of this committee are sensitively treated and always have been. We have no instances of breaches of that kind of information and this is a constitutionally-mandated oversight of a defense contractor which is certainly within our jurisdiction. Under the terms of——

Mr. TROSCH. Mr. Chairman, we're not challenging your oversight role. We really haven't had much dialog between representatives of the committee and us in terms of defining what it is they need, what you're looking for. We are somewhat surprised to hear today that you're now raising serious issues of our challenging the committee's oversight responsibility. We are not, sir.

Mr. CONYERS. If you keep the information that we need in this instance, which I can assure you goes to the heart of the matter of why the deferral was granted, all you're saying is, trust us, that this is exactly what we are trying to receive and it was requested, as my staff tells me, since February 22, and we've been in constant discussion with the Department of Defense legal staff about this. Whether you knew about it or not—the legislative staff, excuse me.

So all I'm saying to you is that proprietary documents come and go in terms of our review and this really gets us to the heart of this deferral because unless it's based on some reasonable basis for which we don't have any information now, the General Accounting Office has been stonewalled up until yesterday afternoon. You're telling us now you're not challenging our jurisdiction, you're just going to keep the proprietary sensitive information. You can't have it both ways, counsel.

I'm just serving you with notice now, because you would have gotten a subpoena, except that I didn't want to execute it so summarily, but believe me, there is no way that we can determine whether $1.35 billion was properly deferred or not until we know the grounds. To tell us that it was a sensitive financial condition is not going to work, and I want to suggest to you that today, being Thursday, we would like you to enter into any discussion with my staff and counsel necessary, but we need that information by next Monday.

After then, understand that we will take whatever steps necessary to get it. I don't like to put this out in the public like this, but for you to come here and suggest that this has just come up and you didn't know about it is not going to wash. We've been working diligently to try to get this information. This is not a new issue and I don't appreciate you suggesting that this came to light just now. It hasn't.

We have to have the information, proprietary documents—we've got a string of cases that have established that a long time ago. We don't think there's much argument one way or the other. We're not trying to put anybody out of business; we need to know why they are getting, in effect, the largest bailout that's ever been granted, a military producer-manufacturer. It's inconsistent with the FAR regulations and that's what this hearing is about.

Mr. TROSCH. Mr. Chairman, we really welcome the opportunity to satisfy you, the public and the General Accounting Office that our analysis and that our conclusions with respect to the deferment are well-founded. We are going to be working with the General Accounting Office in connection with the analysis they're performing at your request.

When Mrs. Spector learned that there were some problems on access to documents, we resolved those problems. We met with the GAO auditors I believe the day before yesterday. They were given an extensive briefing on the review that we performed and that analysis that was conducted by Mrs. Spector and her staff, and I was there also. There were no questions that they asked in connection with our analysis that went unanswered.

At the end of the session, we recognized that because this was the first session we were getting together, they wanted to go back and advise Mr. Math in terms of what had gone on and that there would be further sessions with the auditors.

I can assure you, Mr. Chairman, we do welcome the opportunity to explain our position and we intend to do so with GAO, and if the GAO analysis of what we have done leaves some questions open, we are certainly prepared to discuss with you how we can satisfy your concerns.

Mr. CONYERS. Well, thank you. I think I hear some cooperation coming out of this, and I want you to get a copy of this February 22, 1991, letter that started off this discussion with Mrs. Spector about the information that we need.

Will you furnish the——

Mr. TROSCH. We sent a response to the committee that answered that—we believe answered your questions.

Mr. CONYERS. That is not correct. That information has not been provided. Let me just ask you this simply. Are you prepared to provide this committee by Monday with the information that we have been seeking since February 22 that has not yet come to this committee?

Mr. TROSCH. Sir, you really throw me at a loss. With respect to the information that you wrote to Mrs. Spector and asked for, I am floored. I thought we responded to you in full and provided you the answers to the questions that you asked.

Mr. CONYERS. We want the documents. We don't want the answers to the questions. There were questions here and we also would like to get the documents. Now, if you've misunderstood this up until now, let's just clear the record at this point, can we?

Is it possible for us to seek the contractors' documents in connection with the determination that the deferral was necessary to avoid placing the contractors' in a financial condition that would endanger essential defense programs—all of the documents to be reviewed by my counsel who have top clearance for any and all material that passes to this committee?

Mr. TROSCH. If I may, Mr. Chairman, could I offer an alternative at this point? We are very much concerned because of the unique nature of these documents and the information that they disclose, and the impact that could be had to the contractors. We're very much concerned about making copies and passing that around.

We are not at all concerned with responding to your committee's responsibilities and I would like——

Mr. CONYERS. Well, no one has suggested making copies. What the terms are of us seeing the information can later be determined, because I don't know to what degree it's sensitive or not sensitive, and there is no way I can make that judgment. But the fact of the matter is, we cannot have an oversight hearing on the largest amount of deferral that's ever been granted and told that we will not be able to see the documents, any less than the General Accounting Office is going to have to examine these same documents.

To tell us that our investigative arm can see it and the committee cannot is a contradiction that I'm not prepared to tolerate at this time. I want you to know that we're prepared to discuss this matter with you. I am not operating in an arbitrary fashion but if sensitive, proprietary information is to be cut off from this committee, then the Congress doesn't need a Government Operations Committee to do oversight. We are effectively out of business.

So that is a determination that we have to make and we have ways to go about that to determine the correctness of our position, and that's all we will be doing from this point forward.

Mr. TROSCH. Sir, I would like to arrange a system where we can continue the exchange on this. You mentioned the need to review the documents and determine whether in fact the sensitivity is such that special care should be taken of the documents and perhaps if I could suggest, there might be a basis if perhaps Mrs. Spector and I could come up and meet with you.

Mr. CONYERS. We'd be delighted to do it. I just don't want to take any more time out of this committee. We don't need to negotiate it at the committee session. What we need to do is get to the bottom line on this, and if you're prepared to meet with us, we're happy. Our doors are always open to you for that purpose.

Mr. TROSCH. We certainly are prepared to meet with you because we feel that these are important questions and we do want to satisfy the committee's concern that we have acted appropriately in the matter of the deferment.

Mr. CONYERS. Thank you very much.

I'd recognize now the gentleman from New York, Mr. Horton.

Mr. HORTON. Thank you, Mr. Chairman.

I think another way of putting it is this: For all practical purposes, there's an arrangement made—we don't know with whom—that resulted from discussions apparently between the contractors and some representatives, including Mrs. Spector, between January 7 and February 5, that ended in a signature on three documents at one time. This would indicate, as I said earlier, like closing a house deal on one day. You buy a house and there are a lot of other things that go on before you actually sign all the papers before they get recorded.

All we understand is that you have some document or some information from these companies upon which you based that decision. The Congress is entitled to know what that information is. In other words, our oversight function provides us the opportunity to find the same information that you have and then make a determination as far as the Congress in our oversight responsibility as to whether or not that decision was a good decision.

I have some questions about whether or not there should have been, especially in light of the Beach report and other information which had been furnished by the Department of Defense, as to whether or not you should have been a lot more hardnose with these contractors regardless of what their problems were.

I don't mean to say that we have to throw everybody into bankruptcy but these companies apparently had not performed very well on this contract and there had been a lot of misinformation. As a matter of fact, the Secretary had come up to the Congress and said everything was on target, and then he goes back and finds in less than 30 days, it's not on target.

That's one of the things I want to ask right now on that subject: But the point I'm trying to make, and I think the chairman is also saying, is we need to have that kind of information to determine whether or not this deferment was one that should have been made.

It does bring out other problems. It's been mentioned about the P-7. That was canceled with no deferment granted. The amount was only $125 million in contention and Lockheed says, why don't we get a deferment. That's a fact, isn't it?

Admiral MORRIS. Yes, sir, it is.

Mr. HORTON. Why didn't they get a deferment? They don't have any financial problems?

Admiral MORRIS. That's essentially correct.

Mr. HORTON. In other words, if you're having a financial problem and you've got a big contract, then we'll defer it, is that the idea?

Mrs. SPECTOR. Sir, in our rules, to some extent that's correct. There are several reasons why one would grant a deferment. One, when the fact that it's owed at all is in dispute. The contractors don't agree that they owe that amount back to us.

Mr. HORTON. Well, the Beach report says something is owed here.

Mrs. SPECTOR. The Beach report is discussing whether——

Mr. HORTON. Admiral Morris came to the conclusion it was $1.3 billion, but he didn't do that out of the air, did you, Admiral?

Admiral MORRIS. No, sir.

Mrs. SPECTOR. There are very clear calculations as to where the $1.3 billion comes from and I believe GAO has validated those calculations with our financial people in the field.

The Beach report was saying that the contractors were perhaps progressing too quickly. Instead of getting 80 percent, they possibly should have gotten a lesser amount.

Mr. HORTON. OK, so they got money in advance of what they should have gotten for what they'd done. That's what Beach says.

Mrs. SPECTOR. But let me just say, sir, that they are carrying $300 to $400 million just on this program.

Mr. HORTON. In essence, you've been financing them for some period and if they've got financial problems, I don't think you ought to continue to finance them. That's the point I'm making.

Mrs. SPECTOR. As far as deferring in these circumstances, if the amounts are disputed—and they are in this case—we frequently defer to prevent overpayment. We also defer for contractors who are financially weak, and in this case, because of the very large amount involved, neither contractor could have afforded to repay even half of the amount due and it's clear that were we to demand from either of them an amount, one could have gone bankrupt and the other sue for it, or we may have received nothing. Had they gone under because of this, we would then form in line as another creditor and have not collected at all.

Mr. HORTON. Well, I think it is important for us to have that kind of information and I hope that can be worked out.

Mrs. SPECTOR. We will try to.

Mr. HORTON. Now, I want to ask another question.

Mr. CONYERS. Before you leave that, if the gentleman would just allow me to point out because I heard counsel mention 18 U.S.C. 1905, and I want to assure him in advance that does not prevent us from seeking the information of any proprietary nature that's requested by this committee when the subject matter is within our jurisdiction. I just wanted to get that on the record right at the beginning.

Mr. HORTON. Mr. Chairman, I'd like to ask a couple of more questions.

This has to do with information on the status of the A-12 prior to the decision by the Secretary to cancel. Three analysts working independently on the A-12 costs and schedule data in three separate offices—the DOD Comptroller's Office, Mr. Betti's Acquisition Office, and the Naval Air Systems Command—arrived at the same conclusion in 1989 and 1990, that the A-12 program was substantially over cost and behind schedule. Given the fact that this information was available in all three offices, why was it ignored?

Mrs. SPECTOR. Sir, I'm really not equipped to talk to that. I didn't ignore it. I think you would have to address that to Mr. Betti or to the people involved in that.

Mr. HORTON. Well if, not Mr. Betti, I'm asking why the Office of the Navy, the Department of Defense, with that kind of information available, didn't do anything about it?

Mrs. SPECTOR. I don't know.

Mr. HORTON. Well, who would normally get that kind of information?

Mrs. SPECTOR. The Program Office would get it and——

Mr. HORTON. Would it normally come to your attention or Admiral Morris, would it come to your attention?

Mrs. SPECTOR. No, sir.

Admiral MORRIS. No, sir.

Mr. HORTON. You never get that kind of information?

Admiral MORRIS. No, sir.

Mr. HORTON. Well, you fellows had better get something so the right hand and the left hand know what's going on.

Another question. When Secretary Cheney canceled the A-12 contract, he said he was unwilling to bail out the contractors—which I certainly agree with—who were unable to design, develop, fabricate, assemble and test the A-12 within the contract schedule, and to deliver an aircraft that met contract specs. Yet, the Navy has put out a temporary operational requirement, TOR, for a new plane called the A-X which many are saying is simply a smaller version of the A-12, and they are asking the same team—McDonnell Douglas and General Dynamics—to bid on it. This sounds to me like a bit of a charade. Have you got any comments on that? Are they going to be asked to bid on that?

Admiral MORRIS. Mr. Horton, we've issued the sources sought synopsis asking all of industry or requesting all of industry to express their interest in a concept exploration phase for a potential A-X program. We would have no legal basis whatsoever for precluding General Dynamics or McDonnell Douglas from expressing interest or competing for whatever program evolves.

Mr. HORTON. When is the Navy going to get all the material that they've accumulated with regard to the A-12?

Admiral MORRIS. We've issued a demand for repayment of that which we have deferred, Mr. Horton, and we are intent to pursue that and intend to pursue the termination for default.

Mr. CONYERS. If the gentleman would yield?

Mr. HORTON. Yes.

Mr. CONYERS. You mean it doesn't strike you a bit unusual that a defaulter who is now contesting the amount of how much they owe, are now being invited to rebid on a new project, the successor to this plane? You say that we've invited everybody including them and there's no problem. I see a big problem.

Admiral MORRIS. Mr. Chairman, what I said was that we have no legal way of precluding them from competing. They are contesting our action to terminate for default. We expect that they will pursue litigation in the Court of Claims and/or before the Armed Services Board of Contract Appeals.

Mr. CONYERS. Well, assuming you're right, that there's a $3 billion default, and merely by contesting, this puts them in a lineup now to go for the next model after this one?

Mr. HORTON. Plus they've got a lot of equipment.

Mr. CONYERS. Isn't there going to be any end to this? This looks like a soap opera, it keeps going on and on and you're pleading for their sensitive financial condition at the same time. I don't know how much the American people are supposed to take from this.

Are you saying really that there's nobody else that can build this plane but these two contractors?

Mrs. SPECTOR. Mr. Conyers, I think there is a misunderstanding here.

Mr. CONYERS. Can you answer that question? There's a misunderstanding, yes, ma'am.

Mrs. SPECTOR. We have many contractors who will compete for any ultimate requirement that we have. There will be many competing. We are not going back to McDonnell and General Dynamics for an A-X.

Mr. CONYERS. I just want to make sure though because I've heard this—this has been one of the big defenses raised—that there is nobody else building it.

Admiral MORRIS. Mr. Chairman, we have gone to all of industry and asked for their interest in the concept exploration for the A-X. We have not limited our going to General Dynamics——

Mr. HORTON. How many responses have you had?

Admiral MORRIS. We have received approximately 34 responses to our sources sought synopsis.

Mr. HORTON. How many of them are serious responses? How many of them are viable proposals?

Admiral MORRIS. We have received responses from all of the U.S. aircraft manufacturers and we have yet to evaluate the complete list of companies with the responses.

Mrs. SPECTOR. In those 39, some submit alternative concepts, so it may not be 39 different contractors but all will be considered and there is currently no competition ongoing. Let me just add that we have disputes with a number of contractors at any given time. It doesn't mean they're either suspended or debarred from doing business with us.

Mr. HORTON. Oh, I understand that and I can understand what the admiral said when he said that we have no legal way to prevent or to stop that, but you have a practical way and that's not to make that deferment.

The other thing I wanted to ask was, as I understand it, the development costs for the A-12 were set at about $4.8 billion and there is some conversation that the A-X would be about $11 billion?

Mrs. SPECTOR. I'm familiar with the $4.8 billion.

Mr. HORTON. Admiral, do you know anything about that?

Admiral MORRIS. Mr. Horton, we have not defined the requirement for the A-X yet completely, so I couldn't respond as to what the development costs may be.

Mr. HORTON. Well, first, we need a follow-on plane, don't we?

Admiral MORRIS. Yes, sir. It's my understanding we do need a replacement for the A-6.

Mr. HORTON. And the A-12 was supposed to be the replacement?

Admiral MORRIS. That's correct, sir.

Mr. HORTON. And there ain't no A-12?

Admiral MORRIS. That's correct.

Mr. HORTON. And the contractors weren't even on target to get that plane anywhere near the time that they were supposed to do it, are they?

Admiral MORRIS. That's certainly our position. That's why we terminated the contract.

Mr. HORTON. Thank you.

Mr. CONYERS. Can I just ask you, have you ever heard about a financial ability requirement before you can bid on military systems?

Admiral MORRIS. Yes, sir.

Mr. HORTON. Wouldn't that have any relevance in this discussion that we're having?

Mrs. SPECTOR. They are capable of performing financially. They are capable of performing; they are not capable of paying back $1.35 billion without seriously damaging operations at the company and their ability, if you will, in one case at least, to finance their commercial programs.

Mr. HORTON. Well, what you're telling us is we'll never get the $1.3 billion?

Mrs. SPECTOR. No, sir, I'm not saying that. I'm saying now they are not capable. We are hoping that within the next few years that they will be capable should the judgment go against them and should they have to repay it.

Mr. CONYERS. Well, one company has a tax deferment that goes into the millions and we're talking now about their alternatives. There is no collateral, there's been no discussion of collateral, and now I think you're telling me that you could pull off this caper, and I'm assuming that Government is correct, and end up walking out of the largest contract cancellation in U.S. defense history and then turn around and go right back into the successor plane bid that is required because this one failed, and we find no problem with their financial ability to perform.

Yet, financial ability to perform is an ongoing requirement that neither of you have mentioned in this hearing.

Mrs. SPECTOR. Sir, both contractors are financially capable of performing Government contracts.

Mr. CONYERS. As long as they can default when necessary?

Mrs. SPECTOR. Sir, we will terminate them for default if they are failing to make progress. Neither one could repay the amount we're talking about without severely damaging other Government programs and that was our concern.

Mr. HORTON. Let's quit kidding each other here because if these companies were not doing the job, I don't know how they're qualified to even bid on this thing. You certainly could look at those possibilities, counsel, couldn't you?

Mr. TROSCH. We can, as we look at the qualifications for contractors, look at their past performance records.

Mr. HORTON. Let's don't talk about deferment now. I'm talking about the ability of these companies to build that A-12. They got canceled by default.

Mr. TROSCH. Yes, sir. I'm not responding to you on the deferment issue. In terms of looking at contractor's capability for purposes of a future award, we can look at the record of how they performed on prior work. However, I really have to mention to you that what was undertaken here was a research and development job. The contractors' were developing a new plane and development jobs are not always——

Mr. HORTON. But they've got all this experience, over a period since 1988 they've got experience and the Secretary concluded that they were not on target, not even anywhere near it, and that's why they were terminated by default.

Mr. TROSCH. That is correct, but not all development jobs——

Mr. HORTON. Now, you ought to certainly take that into consideration. Wouldn't you, Admiral?

Admiral MORRIS. Mr. Horton, I think what you're getting at is prior to the award of any successor contract, say for the A-X——

Mr. HORTON. That's what I'm saying.

Admiral MORRIS. We would make a positive financial responsibility determination prior to making an award to any given contractor.

Mr. HORTON. Financial and the ability to perform.

Admiral MORRIS. Absolutely. We'll make a responsibility determination that would encompass that contractor's capability to perform as we see it at that point in time.

Mr. CONYERS. The Chair recognizes the gentleman from Minnesota, Mr. Peterson.

Mr. PETERSON. Thank you, Mr. Chairman. I appreciate it.

Mrs. Spector, I was wondering, you were commenting about the criteria you were using to determine whether they could repay this debt or not and I think you mainly just talked about cash-flows. Did you look at their balance sheet, did you look at their equity, did you look at whether they paid dividends?

Mrs. SPECTOR. Yes, we did.

Mr. PETERSON. And that was part of the determination?

Mrs. SPECTOR. Yes, it was.

Mr. PETERSON. Their equity is gone?

Mrs. SPECTOR. There is not sufficient equity to repay the amounts that we're talking about at this time without impacting on the performance of Government contracts. It's not clear that either could have gotten bank financing or that at least one might not have gotten bank financing in the amounts required to repay this debt at this time.

Mr. PETERSON. Mr. Chairman, is that how you determined that somebody said they weren't going to be able to get bank financing? Is there some level——

Mrs. SPECTOR. Yes, we saw the level of their credit, how much they had, with what banks, and what their capability was of getting additional lines of credit. The fact that this $1.9 billion potential demand was even in the newspapers was scaring their creditors to some extent, and there was concern they would not be able to get additional credit to repay that substantial amount of money.

Mr. PETERSON. So, Mr. Chairman and Mrs. Spector, the procedure here is that if you're in trouble, if you can't cash-flow, and if your ability to proceed is impaired, you can get a deferment from the Government, is that it?

Mrs. SPECTOR. Yes, sir, and if the amount is in dispute.

Mr. PETERSON. Mr. Chairman, the solution to this probably is to put the Department of Agriculture in charge of these defense programs and then transfer the farmer programs to the Department of Defense because we have a situation—I just was at a hearing yesterday where our dairy farmers won't cash-flow because of a Government policy; the Farmers Home Administration, because they won't cash-flow, won't give them a loan and puts them out of business.

Here we have the Department of Defense when you're in that kind of situation, you can get a loan and a deferment and you get 8.38 percent interest, which our farmers can't get. So maybe the solution is just to switch this and we can solve the whole problem. Would you be amenable to taking over a farmer's home and the dairy program? Would the Secretary consider that?

Mrs. SPECTOR. I might. Let me just say here. This is not a loan; this money is spent and gone. It has been expended by the contractors. In fact, they have spent $300 to $400 million in excess of this amount on this program. The money is not there.

Mr. PETERSON. They didn't produce anything.

Mrs. SPECTOR. They produced—this is a R&D contract. When we buy R&D, frequently there are false starts, frequently there are engineers looking into things that don't come to fruition. Almost all our major weapons systems development programs at this point in time have had certain problems. There are unknown unknowns on these programs.

They did produce. They produced the beginnings of design of an aircraft and we didn't feel they were proceeding rapidly enough, but they did produce exploratory research and development on an aircraft.

Mr. PETERSON. I'll yield back the balance of my time. I just think it's ironic that we have a situation like this when we have other people in this country that are doing the best they can and we're putting them out of business.

Mr. CONYERS. I'm sorry the gentleman didn't include the 8A small businessmen while he was at it who have never heard of any kind of opportunities like this. They're checked out from beginning to end. The small and medium businesses, their financial records are gone over with a scrutiny you wouldn't believe. Anything like this would put them out of the running.

It's now being explained to me that there's still a good, ongoing business, they just happen to default and get a deferral and it's in dispute, so stay cool Members of Congress, this will all work out and we'll let them bid on the successor plane that is required because they blew the present A-12 development.

The gentleman from Connecticut, Mr. Shays.

Mr. SHAYS. Thank you, Mr. Chairman.

I was very interested in following up on the questions of the chairman and ranking member. And I just want to say that I found the questions very helpful and the answers somewhat disturbing.

Mrs. Spector, Mr. Trosch, and Admiral Morris, I am told all of you are fine public servants and I think you recognize that we have a job to do. This is a committee that looks at Government contracts with the Defense Department and we wouldn't be doing our job if we weren't here today.

I just would want to preface my questions by saying to you that we all know that in the next 5 years, the defense budget will actually have an absolute reduction in dollars spent, not just in real terms, but in absolute terms. So the whole concept of opportunity costs becomes even more important; if we spend money here, we can't spend it somewhere else because we have limited funds. So we're having to set priorities and we're obviously having to make sure we don't waste money. It's our job to make sure we don't waste money and it's clearly your job.

I look at this contract where we spent $2.6 billion and really what we are saying is the contractor owes us half of the $2.6 billion and we spent half, that we now feel somehow we had some value, but as I listen, I realize we have very little value for the $1.3 billion that we are not asking to be returned. Really what we have is a delay in the program. It makes me wonder, as Mr. Ireland has suggested to me as well, that you really almost have to wonder what are we going to be flying, what's going to be on these aircraft carriers in the years to come?

If I were the Navy, I'd be almost in a panic position because one really has to wonder what planes are going to be on those aircraft carriers we're building.

Mrs. Spector, you said something I found very puzzling. It just makes me want to ask you a question about this. You said the Beach report said that perhaps we were paying too soon. Is there any doubt in your mind that the Beach report said you were paying too soon?

Mrs. SPECTOR. I believe it said that we were.

Mr. SHAYS. Yes, there's no perhaps.

Mrs. SPECTOR. I believe you're right.

Mr. SHAYS. The next question is, do you think you paid too soon?

Mrs. SPECTOR. I don't know the details of that, I'm sorry. I know what the Beach report said, I know what the allegation is, but I don't know——

Mr. SHAYS. Isn't that your job to know?

Mrs. SPECTOR. No, sir. My job is contracting policy by and large. The review of progress payments goes on, in the field they are reviewed by DCAA and the——

Mr. SHAYS. You have no oversight in that regard?

Mrs. SPECTOR. No, sir, I don't, not on the amounts paid for progress payments. I don't.

Mr. SHAYS. OK. Well, it will be interesting to get that person or persons before this committee.

Admiral Morris, do you agree with the Beach report that we were paying too soon?

Admiral MORRIS. Yes.

Mr. SHAYS. Mrs. Spector, you said that even though these letters were dated very clearly to the request. I mean, the request—maybe it's just a term of art but they are asking, in accordance with FAR 32.613, this will consult a request by the contractor team for deferment of repayment. The basis for the request is—this is the letter dated February 5 from McDonnell Douglas and General Dynamics.

The reasons were immediate payment of the amount demanded is not practical and the amount is disputed. Well, we also know that we have demanded in the past that if it's in dispute, you still pay, is that not true?

Mrs. SPECTOR. I imagine that—yes, there have been times when it's been in dispute where we do; there have been times we deferred.

Mr. SHAYS. And obviously this immediate payment of the amount demanded is not practical has greater meaning to you. I mean, it's a one line sentence, there was no documentation in this letter, was there, to back up that argument?

Mrs. SPECTOR. We had already seen the documentation. I believe they say that such repayment would impair the continuing operations on the contract——

Mr. SHAYS. You're quick to answer but I just want to make sure you're clear on my question. Was there extensive documentation in this letter?

Mrs. SPECTOR. Supporting the letter, we had seen documentation prior to its receipt.

Mr. SHAYS. That's not what I asked.

Mrs. SPECTOR. Attached to the letter?

Mr. SHAYS. Yes.

Mrs. SPECTOR. No.

Mr. SHAYS. Do they make reference in this letter anywhere to previous information supplied?

Mrs. SPECTOR. No.

Mr. SHAYS. So it's really a letter that says, immediate payment in the amount demanded is not practical, but we don't have on this letter any documentation that would have accompanied this letter?

Mrs. SPECTOR. I'm sorry, I erred. It says, "In support of these representations"——

Mr. SHAYS. Let me just say something, you don't need to speak——

Mrs. SPECTOR. "Has provided financial data," so I was wrong in my response.

Mr. SHAYS. You don't need to speak quickly and I'm not going to interrupt you because what you say is very important to this committee. The chairman and the ranking member asked very good questions and spent time doing it. You have time to answer, so let me be clear on this. What is your answer and don't read so quickly.

Mrs. SPECTOR. My response is that they did refer to data that they had provided to us and indeed, they had provided data to us.

Mr. SHAYS. And they outlined what that data was in the referral?

Mrs. SPECTOR. No. The sentence is, "In support of these representations, each team member has provided financial data for its respective company."

Mr. SHAYS. But they don't document what day, what time. I find that a little perplexing, frankly. It would seem to me that in a formal request to ask a deferment of $1.3 billion, that accompanying that request would be very precise information and if they didn't have it enclosed they would have been precise as to how they had documented this, not in such general terms as you read.

Let me ask you this, was there any thought that you would ask for a partial payment of $1.3 billion, even $100 million, or $200 million? Was there any request that be done?

Mrs. SPECTOR. Normally, our procedures are, when we defer, we defer until the outcome of litigation. In this case, we put in a revisitation provision. Normally we defer until the outcome of litigation.

Mr. SHAYS. The answer to the question specifically is that you did not give any thought to a partial payment?

Mrs. SPECTOR. Some thought was given to it and we felt that it might damage the contractors' ability to obtain credit if we were collecting against this.

Mr. SHAYS. Even if it was $15 million? See, this is the thing that concerns me. I think you're answering quickly again and this is not a frivolous questions, at least I don't think it is.

The question is, was there a fairly serious attempt to decide, while they couldn't pay the full amount, that they could pay a partial amount?

Mrs. SPECTOR. There was some consideration given to that.

Mr. SHAYS. Some is not clear to me. Is some you thought about it and then said no, or were there extensive meetings where that was debated back and forth?

Mrs. SPECTOR. There were extensive meetings on their financial condition.

Mr. SHAYS. Please think of the question. I just want to know if you gave some time to the consideration of whether there should have been a partial payment or whether it was all or nothing?

Mrs. SPECTOR. I would say that in evaluating the financial condition of the contractors, it became clear that we ought to defer the total amount for the period that we did until litigation settled this amount. We did consider other alternatives but we determined this was the appropriate thing to do.

Mr. SHAYS. I would just react to that by saying to you that I can't tell you whether they could have paid $1.3 billion, but it's hard for me to imagine that they couldn't have paid a few million, and I just find your response rather interesting.

Let me ask you this. Did General Dynamics Corporation pay dividends to its stockholders during the years in question?

Mrs. SPECTOR. I believe they did.

Mr. SHAYS. Did McDonnell Douglas pay dividends?

Mrs. SPECTOR. Yes.

Mr. SHAYS. Do you think the stockholders are entitled to payment on supposed profit when we know that we paid sooner than we should have to both companies? Should they have given dividends when in fact it was really our money that was being advanced to them?

Mrs. SPECTOR. Sir, there is an interlocking between the payment of dividends and credit ratings. In the case of McDonnell Douglas, their dividend was cut in half at the last paying period. We looked into the dividend question and the fact is that there are many institutions that hold the stocks in these companies that would not be allowed to hold the stock if they didn't pay dividends. That factor is tied into their ability to get bank financing.

Mr. SHAYS. I don't mean to be facetious about this, but somehow did we think that it would be secret that they owed us $1.3 billion and don't you think as someone thinking about investing in this company, that I would want to know what their liabilities were?

Mrs. SPECTOR. Certainly.

Mr. SHAYS. So are you saying to me, by the mere fact that we did not object to their paying dividends, that somehow that strengthened their financial condition?

Mrs. SPECTOR. The issue here on the deferment was to provide an environment where these companies could continue to get bank financing to support defense and commercial aircraft sales in the case of one the company's grave financial situation, one of our two commercial aircraft manufacturers in the United States.

Having this sort of a demand outstanding without a deferment might have impaired their ability to get that bank financing. We normally don't particularly worry about stock prices, but we did question the dividend issue and were satisfied that what they were doing was appropriate.

Mr. SHAYS. I guess I would just say that I can't imagine a company with so many liabilities paying dividends. You know, everybody tells me that somehow we should run government the way business runs business and the more I'm in government, the more I begin to think that maybe government sometimes runs its operations better until I come to circumstances like this which may be a plague on both our houses.

I mean no disrespect. I don't know ultimately if they should have or if they could have paid the $1.3 billion. It does seem to me that they should have paid something and it does seem to me that any company that's paying dividends and thinks it has the ability to dispose of, in a sense, and say we're profitable, is really pulling a fast one on its own stockholders. If I were a stockholder, I'd even wonder why they could have paid me a dividend.

I really salute the chairman and ranking member of this committee and Mr. Ireland who, in particular, has focused on this issue because we will get to the bottom of this and hopefully there will be some major changes in the way the Navy does its business.

Thank you, Mr. Chairman.

Mr. CONYERS. Thank you very much for excellent questions.

Mr. Schiff.

Mr. SCHIFF. Thank you, Mr. Chairman. I just have a few areas I'd like to ask about briefly.

The first I'd like to address to Admiral Morris. Admiral, if this is blindsiding you, I'll accept your telling me this because this is not on directly the subject of the hearing. In the packet that we were provided, I was provided a copy of a Washington Times article with the headlines, "Navy to Promote Captain Despite His Reprimand," and the substance of the article is that a captain, who I believe received a letter of reprimand or letter of censure in the course of this A-12 matter in the Defense Department, is still being recommended for promotion within the Department of Navy to rear admiral.

I happen to have a 22-year DOD background myself in the New Mexico Air National Guard, and I'm surprised at that, if that's true. Normally they say you have to start with the firewall on your OER just to be on a par with everybody else before you can even go any farther than that. I wonder if you are familiar with that and if so, can you briefly tell me if that's correct or not?

Admiral MORRIS. I'm not in a position, Mr. Congressman, to evaluate it. The program manager was selected for promotion to rear admiral, and beyond that, I'm not in a position to comment.

Mr. SCHIFF. That's fine, Admiral. This was not a subject of the hearing.

Let me go on then to the subject. A major question about this deferment is whether the Department of Defense granted the deferment to this team in the course of business under its normal procedures or whether this was some kind of special sweetheart deal to these contractors.

If I understand your testimony, Mrs. Spector, you're stating according to the Department of Defense all of the "i's" were dotted and the "t's" were crossed and so forth from the Department of Defense's point of view?

Mrs. SPECTOR. Yes, sir.

Mr. SCHIFF. Not that it shouldn't necessarily, but this remains your position today?

Mrs. SPECTOR. Yes, it does.

Mr. SCHIFF. Let me ask about the amount involved because apparently the amount of this deferment, according to the GAO, is much larger than they've seen in the past. Is that correct?

Mrs. SPECTOR. Yes, it is. We don't normally terminate contracts of this magnitude for default. It's an unusual occurrence, hence the amount of repayment is also high.

Mr. SCHIFF. Well, the fact that the amount is unusual, even if the procedures are normal, doesn't that raise a question by itself of risk to the taxpayers? In other words, we are talking about the Navy having asserted a claim of $1.3 billion. I understand that it's disputed, but still the fact that this is left hanging out there, doesn't that provide an extraordinary risk that if something economically adverse happens to this team, that the taxpayers will never realize this $1.35 billion?

Mrs. SPECTOR. Sir, I am convinced that had we not deferred at that time, one or more of these contractors could have declared bankruptcy right at that point and we would never have been repaid. Bear in mind, we were in the middle of Desert Storm, it had just started 10 days or so before this deferment. These are two of our largest contractors. I think it would have been far more damaging to the taxpayers had either of them gone into chapter 11.

Let me just amplify on that a bit. We have some loss contracts that these contractors are performing and part of the reason for their financial difficulties is that they are performing on these loss contracts on our behalf, thus they don't have the cash that they might ordinarily have.

Had we seen them go into chapter 11——

Mr. SCHIFF. I'm sorry, I don't mean to interrupt. Could you tell me what a loss contract is?

Mrs. SPECTOR. They are "loss," they were losing money——

Mr. SCHIFF. But they were continuing to perform?

Mrs. SPECTOR. They were continuing to perform but losing money. Had they gone into chapter 11, had that eventuality occurred, it's very likely we would not have been able to enforce those contracts, that the receiver would have said, "don't continue to perform losing contracts."

These eventualities were pursued. We did look at what would happen if we said no. That was thoroughly analyzed, I assure you, and the damage to the taxpayer of that would have been far greater than the actions that we're taking now which merely defer repayment. As you suggested earlier, standard commercial practice is to do this when there's a dispute over a debt.

Mr. SCHIFF. So the one factor in granting the deferment was your belief that one or members of this team might have been forced into a bankruptcy reorganization if you had insisted upon a cash payment of $1.3 billion, is that right?

Mrs. SPECTOR. That eventuality was certainly a consideration and also the amount and the fact that it was owed was in dispute.

Mr. SCHIFF. Let me come to the last point then, the effect of all this on future contracts, particularly the future contract for a new A-12 if I can refer to it that way. As you said, these contractors can bid on new contracts; they are not legally prevented from doing so. But you also testified that financial condition is a factor that's looked at in awarding a new contract, is that right?

Mrs. SPECTOR. Yes, it is.

Mr. SCHIFF. Wouldn't there then be an inconsistency in having granted this deferment because of the feeling that $1.35 billion would have set one or both of these team members into Federal bankruptcy court if they are later granted one of the contracts which assumes that they are financially solvent and healthy enough to perform these contracts?

Mrs. SPECTOR. Sir, we are doing business with many contractors who are operating in chapter 11 at this time. That doesn't preclude them from being able to perform contracts. Bear in mind, our provisions state that we finance 80 percent of the amounts that they incur. We do not believe that these two contractors are not capable of performing Government contracts. We do believe that they would not have been capable of paying back $1.35 billion.

Mr. SCHIFF. Let's go back again. If you believe that you can do business with private enterprise companies that are in chapter 11, what was the great concern then that these two team members, or one of them, might have gone into chapter 11 bankruptcy?

Mrs. SPECTOR. The concern was that, as I mentioned, we have several contracts with them on which they are losing money. They are fixed price contracts that we are enforcing and they are performing on, and they will take losses on them. The concern was that on those contracts they might renege on performance in chapter 11 and we would have had to restructure these contracts had we wanted continuation of those programs. That was one concern.

Another is that operation in bankruptcy is an unknown. We would not have known what would have occurred. They might have sold off major components of these companies that are very large defense contractors—whether it be foreign acquisition or other acquisition of those assets. There was concern of the unknown, of what might happen in a bankruptcy for either of them.

Mr. SCHIFF. One last question. Can you tell me since the Navy takes the position, which again I understand is disputed, but the Navy has asserted a claim for default, not termination for convenience against this team, generically does that operate as a black mark against them or anyone else when it comes time to consider the bid for a new contract?

Mrs. SPECTOR. Their past performance is certainly looked at when we award new contracts. That is certainly a consideration in the award of new contracts.

Mr. SCHIFF. I thank the witnesses very much. Thank you, Mr. Chairman.

Mr. CONYERS. Thank you, Mr. Schiff.

The distinguished gentleman from Oklahoma, Mr. English.

Mr. ENGLISH. Thank you, Mr. Chairman.

Mrs. Spector, with regard to aircraft for the Navy, how many companies do we have that bid for this particular contract?

Mrs. SPECTOR. There were two teams of contractors, four contractors altogether in the form of——

Mr. ENGLISH. So other than this team, there was only one other team?

Mrs. SPECTOR. One other team that competed for this particular one, as I understand it.

Mr. ENGLISH. With regard to other aircraft that the Navy or Air Force is looking at for the future, roughly how many companies would you say will be bidding for those contracts?

Mrs. SPECTOR. There are five to seven aircraft companies that normally bid. When I say five to seven, some aren't as interested as they used to be in our business, but five to seven aircraft companies normally bid, assuming we get no foreign contractors interested or that there aren't other business arrangements made.

Mr. ENGLISH. So if we have five to seven, roughly speaking, in this country, that's not many, is it?

Mrs. SPECTOR. No, it's not.

Mr. ENGLISH. Are we getting into a position that the Department of Defense feels that it cannot allow one of these companies to go under?

Mrs. SPECTOR. I wouldn't say that. In fact, one of our large contractors is operating in chapter 11, so I don't know that we would say that. If anything, we're also concerned there may not be enough business for all of them. There are many concerns with the aerospace industry.

Mr. ENGLISH. The point that I am making is that if we get down to the point where you've got one, two, or maybe three companies and that's all we've got producing aircraft for the Air Force and for the Navy, then we're into a situation where in fact there is a serious question, from a technological standpoint, whether we're going to be able to continue to advance and produce advanced aircraft to the same degree as we would say today with five to seven?

Mrs. SPECTOR. You're absolutely right. There is also a concern, certainly on my part, that we treat our contractors fairly and that we don't take advantage of them when they're losing money on our contracts.

Mr. ENGLISH. I appreciate that. The fact of the matter is it seems to me, and maybe we're down to the point that no matter how badly you screw up if you're a contractor, you're pretty much assured Uncle Sam isn't going to let you go under because we got to have you. We can't afford to let you go under; there isn't anybody there to take your place. Certainly in this kind of situation, that comes to bear. Are we just down to the point that we've got such a small number of contractors, the U.S. Government can't allow these contractors to go under, we've got to have them, and no matter what they do, we're going to keep them afloat?

Mrs. SPECTOR. Not in every instance, but that might be a consideration on a case-by-case basis.

Mr. ENGLISH. I was wondering about this particular case. This scenario comes to mind in this particular case. Can you tell us what criteria was used in making this decision, the specific criteria that was used in making this decision?

Mrs. SPECTOR. In making this specific decision, the criteria used were the amount and the fact that it was owed at all were in dispute. Also, the fact that we believed neither of these contractors could afford to pay it back and were we to insist on repayment, that as a minimum, they might have had difficulty with their banks because it would have put the companies in a tenuous financial situation. Worse case, it's conceivable if we insisted on the immediate repayment, they might have gone into chapter 11.

That was our pattern of thinking. It would not have been advantageous to the Department of Defense nor to either of these contractors. There would have been a period of possible disarray during a war—we were at war at that time—and that it would not have been to our advantage to bring about that sequence of events.

Mr. ENGLISH. So in effect, we did have discussion. In this particular instance, we can't afford to let them go broke?

Mrs. SPECTOR. It was more that the chapter 11 would not serve the U.S. Government.

Mr. ENGLISH. Well, what's the difference?

Mrs. SPECTOR. No difference.

Mr. ENGLISH. We can't afford to let them go broke.

Mrs. SPECTOR. It would not be prudent.

Mr. ENGLISH. They've got us over a barrel? We're stuck? We've got to keep them afloat, no matter how bad they are, no matter how much they screw up, no matter how much they overcharge, we can't afford to allow them to go broke?

Mrs. SPECTOR. There was an earlier decision that said we're not going to provide relief on this fixed price contract to enable them to keep performing. That was a decision that was made by the Secretary, so we didn't do what's known as a "bailout" on this contract. We terminated it for default when they were not performing on time.

However, this is merely a deferment of a debt that if pressed would have guaranteed—or we thought might have guaranteed—that we would have never have been paid back. So I can't say that we would have done it if we didn't need them. We mostly do this for small and small disadvantaged businesses. We mostly do it because the Government doesn't take advantage of its contractors when they can't afford to repay and if the amount is in dispute. We don't force them to pay when they can't afford it.

It applies all of the time to all of our contractors and mostly we do it for contractors that arguably are not needed for the defense base. It's for small and small disadvantaged contractors that we usually do this.

Mr. ENGLISH. Well, since the analogy was made with regard to agriculture, I am on the Agriculture Committee. I do chair the subcommittee over Farmer's Home and I can guarantee you they don't do business that way. I'll guarantee you that if a farmer can't pay, most likely he's going to get foreclosed.

Now, we do have a situation if it's cheaper for the Federal Government, well, we'll try to arrange some kind of write-down and make some kind of adjustment, but that isn't what we're talking about, what's cheaper for the Federal Government in this particular case, are we?

Mrs. SPECTOR. Yes, it is.

Mr. ENGLISH. Can you explain that?

Mrs. SPECTOR. Yes, I can. Both of the contractors are performing several of our contracts on which they are taking big losses. In the case of one of them, they are now losing about $900 million on at least three of our contracts.

We believe that if they were to go into chapter 11, it's possible that they would not have continued performing those contracts at those prices and we would have had to reform the contracts and pay more money for them. So that, yes, it is cheaper to have done this than to force them into chapter 11.

Mr. ENGLISH. In those particular cases then, what were the losses going to be? Give me the magnitude of the loss? What is the bottom line from an accounting standpoint?

Mrs. SPECTOR. I don't know the answer. I know it on one or two of them, but I don't know the aggregate amount of their losses, but——

Mr. ENGLISH. Well, I have a hard time really believing that this was what we came down to, trying to do what's cheapest for the taxpayer because then you've got to weigh down what is the bottom line from an accounting standpoint; where are we in black and white; what's it going to cost us if we let these folks go under; and what is it going to cost us if we have to bail them out? Where is the taxpayer better off?

Mrs. SPECTOR. The amounts, I suspect, for both contractors would have been in excess of the $1.35 billion.

Mr. ENGLISH. But see that's what troubles me, you suspect. You should know.

Mrs. SPECTOR. I do know that it would have been in excess of that amount.

Mr. ENGLISH. You can't give me the numbers.

Mrs. SPECTOR. I don't have them here today, sir.

Mr. ENGLISH. Can you give me a ballpark figure, can you come within $100 million either way?

Mrs. SPECTOR. No, I can't right now.

Mr. ENGLISH. If you can't come within $100 million, I've got to really believe that was not a serious criteria in making this decision.

Mrs. SPECTOR. It was, sir.

Mr. ENGLISH. Well, there's one way we can get to the bottom of this, Mr. Chairman. I understand that you all got into this a little bit earlier and that is the question of documentation. I see no way to resolve this matter from the standpoint of the Congress making an evaluation unless we have the documentation.

Will you provide the documentation to this committee so it can be determined whether or not this decision was made in the best interests of the taxpayers?

Mr. TROSCH. I think we've just had that discussion earlier with the chairman.

Mr. ENGLISH. What was your response?

Mr. TROSCH. I think we have worked out what our next step is in terms of identifying to the chairman what the basis is to satisfy the questions that you're going to have.

Mr. ENGLISH. Well, Mr. Chairman, I certainly don't want to step in if you've worked out some arrangement, but it just seems to me there's not a question of you working out an arrangement. The chairman has requested that you turn the documents over to the chairman and let this committee determine what took place. Will you or will you not turn over the documents, answer me, yes or no?

Mr. TROSCH. Certainly the documents that deal with——

Mr. ENGLISH. Is that a yes or no?

Mr. TROSCH. I think my answer is a yes, but.

Mr. ENGLISH. Well, Mr. Chairman, like I said, I certainly appreciate your situation. I've got to say that I think you're being a bit unreasonable about this. If you, in fact, are confident of the decisions that you made, you should be delighted to turn the documents over to the chairman and certainly allow the committee to make the determination. I'd think you'd be anxious to do that.

Mr. CONYERS. Would the gentleman yield?

Mr. ENGLISH. Yes, Mr. Chairman.

Mr. CONYERS. If I might observe, this committee does not move precipitously on the important question of issuing subpoenas to enforce compliance with documents and consistent with that policy, since there has been a claim it wasn't clear what we wanted, we're going to enter into negotiations.

I have asked, I would say to my friend from Oklahoma, that by Monday we have this matter cleared up. If there's a question of our legislative authority or statutory right to these documents, the care in which this committee is historically known for treating sensitive information, we'd be happy to cooperate.

Beyond that, we can negotiate from now on but there is an end to which we come in these matters and we have a way of testing our right to these documents. As most people in the executive branch know, the Government Operations Committee has very little reluctance about that. Our jurisdiction would be effectively crippled if sensitive, proprietary information was a test as to whether we should be entrusted with this information, and I appreciate the gentleman raising this question once more.

Mr. ENGLISH. I can only say to our witnesses that you should be very thankful you've got a kind and understanding chairman here. I just want to say, Mr. Chairman, if your patience wears thin, you let me know. I'll be happy to move for the subpoena if you'd like for someone to make that motion.

Mr. TROSCH. Mr. English, we do appreciate the chairman's kindness, cooperation, and consideration. We also, as we said earlier, and I believe it may have been before you arrived, we welcome the opportunity to explain and to justify how we arrived at our decision.

Documents that we prepared ourselves, documents that assess the balance, the pros and the cons, all of our own documents that we worked up, we have no reservation whatsoever in disclosing to the committee, to its staff, to the GAO, to anyone.

We did receive some extremely sensitive documents from the corporations in question, documents that could well impair their ability to compete fairly in a worldwide market and it's with respect to those documents that we are very, very sensitive in terms of what happens to them, but we welcome our opportunity to explain to the chairman and to work out with the committee how we can satisfy the committee's concerns that we've done the right thing. We believe that we have, and we believe we can satisfy you.

Mr. ENGLISH. Mr. Chairman, just one final comment, if I could. I just want to say that as I said, the chairman is kind, understanding, and patient. I don't know how long his patience will go. I would suggest to you that you be very forthcoming and very eager in providing the information. If he's not, some of the rest of us on this committee are not as kind and understanding and patient. I, for one, am going to be doing all I can to make sure that all the information that this committee needs to deal with this problem is forthcoming. I'm going to give the chairman every bit of support that I possibly can. So Mr. Chairman, you just let me know whenever your patience wears thin, and we'll see if we can take other steps. I don't think a subpoena is out of the question at all.

Mr. CONYERS. Well, might I say to the gentleman from Oklahoma, when I said negotiate, I meant to keep open the discussion of which documents we want. Our authority is not negotiable and we're not here to work out a deal. We either have the right to these documents or we don't. If we don't, I'd be the first to admit it and find some other way to do it.

But obviously I think perhaps counsel may not be familiar with the line of cases that back up the Government Operations Committee, and to that extent, we're going to make our information available to him. I thank the gentleman.

I'd like to recognize the gentleman from the Armed Services Committee, a former member, Mr. Ireland, for 5 minutes.

Mr. IRELAND. Thank you, Mr. Chairman.

Mrs. Spector, it's my understanding that at the point at which this contract originated, you were read into the program and asked to make a decision whether it was the correct thing to do to enter into this fixed price contract within a 24-hour period, is that correct?

Mrs. SPECTOR. It wasn't exactly a decision; it was a recommendation to the Under Secretary, but yes, I was read into it.

Mr. IRELAND. You were read into the program and asked to give your recommendation 24 hours later, roughly speaking?

Mrs. SPECTOR. Yes, Mr. Ireland.

Mr. IRELAND. It is also my understanding that your recommendation was that we should not enter into a fixed price contract, is that right?

Mrs. SPECTOR. I expressed reservations about the type of contract for this type of effort.

Mr. IRELAND. And you presented that in writing to the Assistant Secretary of Defense, Dr. Costello?

Mrs. SPECTOR. Under Secretary, yes, sir.

Mr. IRELAND. Under Secretary, excuse me. Your recommendation was this was not a proper contract?

Mrs. SPECTOR. I expressed reservations about the type of contract.

Mr. IRELAND. Was there any discussion about your recommendation?

Mrs. SPECTOR. Not with Dr. Costello, there was not.

Mr. IRELAND. Was there any discussion with anybody else about your recommendations?

Mrs. SPECTOR. Yes.

Mr. IRELAND. With who?

Mrs. SPECTOR. With the Navy.

Mr. IRELAND. With who in the Navy? You've got to understand that as you well know, because you and I have discussed before, I'm interested in people. I get up to here and all this committee here has heard from any of the three of you on the witness stand is "we" this, "we" this, "we this" and that avoids responsibility. I want to know who. You wrote a recommendation, you gave it to Dr. Costello, you gave it to the Navy; who in the Navy did you give it to?

Mrs. SPECTOR. I discussed the recommendations or the reservations with Admiral Morris at the time.

Mr. IRELAND. With Admiral Morris at the time. He had that document, is that correct?

Mrs. SPECTOR. No, he did not have the document.

Mr. IRELAND. Who has the document?

Mrs. SPECTOR. The Under Secretary. It was a special access document at the time, sir, there were two copies that I knew of. One went to the Under Secretary and one was retained in the file of the office that maintained the special access documents in the Office of the Secretary of Defense.

Mr. IRELAND. You're aware that—the Armed Services Committee has asked for those documents, right?

Mrs. SPECTOR. Yes, sir.

Mr. IRELAND. I would ask, if permissible, that a copy of it be furnished to this committee as well.

Mr. CONYERS. Would you agree to extending the supplying of those documents?

Mrs. SPECTOR. I believe Mr. O'Donnell is currently assessing the furnishing of those and certainly if we furnish it to Armed Services, you may have it as well.

Mr. CONYERS. So Armed Services is in limbo on this also?

Mr. IRELAND. We have gotten some of the same kind of answers about getting things from the DOD that you have, which is perhaps some comfort to you, Mr. Chairman. We'll bird dog this one if you'll bird dog the other one.

Admiral Morris was the only one that you discussed your reservations with in the Navy, remembering you're under oath here now, because I'm deep into who and we're going to find out who is in some of these things.

Mrs. SPECTOR. I'm just trying to recollect. I met with approximately four or five people at the Navy on this issue. I asked a number of questions at the meeting. Whether I discussed my reservations specifically there, I may have.

Mr. IRELAND. And who are some of those four or five people?

Mrs. SPECTOR. They were the contracting officer, the lawyer——

Mr. IRELAND. Put names on those. Times change, I want to know who they were. The contracting officer?

Mrs. SPECTOR. The contracting officer was named Bonnie Jones. The lawyer was named Margaret Olsen. The program manager was Larry Elberfeld and Admiral Morris. I don't recall if there was anybody else present.

Mr. IRELAND. I see. To follow up, I think the committee chairman and others have done an excellent job of outlining to you the need of this committee and indeed the Congress to be able to examine materials which you used to make your decision to grant this generous deferment. That's a great deal of material and I think it's essential that the committee have it.

At the same time, there was a decision made which again each of you have used the word "we." I would like to know if that decision as you made it was put in writing. Was it put in writing, Admiral Morris? Yes or no.

Admiral MORRIS. Let me understand the question, Mr. Ireland.

Mr. IRELAND. Let me explain the question. You got all this material that we've had a wide-ranging discussion on of proprietary interest, but you all used the "we" and we are going to find out who "we" is, a decision was made to defer—extend this deferment. You signed it as a matter of fact. Now that decision, was that a bunch of the boys in the backroom clucking it up a little bit or did somebody write up a memorandum that says, this is what ought to be done, Admiral Morris ought to sign this, and these are the reasons, and that circulated and people get together and say, if so, was there a written recommendation, a piece of paper, and who examined it, who discussed it, who signed off on it, and whose decision was it? I don't want any more "we's," no more "we's." Was there a piece of paper, yes or no?

Admiral MORRIS. I did not prepare a piece of paper.

Mr. IRELAND. Did you see a piece of paper?

Admiral MORRIS. I signed the demand letter. I recommended that the deferral be approved on the basis——

Mr. IRELAND. Was it a recommendation in writing?
Admiral MORRIS. I don't believe so, Mr. Ireland.
Mr. IRELAND. And who did you recommend it to?
Admiral MORRIS. I discussed it in conjunction with the——
Mr. IRELAND. Who did you discuss it with?
Admiral MORRIS. I discussed it with my in-house attorney, I discussed it with the Assistant Secretary for Financial Management and staff——
Mr. IRELAND. Who was that?
Admiral MORRIS. Mr. McCormack. With his staff, individuals, and I took part in several meetings with Eleanor and her staff.
Mr. IRELAND. Whose decision was it to make? Whose decision was it?
Admiral MORRIS. The deferment agreement was signed on behalf of the Department by the Assistant Secretary of the Navy for Financial Management, Mr. McCormack.
Mr. IRELAND. In other words, it was his decision? You're saying he signed it, was it his decision?
Admiral MORRIS. Yes, sir.
Mr. IRELAND. OK, he's responsible, a man named McCormack. It was his decision, is that correct?
Mrs. SPECTOR. That is correct. There was discussion certainly at the Secretary of Defense level on the subject but it was his final decision.
Mr. IRELAND. And that's the proper place for it. In other words, he's accountable for it. If we want to go and say, who is accountable for this deferment, it's his?
Mrs. SPECTOR. He signed it, yes, sir.
Mr. IRELAND. And you all discussed it with him, right?
Mrs. SPECTOR. Yes. The analysis was certainly discussed with him.
Mr. IRELAND. You all are very confident that your analysis of this was a proper one based on this material. Was all this analysis and this discussion done orally and did anybody put anything down and say, Mr. McCormack, this is our recommendation?
Mrs. SPECTOR. There were briefings. It's in the form of briefing charts and there were briefings provided. There's extensive data. There is a lot of——
Mr. IRELAND. Oh, I know there's a lot of data and we're going to see it. I know that.
Mrs. SPECTOR. There were briefings provided, culling through that data——
Mr. IRELAND. And who made those briefings?
Mrs. SPECTOR. I made some of them.
Mr. IRELAND. You made them and you wrote them up and they were in a memorandum form?
Mrs. SPECTOR. No, they were in briefing form.
Mr. IRELAND. What is briefing form? It looks like it's something nobody can be responsible for.
Mrs. SPECTOR. Vugraphs with data. That's not the case, sir. The briefing was provided by several people on the condition of McDonnell Douglas and General Dynamics——
Mr. IRELAND. I know that you got that information but I want to know—you say you gave a briefing, did you hand out a memoran-

dum to these people saying—I had to present a lot of loans to a loan committee at a bank in my younger days and I had to come in there with a piece of paper saying this is it, this is how I analyzed these financial statements, and this is my recommendation. Sometimes they bought it, sometimes they didn't.

Mr. McCormack is on the hook, as far as what you all have said here, for having made this decision based on information you gave him. In what form did you give it to him and can we have it, your recommendation?

Mrs. SPECTOR. They were provided in briefings.

Mr. IRELAND. They?

Mrs. SPECTOR. The data.

Mr. IRELAND. You provided?

Mrs. SPECTOR. Yes—that had recommendations that the conclusion of the briefings and——

Mr. IRELAND. OK. Where is that, your recommendations?

Mrs. SPECTOR. I have them.

Mr. IRELAND. Would you please submit them to this committee?

Mrs. SPECTOR. They will certainly be part of the data.

Mr. IRELAND. Because when the chairman gets this data, he's going to want to look at it and come up with what his analysis is and we want to compare it to your analysis. See what I mean?

Mrs. SPECTOR. I understand.

Mr. IRELAND. The GAO earlier, we asked them the question—they were not privy to your recommendations.

Mrs. SPECTOR. I believe they are now.

Mr. IRELAND. That's distressing to me that they were not.

Mrs. SPECTOR. That's not accurate at this point. They are privy to our recommendations and to all of our data. We've shown everything to them on Tuesday. Everything that we had was shown to them; they did not take it away but it was all shown to GAO representatives on Tuesday of this week—all of the briefings, all of the recommendations.

Mr. IRELAND. All those recommendations.

Mrs. SPECTOR. Yes.

Mr. IRELAND. Well, I understand you had been told in 24 hours you had to say whether it was worthwhile going into a $4.4 billion contract, I understand the difficulty. Here we have multibillion dollar operations, multibillion dollar audit procedures and we're giving people 36 and 24 hours to do it which in itself is a condemnation of this whole matter.

So you recommended to Mr. McCormack in your recommendation based on this material, that this thing be signed, right?

Mrs. SPECTOR. The service Secretaries recommended to the Deputy Secretary——

Mr. IRELAND. Wait a minute. You just a minute ago told me you, in your analysis, recommended, right, and we're going to see that?

Mrs. SPECTOR. That's correct.

Mr. IRELAND. You sent that recommendation to whom, just Mr. McCormack?

Mrs. SPECTOR. The briefings were given——

Mr. IRELAND. I don't care where the briefings are concerned, what's the paper—your recommendation went to whom?

Mrs. SPECTOR. They were given to representatives of the three services.

Mr. IRELAND. Representatives of the three services?

Mrs. SPECTOR. Yes, and the Under Secretary of Defense.

Mr. IRELAND. Who were the representatives of the Army and why would they want to know this? You said three services.

Mrs. SPECTOR. These contractors do business with all three services and we were initially, before this deferment came up, concerned with losses on contracts involving at least one of the other services, so there had been discussions with them before.

In addition, the three services reviewed the financial data to be certain that the information provided to us regarding their contracts was, in their opinion, accurate, that we were getting information that they agreed was correct. So they had been included in the discussions.

Mr. IRELAND. But that, as we all know, is just a little piece of these companies business, but you had the analysis of the whole company, right? You did the analysis of each of these two full companies and you presented a recommendation to defer, right?

Mrs. SPECTOR. The analysis was done by my office and, yes, I certainly participated in it and I presented——

Mr. IRELAND. But it's your responsibility and your recommendation, don't pawn it off on these other people.

Mrs. SPECTOR. No, I'm not pawning it off on anybody. I believe it was very good analysis and I'm proud of it.

Mr. IRELAND. And you gave it to these three service Secretaries?

Mrs. SPECTOR. It was given to representatives of the services. I didn't personally brief the service Secretaries.

Mr. IRELAND. What was their responsibility? What is their authority? Do you remember who they were?

Mrs. SPECTOR. Yes. It was given to many people over a period of time, but yes, I certainly remember——

Mr. IRELAND. And those people looked at what you did and then they recommended to McCormack too?

Mrs. SPECTOR. There were recommendations on the part of the three service Secretaries and the controller to the Deputy Secretary of Defense.

Mr. IRELAND. That's McCormack?

Mrs. SPECTOR. No. In this case, it was——

Mr. IRELAND. I thought you said McCormack was the one that was responsible.

Mrs. SPECTOR. He signed the deferment agreement——

Mr. IRELAND. Well, who is responsible? Can't you understand I'm trying to find out who is the person that made this decision?

Mrs. SPECTOR. Mr. McCormack made the decision.

Mr. IRELAND. Mr. McCormack.

Mrs. SPECTOR. But it was supported by the whole Department.

Mr. IRELAND. And each one of these other people recommended it?

Mrs. SPECTOR. Yes.

Mr. IRELAND. Did they sign anything saying, I recommend this?

Mrs. SPECTOR. I believe they did.

Mr. IRELAND. What is it that they signed that said, I recommend this?

Mrs. SPECTOR. They signed a recommendation to the——
Mr. IRELAND. The recommendation, and what would that be, a note on your recommendation or what?
Mrs. SPECTOR. It was a document recommending that the deferment——
Mr. IRELAND. Where is that document?
Mrs. SPECTOR. It's within the Department.
Mr. IRELAND. Would you furnish that to this committee?
Mrs. SPECTOR. I'll have to defer to my counsel.
Mr. TROSCH. That will be part of the package. Anything that the chairman wants to consider as part of the discussions we have, that will be a part.
Mr. CONYERS. Thank you very much.
Mr. IRELAND. Thank you, Mr. Chairman.
Mr. CONYERS. I want to thank the gentleman from the Armed Services Committee whose experience in this matter has been augmented by having the witnesses come before him and we appreciate him joining us.
I have one question and so does Mr. Shays. The one question that I need to get on the record is, Mrs. Spector—and we thank you for the prolonged discussion that this subject matter has generated—have you talked to the two contractors here today about their cooperation with this committee in terms of the hearing?
Mrs. SPECTOR. No, sir.
Mr. CONYERS. Or have you talked with them in any way about their testimony that they would give here prior to today?
Mrs. SPECTOR. I believe I spoke to the lawyer at General Dynamics about the hearing, but it was fairly general.
Mr. CONYERS. But not to the two witnesses from the corporations that are present?
Mrs. SPECTOR. I've spoken to neither of the witnesses about the hearing or about their testimony.
Mr. CONYERS. Thank you very much.
Mr. Shays.
Mr. SHAYS. Thank you.
Mrs. Spector, to your credit, if you did write a memo questioning whether it was a fixed contract, you should have been congratulated for that and you're taking a little heat on this but if in fact that exists, and I say in fact because I would like to see that document, I have to tell you I feel like we're playing a game and it's a very serious game. But it's as if we don't ask the right question, we don't get the answer to a question.
It would seem to me that you voluntarily would have wanted this committee to see your analysis and we shouldn't have had Mr. Ireland have to discover, in a sense, that there is this document.
I still don't know what briefing means. I want to be clear, does a briefing mean a memo with a specific title or does briefing mean slides?
Mrs. SPECTOR. Sir, there are two different documents involved here. One document Mr. Ireland is referring to I wrote 3 years ago.
Mr. SHAYS. I understand that one and that one you will give us because that's of interest to this committee. Then the other document is the so-called briefings as to the deferment?

Mrs. SPECTOR. Yes, and it's hard copies of what you might say are vugraph format of recommendations and data.

Mr. HORTON. Would you yield?

Mr. SHAYS. Yes.

Mr. HORTON. I don't think she has the authority to give us that letter.

Mrs. SPECTOR. I don't right now.

Mr. HORTON. It's in two different places. There has been a request, as I understood from what Congressman Ireland said, by the Armed Services Committee requesting that and that has not been determined yet.

Mrs. SPECTOR. That's correct.

Mr. TROSCH. That's correct. The letter——

Mr. HORTON. That's what we're talking about, the first letter. She wrote it but she doesn't have a copy of it, and she won't make the decision as to whether or not it would be furnished.

Mr. SHAYS. You know, I hear what you're saying. I guess even if she's not going to give it to us, or even if she doesn't have the authority, she certainly has the ability to tell us without our asking that such a document exists.

Mr. HORTON. Well, she did do that.

Mr. SHAYS. In the questioning of Mr. Ireland, but we would not have learned had Mr. Ireland not asked the question.

Mr. HORTON. We knew that. We have that in our briefing papers.

Mr. SHAYS. Excuse me. I am talking about the briefing comments suggesting that the deferment be postponed, that there be a deferment. That's the document I'm talking about.

Mrs. SPECTOR. I'm sorry, I misunderstood which document you meant.

Mr. SHAYS. That is the document I am talking about, and I did not read it in any of my briefing papers.

Mrs. SPECTOR. I'm not sure what your question is.

Mr. SHAYS. My question is simply this. When you say briefings, it means it is one document, correct?

Mrs. SPECTOR. I believe I have two briefings, two separate briefings.

Mr. SHAYS. Regarding the deferment?

Mrs. SPECTOR. Yes, sir, regarding the deferment and some other issues.

Mr. SHAYS. I just want to make sure we know there are two documents and those are two documents that we both want and my question to you is, I want to know if it is in slide form or in memorandum form?

Mrs. SPECTOR. It's in vugraph format, slide form.

Mr. SHAYS. Thank you. Now, the only other question I want to ask you is, and I want to ask both of you for the record, do you, Mrs. Spector, agree that the Navy's contract with McDonnell Douglas and General Dynamics was in default and needed to be canceled?

Mrs. SPECTOR. In my opinion, having read what the Navy wrote in support of what they did, I agree with what the Navy did. It was a contracting officer decision at this point and it was Admiral Morris——

Mr. SHAYS. I understand but you are right closely involved in this whole process and your view is important.
Admiral Morris.
Admiral MORRIS. Absolutely. I took the action, sir.
Mr. SHAYS. Thank you, Mr. Chairman.
Mr. CONYERS. Thank you very much.
Mrs. Spector, because of the fact that you did talk to the attorney from General Dynamics about this hearing and before it, what was the nature of that discussion?
Mrs. SPECTOR. Generally——
Mr. CONYERS. If you can remember specifically what you talked about?
Mrs. SPECTOR. Generally the subject of what would be included in our prepared statement.
Mr. CONYERS. More or less how to proceed?
Mrs. SPECTOR. No, not really. Just that what did we think the hearing was about and what were we going to say in our prepared statement, and I generally outlined that, that we planned to just state the facts of what had occurred and that was the entire substance. It was the first time I'd ever spoken to the man and it was the entire substance of our discussion.
Mr. CONYERS. Was it in person or by phone?
Mrs. SPECTOR. No, it was on the phone.
Mr. TROSCH. Mr. Chairman, let me say because you're talking on this subject, I had some conversations I believe yesterday with the attorney for McDonnell Douglas. They had to do with the nature of the information that McDonnell Douglas had submitted to us and its sensitivity to the corporation, and essentially the conversations that we had dealt with the concerns of the company over their disclosure.
Mr. CONYERS. Thank you. You did not talk to any of the witnesses that are here from the company?
Mr. TROSCH. I'm not sure who the witnesses from the companies are going to be. I believe that the general counsel for McDonnell Douglas may accompany them, but I have not seen the witness list.
Mr. CONYERS. Did you give them any direction in terms of what they might be prepared to relate to the committee?
Mr. TROSCH. No, sir. It's not my position to give them direction. I was very much concerned though about the sensitivity and about the discussions we were going to have today about the sensitivity of the documentation and I wanted to reconfirm the nature of those documents with the company and their concerns over the documents and what they felt potential impact might be if the documents were disclosed.
Mr. CONYERS. Thank you very much. You've been very, very helpful.
[Mrs. Spector's submissions to additional questions of Congressman Conyers follow:]

INSERT FOR THE RECORD							
HOUSE	APPROPRIATIONS COMMITTEE	HOUSE	ARMED SERVICES COMMITTEE	X	HOUSE	OTHER	Govt Operations
SENATE		SENATE			SENATE		
HEARING DATE 11 April 91	TRANSCRIPT PAGE NO.	LINE NO.			INSERT NO. Question No. 1		

Financial Analysis

Congressman Conyers. Who specifically made the analysis regarding deferment? What was the result for each contractor?

Mrs. Spector. Ms. Carol Covey, Deputy Director for Cost, Pricing, and Finance in the Office of the Director of Defense Procurement performed the analysis. The analysis focused on the financially weaker contractor, McDonnell Douglas. The analysis found that McDonnell Douglas did not have sufficient credit or liquid assets available to repay its share of the debt. Additionally, the company had been notified by some of its banks that the termination of the A-12 contract may have resulted in a material adverse change in the company's financial condition, which could preclude the company from borrowing any additional amounts on current lines of credit. General Dynamics appeared to have adequate credit available to repay its share of the debt, but the company had recently had its credit rating downgraded and it would likely have been downgraded further to the "junk bond" level if the Department demanded immediate repayment, which would reduce the company's access to financial markets and leave it less capable of supporting current operations.

INSERT FOR THE RECORD						
HOUSE / SENATE	APPROPRIATIONS COMMITTEE	HOUSE / SENATE	ARMED SERVICES COMMITTEE	X HOUSE / SENATE	OTHER Govt Operations	
HEARING DATE 11 April 1991	TRANSCRIPT PAGE NO.	LINE NO.		INSERT NO. Question No. 2		

Financial Analysis

Congressman Conyers. How long did it take to perform the analysis used in making the decision to defer the amount owed?

Mrs. Spector. Approximately one week. However, the Department had been tracking the financial capability of these firms for about five months because of their deteriorating financial conditions.

INSERT FOR THE RECORD						
HOUSE	APPROPRIATIONS COMMITTEE	HOUSE	ARMED SERVICES COMMITTEE X	HOUSE	OTHER Govt Operations
SENATE		SENATE		SENATE	
HEARING DATE 11 April 1991	TRANSCRIPT PAGE NO.	LINE NO.		INSERT NO. Question No. 3	

Deferment

Congressman Conyers. On what date did you inform the contractors that the deferment had been granted?
Mrs. Spector. The Navy informed the contractors on February 5, 1991.

INSERT FOR THE RECORD							
HOUSE	APPROPRIATIONS COMMITTEE	HOUSE	ARMED SERVICES COMMITTEE	X	HOUSE	OTHER	
SENATE		SENATE			SENATE	Govt Operations	
HEARING DATE 11 April 1991	TRANSCRIPT PAGE NO.	LINE NO.		INSERT NO. Question No. 4			

Deferment Standards

Congressman Conyers. What standard did you use to decide whether to grant a deferment?

Mrs. Spector. Subpart 32.6 of the Federal Acquisition Regulation sets forth standards to be used to determine if a deferment of collection should be granted. When a contractor has appealed the debt in accordance with the procedures of the Disputes clause of the contract, the Department may grant a deferment if the contractor is considered to be financially weak; additionally, consideration must be given to achieving a reasonable balance of the need for Government security against loss with undue hardship on the contractor. The Department determined that the companies would be unable to repay the amount owed at this time and that the contractors' operations under national defense contracts would be seriously impaired if the Department did not grant a deferment.

INSERT FOR THE RECORD						
HOUSE	APPROPRIATIONS COMMITTEE	HOUSE	ARMED SERVICES COMMITTEE	X HOUSE	OTHER	
SENATE		SENATE		SENATE	Govt Operations	
HEARING DATE 11 April 1991	TRANSCRIPT PAGE NO.	LINE NO.	INSERT NO. Question No. 5			

Potential for Bankruptcy

Congressman Conyers. Was the deferment warranted if there would have been no resulting bankruptcy?

Mrs. Spector. Yes, the deferment was warranted because the companies intended to appeal the debt, were not able to repay the Department $1.352 billion, were financially weak, and operations under national defense contracts would have been seriously impaired if the Department had not granted a deferment. An additional consideration was whether deferment of the debt was advisable to avoid possible overcollection by DoD pending the resolution of the appeal. The outcome of litigation is always uncertain. As a result of the litigation, it may be determined that the companies do not owe DoD a significant portion of the amount currently believed to be due. In as much as the companies are challenging the termination for default decision and are unable to repay the amount demanded, we believe it would be unfair to force them to repay.

INSERT FOR THE RECORD							
HOUSE	APPROPRIATIONS COMMITTEE	HOUSE	ARMED SERVICES COMMITTEE	X	HOUSE	OTHER	
SENATE		SENATE			SENATE	Govt Operations	
HEARING DATE 11 April 1991	TRANSCRIPT PAGE NO.	LINE NO.		INSERT NO. Question No. 6			

Interest Payments

    Congressman Conyers. On what basis did you waive the interest payments?
    Mrs. Spector. Interest payments were not waived. Interest will be collected along with the principal.

INSERT FOR THE RECORD							
HOUSE	APPROPRIATIONS COMMITTEE	HOUSE	ARMED SERVICES COMMITTEE	X HOUSE	OTHER Govt Operations
SENATE		SENATE		SENATE	
HEARING DATE 11 April 1991	TRANSCRIPT PAGE NO.	LINE NO.		INSERT NO. Question No. 7	

Executive Bonuses

Congressman Conyers. Is it the position of the Department of Defense that the executives of these two companies should receive cash bonuses adding up to millions of dollars when there are no interest payments being made?

Mrs. Spector. Interest will be collected along with the principal as soon as a decision is made by the Claims Court on the contractors' appeal. In the meantime, the companies are required to maintain sufficient assets or available credit to pay the Government the full amount of the debt. The companies' overall compensation should be adequate to attract and maintain good executives.

INSERT FOR THE RECORD						
HOUSE	APPROPRIATIONS COMMITTEE	HOUSE	ARMED SERVICES COMMITTEE	X HOUSE	OTHER	
SENATE		SENATE		SENATE	Govt Operations	
HEARING DATE	TRANSCRIPT PAGE NO.	LINE NO.		INSERT NO.		
11 April 1991				Question No. 8		

Financial Data

Congressman Conyers. Did anyone at the Department of Defense suggest in any way to the contractors that they not share the financial data with the Subcommittee?

Mrs. Spector. We do not know of any person within the Department of Defense who suggested to the contractors that they not share financial data with the Subcommittee.

INSERT FOR THE RECORD						
HOUSE / SENATE	APPROPRIATIONS COMMITTEE	HOUSE / SENATE	ARMED SERVICES COMMITTEE	X	HOUSE / SENATE	OTHER Govt Operations
HEARING DATE 11 April 1991	TRANSCRIPT PAGE NO.	LINE NO.		INSERT NO. Question No. 9		

Reprocurement Rights

Congressman Conyers. Does the Department of Defense intend to pursue its reprocurement rights under the contract? If not, why not?

Mrs. Spector. The contractors' liability for reprocurement costs will depend on the similarity between the AX and A-12 scopes of work. The concept for the AX has not yet been established.

INSERT FOR THE RECORD						
HOUSE	APPROPRIATIONS COMMITTEE	HOUSE	ARMED SERVICES COMMITTEE	X HOUSE	OTHER	
SENATE		SENATE		SENATE	Govt Operations	
HEARING DATE 11 April 1991	TRANSCRIPT PAGE NO.	LINE NO.		INSERT NO. Question No. 10		

Contractor Monitoring

Congressman Conyers. What systems are in place to monitor the contractors' financial stability?

Mrs. Spector. The Corporate Administrative Contracting Officers (CACOs) at the two companies regularly monitor financial stability, and obtain the advice and assistance of Defense Contract Audit Agency auditors in order to perform their analyses. Additionally, the Navy contracting officer for the A-12 contract has asked the CACOs to provide periodic status reports to him.

INSERT FOR THE RECORD							
HOUSE	APPROPRIATIONS COMMITTEE	HOUSE	ARMED SERVICES COMMITTEE	X	HOUSE	OTHER	
SENATE		SENATE			SENATE	Govt Operations	
HEARING DATE	TRANSCRIPT PAGE NO.	LINE NO.		INSERT NO.			
11 April 1991				Question No. 11			

Reports

Congressman Conyers. Will you provide those required reports with the Subcommittee? If not, on what legal basis are you withholding them?

Mrs. Spector. The Committee has already been given 52 documents, including those documents on which we relied for our analysis.

INSERT FOR THE RECORD						
HOUSE SENATE	APPROPRIATIONS COMMITTEE	HOUSE SENATE	ARMED SERVICES COMMITTEE	X HOUSE SENATE	OTHER	Govt Operations
HEARING DATE 11 April 1991	TRANSCRIPT PAGE NO.	LINE NO.		INSERT NO. Question No. 12		

Contractor Monitoring

Congressman Conyers. How do you justify granting a deferment to "financially weak" contractors, and then say that you are monitoring their financial stability so that you can demand the money if they show signs of slipping?

Mrs. Spector. The deferment agreement states that it shall remain in effect unless the Government determines, within its sole discretion, that the contractors have failed to diligently pursue their appeal or there is a substantial change in either contractors' financial condition such that deferment is no longer in the best interest of the Government. The change in financial condition envisioned by this provision would be an improvement in financial condition, such that the Department could decide to terminate the deferment agreement and require immediate repayment without placing the companies in financial jeopardy.

INSERT FOR THE RECORD						
HOUSE ☐ SENATE ☐	APPROPRIATIONS COMMITTEE	HOUSE ☐ SENATE ☐	ARMED SERVICES COMMITTEE	X HOUSE ☐ SENATE	OTHER Govt Operations	
HEARING DATE 11 April 1991	TRANSCRIPT PAGE NO.	LINE NO.		INSERT NO. Question No. 13		

Interest

Congressman Conyers. Does the accrued interest compound annually? If not, why not?

Mrs. Spector. In accordance with the Federal Acquisition Regulation (FAR), Federal Agencies <u>charge</u> simple interest on contract debts in accordance with the Interest clause included in contracts (FAR 52.232-17), in the same manner that the Federal Agencies <u>pay</u> simple interest on contractor claims in accordance with the Disputes clause included in contracts (FAR 52.233-1).

Mr. CONYERS. Our final panel consists of the representatives from the two corporations, McDonnell Douglas and General Dynamics, Mr. Herbert Lanese and Mr. Donald W. Putnam. If you gentlemen and your counsel will come forward, I'd like to separate out the counsel from the witnesses so that I can administer the oath to the witnesses.
[Witnesses sworn.]
Mr. CONYERS. Thank you very much. Please be seated.
We have both of your prepared statements and without objection, they will be incorporated in the record. We would ask that you summarize. As you can see, we've gone much longer than we intended to with the previous panel, so your summaries will be helpful to us getting to a few questions that will put to you and that will conclude this hearing for today.
Welcome, and we invite Mr. Lanese to proceed, if you will.

STATEMENT OF HERBERT J. LANESE, SENIOR VICE PRESIDENT, FINANCE, McDONNELL DOUGLAS CORP.

Mr. LANESE. If I may, at the end of my prepared remarks I give a summary paragraph and I'd like to refer to that paragraph, if I may.
Mr. CONYERS. Please do.
Mr. LANESE. It's the final page in the prepared remarks. In summary, I'd like to say that McDonnell Douglas has taken a number of actions to improve its cash situation in order to retain the confidence of its lenders, but nonetheless there was a critical element in maintaining the confidence of our lenders and this deferment agreement played a critical role in that process.
It also played a critical role in the current rating that McDonnell Douglas has received from the rating agencies; namely, Moody's and Standard and Poors, in maintaining our investment grade status. That's very critical if we are to fund the company's needs over the next year.
In addition, our cash outlook, I would say, is improving but it is still very tight. To this committee we supplied some public information which, I believe, consisted of our annual report, and possibly our 10K, as well.
In our annual report, it's very easy to look at the financial condition McDonnell Douglas was in at the end of the year. We had $550 million left in our legal lines of borrowing and it stated in the annual report, which is true, that we anticipated that our borrowing needs would increase through the first 6 months of 1991. That, in fact, has happened and under those same credit agreements as of the end of the first quarter, our remaining borrowing from a legal borrowing standpoint currently is approximately $200 million.
That concludes my summary remarks, Mr. Chairman.
[The prepared statement of Mr. Lanese follows:]

The testimony of

Herbert J. Lanese

Senior Vice President - Finance

McDonnell Douglas Corporation

before

Legislation and National Security Subcommittee

of

The Committee on Government Operations

11 April 1991

My name is Herb Lanese. I am Senior Vice President - Finance for McDonnell Douglas Corporation. I am here to provide testimony requested by the Subcommittee concerning the deferment of the collection of approximately $1.3 billion which the Government has claimed it is owed jointly by McDonnell Douglas Corporation and General Dynamics Corporation as a result of the termination for default by the Government of the A-12 development program. MDC and GD were joint prime contractors for development and initial production of the A-12 stealth aircraft for the Navy. I trust that this testimony will be helpful to the Subcommittee in its consideration of this matter.

The Deferment Agreement was executed on February 5, 1991. It recites that:

(a) the Contracting Officer has demanded payment of $1,352,495,644 arising out of the default of the Contractors;

(b) the Contractors have represented that they will appeal to the Armed Services Board of Contract Appeals or file suit in the Claims Court to contest this default termination;

(c) the Contractors have requested that the Government defer collection of the amount demanded by the Government pending the outcome of the litigation;

(d) the Contractors have presented financial information which shows that, absent deferment, one or both contractors may be placed in a financial condition that could endanger essential defense programs; and

(e) the Contractors are jointly and severally liable under the contract and the Department of Defense has determined that it is not in the best interests of the Government to have either of the Contractors in a financial condition that endangers essential defense programs.

I believe it is important to emphasize that under the Agreement the Government has not waived its rights to any amounts ultimately determined to be due it. The Contractors have also agreed to pay interest from the date of the Agreement at the statutory rate on any such amount and agreed diligently to prosecute the litigation. The Government has an immediate right to enforce collection in case of default and has the right to review the deferment on 1 December 1992 and annually thereafter. The Government also has the right to terminate the Agreement if the litigation is not being diligently pursued or there is a substantial change in the Contractors' financial condition such that deferment is no longer in the best interest of the Government.

The disputed $1.352 billion represents payments under the contract in excess of the price of goods and services delivered and accepted prior to termination. Contractors under fixed price contracts with DoD of the type here involved have normally been paid, on a monthly basis, 80% of the costs they incur in performance of the contract. Such payments are necessitated by the tremendously large expenditures required in performance of the contracts, the extended periods of time before end items are delivered, and the fact that interest payments to finance work in process are not allowable costs under government contracts. At the time of termination of the A-12 contract, the prices for A-12 development effort and Lot 1 production totaled approximately $6.05 billion; the Contractors had been paid approximately $1.335 billion for end items which had been delivered and accepted; and the Contractors had been paid $1.352 billion in progress payments for additional work performed. The Contractors also had incurred an additional $1.42 billion for which they had not been paid. The deferred $1.352 billion had all been spent in performing work under the contract.

The progress payments clause of the contract provides that in the event of termination of the contract for default the Government may demand repayment of progress payments made in excess of the price of delivered items. These amounts are called "unliquidated" progress payments. The A-12 contract also provides that in case of termination of a contract for the convenience of the Government the Contractors will be paid the costs they have incurred in performance of the contract plus an allocable portion of the earnings provided under the contract. Thus, if the Contractors are correct in their belief that the termination for default was not appropriate and will be converted to a termination for convenience of the Government, they are entitled under the termination for convenience provision to retain the progress payments, to receive additional payments for costs not paid by the Government under the progress payments clause, and to be paid a reasonable profit. These amounts are subject to reduction if the contract is determined to have been in an overrun condition at the time of termination. Although the estimated cost at completion exceeds the contract price, the Contractors believe they are entitled to substantial increases in the contract price and prior to contract termination had submitted claims for over $1.4 billion in contract price increases.

The Federal Acquisition Regulations (FAR) provide discretion for the Government to enter into deferment agreements if requested by the contractor when a debt is disputed and in other circumstances. The regulations require contractors requesting deferment to provide information as to financial condition. The essence of the information provided by McDonnell Douglas is reflected in the Company's Annual Report to Shareholders which was publicly released several weeks ago. MDC had $2.97 billion of debt at year end. Approximately $550 million was available to borrow under bank credit agreements and approximately $100 million was available to borrow under an asset backed financing agreement. MDC was financing over $2 billion of Government work in process and inventories and nearly $600 million in Government accounts receivable. This financing primarily had to do with the F-15, F-18 and AV-8B fighters, the T-45 trainer, the Harpoon and Tomahawk missiles and the C-17 transport. As stated in the Annual Report, cash requirements were projected to increase during 1991 as the MD-11 aircraft entered production. In these circumstances, to have paid the Government the disputed $650 million (half of the $1.352 billion claimed by the Government to be owing by the Contractor) obviously would have been extremely difficult, have seriously strained MDC's financial capabilities, and have jeopardized continued performance of other Government contracts.

We believe that there was a more than adequate record for the Department of Defense to determine that, absent deferment, one or both contractors might be placed in a financial condition that could adversely affect critical defense programs. We further believe it would have been grossly inequitable to attempt to enforce collection of such a large disputed amount prior to determination of ultimate liability or settlement.

As a final point, I wish to emphasize that McDonnell Douglas has taken numerous actions to improve its cash flow and retain the confidence of its lenders. A very critical element in maintaining this confidence, and in gaining the recent affirmation for McDonnell Douglas as an investment grade credit by both Moody's and Standard and Poors rating agencies, was the execution of this deferment agreement. Although our cash outlook is improving, we continue to believe this deferment is still very much needed.

Mr. Chairman, this concludes my prepared remarks.

Mr. CONYERS. Thank you very much.
Welcome, Mr. Putnam.

STATEMENT OF DONALD W. PUTNAM, CORPORATE DIRECTOR, CONTRACTS AND TECHNICAL ANALYSIS, GENERAL DYNAMICS CORP.

Mr. PUTNAM. Thank you, sir. My statement primarily recites facts that you've already, I think, heard today. Perhaps I would touch on the point that we did meet the Navy. The date of that meeting was January 16. I don't think that's been entered prior to my statement.

Mr. CONYERS. Who in the Navy?

Mr. PUTNAM. On the 16th of January, sir? We met with the contracting officer, Admiral Morris. I believe at that meeting also—yes, I'm also quite certain—Mr. McCormack attended that meeting and there were members of both of their staffs present.

Mr. CONYERS. Thank you.

Mr. PUTNAM. We consider that our agreement regarding the deferral is completely in accordance with and pursuant to Federal Acquisition Regulations and that it properly protects the interests of the Government and protects our companies as well, and that we think it a proper agreement under the circumstances.

[The prepared statement of Mr. Putnam follows:]

Statement by:

Mr. Donald W. Putnam
Corporate Director, Contracts and Technical Analysis
General Dynamics Corporation

Before the
Subcommittee on Legislation and National Security
House Government Operations Committee

United States House of Representatives

First Session, 102nd Congress

11 April 1991

MR. CHAIRMAN AND MEMBERS OF THE SUBCOMMITTEE:

MY NAME IS DONALD PUTNAM. I AM CORPORATE DIRECTOR OF CONTRACTS AND TECHNICAL ANALYSIS FOR GENERAL DYNAMICS. I AM PLEASED TO BE PRESENT HERE AND TO PRESENT, ON BEHALF OF GENERAL DYNAMICS, THESE BRIEF COMMENTS. IT IS MY UNDERSTANDING THAT IT IS THE INTEREST OF THE SUBCOMMITTEE TO HAVE OUR VIEWS CONCERNING THE DEFERMENT AGREEMENT EXECUTED BETWEEN THE DEPARTMENT OF THE NAVY AND THE A-12 CONTRACTORS, MCDONNELL DOUGLAS AND GENERAL DYNAMICS. THESE COMMENTS ADDRESS THAT SUBJECT.

GENERAL DYNAMICS AND MCDONNELL DOUGLAS WERE BOTH PARTIES TO A SINGLE CONTRACT WITH THE NAVY FOR THE FULL-SCALE DEVELOPMENT, AND INITIAL PRODUCTION OPTIONS, OF THE NAVY A-12 AIRCRAFT. THE CONTRACT WAS AWARDED IN JANUARY 1988. ON JANUARY 7 OF THIS YEAR, THE NAVY TERMINATED THE A-12 PROGRAM AND CONTRACT.

DURING PERFORMANCE OF THE CONTRACT, APPROXIMATELY $2.7B HAD BEEN PAID TO THE CONTRACTORS. OF THAT AMOUNT, APPROXIMATELY $1.4B WAS PAID FOR DELIVERABLES RECEIVED BY THE GOVERNMENT. THE BALANCE OF PAYMENTS RECEIVED BY THE CONTRACTORS, OR, APPROXIMATELY $1.3B PRESENTS UNLIQUIDATED PROGRESS PAYMENTS. UNDER THE PROGRESS PAYMENT CLAUSE OF THE CONTRACT, AS PROVIDED FOR IN THE FEDERAL ACQUISITION REGULATIONS, THE NAVY HAD THE AUTHORITY TO DEMAND THE RETURN OF THE UNLIQUIDATED PROGRESS PAYMENTS IN THE EVENT OF A TERMINATION FOR DEFAULT.

THE TERMINATION OF THE A-12 CONTRACT WAS FOR DEFAULT. AS YOU KNOW, THE CONTRACTORS ARE IN DISAGREEMENT WITH THE GOVERNMENT CONCERNING THE DEFAULT ISSUE AND ARE PROCEEDING TO CHALLENGE THAT DECISION. THE CONTRACTORS ARE CONFIDENT OF THEIR POSITION, AND SHOULD THEY PREVAIL, THE CONTRACTORS MAY HAVE NO OBLIGATION TO RETURN ANY UNLIQUIDATED PROGRESS PAYMENTS TO THE GOVERNMENT. IT MAY BE, ALSO, THAT ADDITIONAL PAYMENTS WOULD BE OWING TO THE CONTRACTORS. IT IS FAIR AND REASONABLE TO DEFER COLLECTION OF A POTENTIAL DEBT (THE DEBT, IN THIS INSTANCE, REPRESENTED BY THE UNLIQUIDATED PROGRESS PAYMENT OBLIGATION) UNTIL THE ISSUE OF WHETHER IT IS OWING OR NOT IS RESOLVED.

CONDITIONS FOR THE REQUEST, CONSENT TO, AND ACQUISITION OF A DEFERRAL AGREEMENT ARE PROVIDED FOR UNDER CONTROLLING FEDERAL ACQUISITION REGULATIONS. A CONTRACTOR'S FINANCIAL CONDITION IS IMPORTANT TO A DECISION TO GRANT A DEFERRAL AGREEMENT. IT IS ALSO IMPORTANT THAT THE DECISION ESTABLISHING A DEBT HAS BEEN APPEALED. ALTHOUGH THE EXISTENCE OF A CONTRACTOR APPEAL DOES NOT OF ITSELF REQUIRE THE GOVERNMENT TO DELAY ENFORCING THE RETURN OF UNLIQUIDATED PROGRESS PAYMENTS, THE FACT OF THE APPEAL IS TO BE CONSIDERED FOR THE PURPOSE OF AVOIDING POSSIBLE OVERCOLLECTION. IF A DECISION ESTABLISHING A DEBT IS NOT APPEALED, THE GOVERNMENT STILL MAY DECIDE TO DEFER COLLECTION IF A CONTRACTOR CANNOT PAY OR A CONTRACTOR'S OPERATIONS UNDER NATIONAL DEFENSE CONTRACTS MAY BE SERIOUSLY IMPAIRED.

THE NAVY DEMAND FOR THE RETURN OF THE UNLIQUIDATED PROGRESS PAYMENTS WAS OFFICIALLY MADE BY A LETTER DATED 5 FEBRUARY 1991. HOWEVER, THE PROSPECT FOR SUCH A DEMAND WAS RECOGNIZED IMMEDIATELY FOLLOWING THE TERMINATION, AND CONTACT WAS MADE WITH APPROPRIATE AUTHORITIES TO EXPLORE BOTH THE TIMING FOR SUCH A DEMAND, AND THE POSSIBILITIES REGARDING A DEFERRAL. IT WAS MY UNDERSTANDING THAT MCDONNELL DOUGLAS HAD ALSO MADE SIMILAR CONTACTS WITH THE NAVY. IN RESPONSE, THE NAVY AGREED TO BEGIN ITS REVIEW OF INFORMATION IN SUPPORT OF A REQUEST FOR DEFERMENT WHILE IT WAS STILL IN THE PROCESS OF VERIFYING THE AMOUNTS DUE.

ON JANUARY 16, 1991, THE CONTRACTORS MET WITH REPRESENTATIVES OF THE GOVERNMENT TO REVIEW WITH THE GOVERNMENT THE FINANCIAL STATEMENTS OF THE CONTRACTORS AND THE IMPACT THE FAILURE TO EXECUTE A DEFERRAL AGREEMENT MAY HAVE UPON THE CONTRACTORS. THESE PRESENTATIONS WERE MADE IN SEPARATE MEETINGS, ON THE SAME DATE, BETWEEN THE TWO COMPANIES WITH THE GOVERNMENT. BASED UPON THESE PRESENTATIONS, AND, PRESUMABLY, OTHER CONSIDERATIONS AND FURTHER DELIBERATIONS WITHIN THE GOVERMENT, IT WAS CONCLUDED BY THE GOVERNMENT THAT THE CONTRACTORS HAD MADE A SHOWING TO THE DEPARTMENT OF DEFENSE THAT, ABSENT DEFERMENT, ONE OR BOTH OF THE CONTRACTORS MAY BE PLACED IN A FINANCIAL CONDITION THAT WOULD ENDANGER ESSENTIAL DEFENSE PROGRAMS.

WHEN THE DEMAND WAS MADE, THE CONTRACTORS WERE PREPARED TO RESPOND IMMEDIATELY TO THE GOVERNMENT WITH A RESPONSE REQUESTING

A DEFERMENT AGREEMENT. THE REGULATIONS PRETTY WELL SPELL OUT WHAT SUCH AN AGREEMENT IS TO PROVIDE. ON FEBRUARY 5, THE DEFERMENT AGREEMENT WAS READY AND WAS EXECUTED BY THE GOVERNMENT AND THE TEAM. THE AGREEMENT RECOGNIZES THAT THE TEAM IS APPEALING OR WILL FILE A COMPLAINT IN RESPECT TO THE TERMINATION FOR DEFAULT, THAT COLLECTION OF THE UNLIQUIDATED PROGRESS PAYMENTS CAN BE DEFERRED PENDING RESOLUTION OF AN APPEAL, THAT ABSENT DEFERMENT, THE CONTRACTORS MAY BE PLACED IN A FINANCIAL CONDITION THAT WOULD ENDANGER ESSENTIAL DEFENSE PROGRAMS, AND THAT IT IS NOT IN THE BEST INTEREST OF THE GOVERNMENT TO CAUSE SUCH PROGRAMS TO BE ENDANGERED.

THE AGREEMENT IS TO REMAIN IN EFFECT UNTIL RESOLUTION OF APPEAL OF THE TERMINATION OR A NEGOTIATED SETTLEMENT IS MADE, SUBJECT TO A REVIEW ON DECEMBER 1, 1992, AND ANNUALLY THEREAFTER. THE TEAM IS OBLIGATED TO PAY INTEREST ON THE AMOUNT, IF ANY, ULTIMATELY DETERMINED TO BE PAYABLE TO THE GOVERNMENT.

THE GOVERNMENT IS AT VIRTUALLY NO RISK UNDER THE DEFERMENT AGREEMENT. ENFORCEMENT OF REPAYMENT OF THE UNLIQUIDATED PROGRESS PAYMENTS LIABILITY WOULD BE STRESSFUL TO BOTH CONTRACTORS. IT WOULD STRAIN GENERAL DYNAMICS BORROWING CAPACITY AND COST OF BORROWING. IT WOULD NOT BE IN THE INTEREST OF THE NATIONAL DEFENSE. A DETERMINATION OF RESPONSIBILITY, THAT IS, OF LIABILITY FOR AN AMOUNT AS LARGE AS THAT INVOLVED HERE, SHOULD PROCEED FIRST.

MR. CHAIRMAN, THIS CONCLUDES MY PREPARED REMARKS. ONCE AGAIN, WE THANK YOU FOR THIS OPPORTUNITY TO PRESENT THE VIEWS OF GENERAL DYNAMICS ON THIS ISSUE.

Mr. CONYERS. Let's see if we can take less time with you than we did the previous panel. First of all, I appreciate your coming, appreciate your cooperation, and Mr. Lanese, you submitted to DOD for the consideration of the deferment a financial statement?

Mr. LANESE. That's correct.

Mr. CONYERS. Was there anything else or was that the essential ingredient?

Mr. LANESE. We submitted financial information that outlined McDonnell Douglas' financial condition at the yearend of 1990 as well as projections of cash-flow and program cash-flow throughout 1991.

Mr. CONYERS. How many documents did that take?

Mr. LANESE. I don't recall.

Mr. CONYERS. Let's start counting then. It took one?

Mr. LANESE. I don't recall.

Mr. CONYERS. It took two?

Mr. LANESE. It was an amount between 10 and 20 and then based on those documents, there were some followup questions that the Department of Defense had and we supplied further data.

Mr. CONYERS. Somewhere between 10 or 20. There may been some further documents after that?

Mr. LANESE. There, in fact, were; there were followup questions.

Mr. CONYERS. Which you could respond to inside of one document?

Mr. LANESE. I really don't remember the amount of detail that was requested. I know that we were responsive in providing backup information and there was a further review that was requested by the DCAA—excuse me, by the Department of Defense that the DCAA also review and audit the information that we had sent in to the Department of Defense. That resulted in some amount of information being prepared and submitted as well. I'm not sure of the detail or the amount.

Mr. CONYERS. Well, as senior vice president of finance, you probably had someone helping you prepare these documents?

Mr. LANESE. In fact, they were prepared by people in my organization.

Mr. CONYERS. Who was the principal person that helped put these together for your organization?

Mr. LANESE. Our director of financial planning, a gentleman named Ken Velton, and the treasurer of our company at the time, a gentleman named Bill Chase.

Mr. CONYERS. Were there other principals in addition to those two?

Mr. LANESE. Our vice president of contracts administration, James Gardner, also participated to some degree.

Mr. CONYERS. We've been acquainted with the IRS obligation that you have and there's a deferment agreement with the IRS, is that correct?

Mr. LANESE. Yes, there is.

Mr. CONYERS. Can you relate the terms or the conditions of that agreement with your corporation and IRS?

Mr. LANESE. I can tell you generally what occurred. The tax returns for the years 1977 to 1980 were submitted and reviewed and audited by the IRS and based on that review, there was a sum of money that would have been owed by McDonnell Douglas, and I'd place that sum of money in the $300 million range.

However, there were subsequent returns for the years 1981, 1982 and possibly beyond that were also submitted but had not yet gone through audit. Based on those returns, there would be created a loss carryback and based on that loss carryback, we would owe only a portion of the funds that were identified in the 1977 to 1980 returns.

Therefore, we requested—which is a reasonable request—that any payment made to the IRS be postponed until we complete these earlier tax year returns.

Mr. CONYERS. Did they grant that?

Mr. LANESE. They granted that but they granted that with some form of security and they requested that some security be provided because they would have been a general obligor, and that security was the stock of one of our subsidiary companies which is our helicopter company.

Mr. CONYERS. It was the helicopter company?

Mr. LANESE. That's correct.

Mr. CONYERS. In your opinion, Mr. Lanese, as the finance person for your corporation, can you look back and project whether or not McDonnell Douglas would have filed bankruptcy if your share of this deferment had not been granted?

Mr. LANESE. It was certainly not our intention to file bankruptcy but without this deferment, we would have been placed in a very difficult position. Again, I'd refer to one obvious fact and that's our yearend financial position. Although we had $550 million left on our borrowing capability through legal lines, that certainly is not as great as the $676 million, which is half of the $1,352 million that was identified in earlier testimony.

That certainly would have strained our financial condition a great deal, but over and above that, we had indication from some of our banks that a demand payment on this deferred amount would be viewed in their mind as a material adverse change, and a material adverse change from a lending standpoint means that the institutions feel there has been such an adverse change in the financial condition of the company or there may be, that they no longer are obligated to lend under their current agreements.

That ran the prospects for us, Mr. Chairman, of being placed in a position where even the $550 million that was available for borrowing may evaporate given that our banks perceived that we may be forced to pay an amount of $676 million related to the A-12 cancellation.

So from our standpoint, that would have put us in a very serious financial condition.

Mr. CONYERS. It still isn't clear whether you would have gone into bankruptcy. It certainly wouldn't have improved your condition, nobody would argue that, but whether or not you'd go into bankruptcy or not, is it unclear what your course would have been under those circumstances?

Mr. LANESE. It was certainly not our intention. I think it's fair to say that we do not believe—we strongly do not believe that this can be a cancellation for default. We believe strongly that it will be a cancellation for the convenience of the Government and it's our intention to pursue that in the courts.

Had this demand taken place, we would have sought whatever relief that we could have sought to defer payment of this amount until the dispute was settled. So from our standpoint, had the demand been made, had we not been granted a deferment, we would have sought an injunction to prohibit the Government from trying to collect funds that we felt were in dispute and not readily owed the Department of Defense.

Mr. CONYERS. Well, Secretary Cheney isn't more agreeable with your position.

Mr. LANESE. I understand.

Mr. CONYERS. Would you have been willing to consider putting collateral up as you did with IRS to satisfy the demand even though it was in dispute?

Mr. LANESE. The difference between the IRS dispute and the one on the A-12 very simply is that the IRS was a general creditor of the corporation; the Department of Defense is not a general creditor, it's a preferred creditor. As a result, if you look at the balance sheet of our company, there is approximately $2 billion of work in process that we carry on our books that the U.S. Government has first call on. In addition to that, there is another $600-plus million of amounts that McDonnell Douglas has paid for based on the way the progress payments work—80 percent being paid, 20 percent being held back. Based on that, the Government has first call on that as well.

So from a protection standpoint, the Government was protected to a tune of at least $600 million against this supposed amount of $676 million that was owed it. That being the case, they were in a very different position from the IRS which is just a general creditor.

Mr. CONYERS. Well, as a preferred creditor, it would seem to me that you would be more anxious to put up collateral if they had insisted?

Mr. LANESE. No, in fact, it says they already have the collateral. It says that collateral is already there. To put up more collateral beyond that, I feel, isn't proper because they are already protected.

Mr. CONYERS. Well, let me ask you about a partial payment. Was there any discussion about that, making a partial payment toward this amount?

Mr. LANESE. Not that I'm aware of.

Mr. CONYERS. Was there any discussion about collateral?

Mr. LANESE. Not that I'm aware of.

Mr. CONYERS. If you had been required to pay your share of the interest on a regular basis, would that have had any destabilizing effect?

Mr. LANESE. Our feeling is that it would be improper to do that. It would be improper because the amounts really are in dispute. We feel we have very strong legal arguments that show that we are owed money and not the Department of Defense. I'd go back to the comment I made earlier that we believe it can only be a cancellation for convenience and not default.

Given those circumstances, I think it would be very inequitable to have us pay interest on a current basis on the amounts until this dispute is resolved.

Mr. CONYERS. Well, you've already agreed to pay the interest in the deferment agreement.

Mr. LANESE. The interest if it's owed.

Mr. CONYERS. Right. So you could pay your interest share without going into bankruptcy?

Mr. LANESE. If your question is were we able to pay interest if we were asked to pay interest?

Mr. CONYERS. Yes.

Mr. LANESE. We probably had funds available to do that on an ongoing basis.

Mr. CONYERS. And that would not have forced you into bankruptcy?

Mr. LANESE. Once again, we would have contested that. Again, we feel that the Government is not justified in canceling this contract for default. We feel the amounts they claim they are owed were owed to us in that amount plus amounts beyond it. For that reason, I think it would have been contested.

So from a very practical standpoint, I think if a demand was made to make interest payments, we would have resisted that pending the outcome of this dispute in the courts.

Mr. CONYERS. That would not have been though for financial reasons.

Mr. LANESE. That's correct.

Mr. CONYERS. It would be part of the overall dispute?

Mr. LANESE. That's correct.

Mr. CONYERS. Let me turn to Mr. Putnam and just raise a couple of questions here. Before we leave, Mr. Lanese, can you remember about how many pages of this information—you said there was between 10 to 20 documents—about how many pages did that comprise?

Mr. LANESE. I'm sorry, there were about 10 to 20 pages.

Mr. CONYERS. There were about 10 to 20 pages?

Mr. LANESE. There were about 10 to 20 pages provided. We may have also though provided other information like, for example, our 10Q from the third quarter, our bank agreements.

Mr. CONYERS. Would the 10 to 20 pages have included the financial statement?

Mr. LANESE. Yes, they would have.

Mr. CONYERS. Mr. Putnam, let me just ask you about the information you gave DOD. Did you give them a financial statement?

Mr. PUTNAM. Yes, sir.

Mr. CONYERS. Was there anything beyond that?

Mr. PUTNAM. We gave them a narrative discussion of our company's financial situation, accompanied by some charts that contained various information such as capital expenditures, that sort of information, and then in addition, attached to it were the filings with the SEC and a copy of our 1989 annual report.

Mr. CONYERS. Would that have exceeded 10 to 20 pages?

Mr. PUTNAM. I would estimate it was in the range of 10 to 20 to 30 pages of material, sir, and that would exclude the annual report.

Mr. CONYERS. Excluding the annual report. When were those documents turned over, Mr. Putnam?

Mr. PUTNAM. On the 16th of January, sir.

Mr. CONYERS. Let's approach the possibility of bankruptcy. What's your feeling about General Dynamics possibly being forced to consider bankruptcy if their share of the amount in dispute had been demanded?

Mr. PUTNAM. May I clarify first, sir, that I'm not a financial expert so my answer is more from a layman's point of view and from my knowledge generally of what is going on in the company.

Mr. CONYERS. All right, we'll accept that qualification.

Mr. PUTNAM. I am not aware that there has been any serious discussion or even serious speculation in the press that our company is on the verge of bankruptcy. There certainly has been no discussions that I'm aware of within the company regarding bankruptcy.

Mr. CONYERS. Thank you very much.

Mr. Horton.

Mr. HORTON. Thank you very much, Mr. Chairman.

Mr. Lanese, on page 5 of your statement, you've indicated in about the fifth or sixth sentence, in essence, you say, "The essence of the information provided by McDonnell Douglas is reflected in the company's annual report to shareholders which was publicly released several weeks ago" et cetera and so forth.

I assume from what you've said to the chairman, that you did furnish other material other than what was in the annual report, is that correct?

Mr. LANESE. In fact, the annual report at the time wasn't prepared. It was not ready.

Mr. HORTON. So that was not available at all?

Mr. LANESE. That's correct. It was still early January and the annual report really doesn't get prepared until sometime in mid- to late-February, so we had to provide supplemental information based on our third-quarter performance.

Mr. HORTON. So what you're saying now though with this statement is that basically the information that was furnished at that time was later put into the report so for all practical purposes it was public information at this point?

Mr. LANESE. Very consistent with the annual report. Some of the information is, not all of the information. Certainly our projections are not part of the public information.

Mr. HORTON. When we requested that you provide us with a list of documents, we were told there was no such list. That doesn't make sense to me, that you would furnish documents and not have a list. Do you have a list of documents?

Mr. LANESE. We have a copy of the documents. I don't have a list.

Mr. HORTON. How many documents?

Mr. LANESE. Ten to twenty pieces of paper in one document.

Mr. HORTON. That's the 10 to 20 pages you were talking about?

Mr. LANESE. That's correct.

Mr. HORTON. And that's all?

Mr. LANESE. No. There was followup by the Department of Defense. After we gave the Department of Defense the initial financial information, they had a number of questions, in essence going through a due diligence process where they came back, asked for additional information and also had that information audited by the DCAA.

From that process, I'm sure there was other paperwork generated, a great deal of which may have been by the DCAA or the Department of Defense itself.

Mr. HORTON. Do you have copies of all the information you furnished?

Mr. LANESE. I believe we do. I personally do not, but in our organization, I believe we did keep copies and a record.

Mr. HORTON. Can you furnish that to the committee?

Mr. LANESE. Meaning am I able to furnish that or will I furnish that?

Mr. HORTON. Let me ask you first, are you able to furnish it?

Mr. LANESE. I'm able to furnish the information that's public information to the committee. There is certain other information in that package that is very sensitive to us that goes beyond our defense business, goes into our commercial, and there is some sensitivity there. That information I think we have to take under advisement and we have to talk about with counsel.

Mr. HORTON. Did any Government official ever discuss the possibility that you post some collateral?

Mr. LANESE. Not that I recall.

Mr. HORTON. Were you here in the room this morning when Admiral Morris did say that collateral was required? I'm a little confused because you indicated that there's already collateral, and I thought he said there was collateral to be required.

Mr. LANESE. No, I'm confused on that. I was here this morning when the admiral spoke. I don't personally remember any discussions regarding collateral. Certainly there were none with me.

Mr. HORTON. Is it your understanding that you do have to furnish collateral at this stage?

Mr. LANESE. No, it is not, but it is my understanding though, and in fact is true, that the Government has a preferred creditor position with all defense contractors.

Mr. HORTON. Is that what we talk about when we talk about collateral, the preferred position?

Mr. LANESE. Well, collateral gives a creditor a position over and above creditors, other general creditors.

Mr. HORTON. I understand that, but I'm asking about specific collateral. Is there any other collateral other than that?

Mr. LANESE. Collateral that's been committed?

Mr. HORTON. Either contemplated or is in the deferment agreement?

Mr. LANESE. No, not that I'm aware of.

Mr. HORTON. In other words, your company is not expecting any requirement for any collateral?

Mr. LANESE. That's correct.

Mr. HORTON. You also indicated something about interest. The admiral, I think in response to a question I asked about interest, indicated that there was interest or there would be interest paid. What you're saying is that interest wouldn't be due until there's been a determination as to what is owed?

Mr. LANESE. That's correct. The way the agreement reads, upon dispute any moneys that are found to be owed to the Government will be paid to the Government with interest over that period and certainly any moneys that are due to be paid to us will be paid to us but the clause calls for it not being paid with interest.

Mr. HORTON. As I understand it also, you dispute, first, the termination by default. You think it should have been a termination by convenience. Then you also disputed the amount, $1.3-plus billion, is that correct?

Mr. LANESE. We do not dispute the $1.35 billion in terms of unliquidated progress payments, which is the way it's been defined here.

Mr. HORTON. What do you dispute?

Mr. LANESE. We dispute the cancellation of the contract for default and we take exception with the fact that we owe the Federal Government money on this canceled contract. We, in fact, have a position that we will take to the courts that claims that we, in fact, have claims that need to be considered on the contract as well as we have an opinion that the contract can only——

Mr. HORTON. In other words, you claim that they owe you?

Mr. LANESE. That's exactly right.

Mr. HORTON. Has that been presented to the Department of Defense?

Mr. LANESE. We've presented our claims to the Department of Defense; the Department of Defense has asked for a recertification of those claims. I'm not aware of what the reason is for that recertification.

Mr. HORTON. What bonuses, if any, did McDonnell Douglas give its employees last year?

Mr. LANESE. It paid bonuses to virtually all employees who were in the incentive compensation group. Are you interested in the amounts?

Mr. HORTON. Pardon?

Mr. LANESE. Are you interested in the amounts?

Mr. HORTON. Yes.

Mr. LANESE. The amounts of those were substantially less than the aerospace industry and in fact, if you look at McDonnell Douglas' compensation of its 10 highest paid people, that compensation is approximately 20 percent less than the average paid in the aerospace industry and substantially less than industry in general.

Mr. HORTON. Let me ask you the question, how much was paid for bonuses and what was the largest?

Mr. LANESE. The amount that was paid, I would estimate, is approximately $18 million throughout the entire corporation. Of that amount, the largest bonus was probably paid, as best I can determine, to our chairman, John McDonnell, and if you care, I have a proxy here and I'll be glad to look in that and tell you the exact amount of that.

Mr. HORTON. If you could. Is that public information?

Mr. LANESE. Yes, it is public information. Excuse me, in fact, I was going to say my copy is in my briefcase. If you'll wait a second, I'll get another. Congressman, it's not broken out in detail in the current proxy, I thought it was. I would estimate for you though that it's approximately $200,000. The total compensation of our chairman last year was $578,000.

Mr. HORTON. Under the deferment agreement, McDonnell Douglas has agreed to maintain sufficient assets or available credit to pay the Government for the full amount of the debt. What are you doing to comply with that provision?

Mr. LANESE. No. 1, McDonnell Douglas has $3.5 billion in equity currently on its balance sheet. Two, the cash-flow situation that McDonnell Douglas finds itself in is very directly an effect of three circumstances, the first of which is an extremely tight capital market. Capital markets in this country have become so tight that lower grade investment credits like ourselves have a very difficult time accessing the market and as a result, have been forced almost entirely to go to the banking industry in order to meet its funding needs. As I'm sure you all know, the banking industry is not on the most solid of ground either.

Two, we launched a new aircraft called the MD-11 which is a widebody commercial aircraft that requires substantial upfront funding. We just completed the development and first deliveries of that aircraft late last year in December.

The way these development programs work, there is a significant cash outlay required to fund the program and begin initial production work. That cash outlay for us continues through the first 6 months of 1991. As we enter into full production, that cash begins to come back to us so if you look later in 1991 and certainly in 1992, our cash position is much improved over where it is now.

Mr. HORTON. So what you're telling me is that when this deferment agreement matures, and assuming that as a result of the court cases and all that sort of thing, and assuming the $1.3-plus billion, that you would be in a better financial situation to pay that than you were when it occurred in January?

Mr. LANESE. It's our belief that in 1½ years or toward the end of year 1992, we'll be in a significantly better cash position than we are today.

Mr. HORTON. Mr. Putnam, in your statement on page 4, you've talked about the deferment agreement, and you indicated you had a financial problem. When did you first realize you had a financial problem in your company?

Mr. PUTNAM. Again, sir, my expertise is not the financial side. As to a first recognition, I believe that one makes those determinations incrementally and not on a given day. That is to say, we naturally look on a quarterly basis at our earnings and at our performance, and evaluate that situation and progressively make a determination as to how we are doing financially.

Mr. HORTON. One other question for you. You said on that statement, "The Government is at virtually no risk under the deferment agreement." What do you base this on?

Mr. PUTNAM. I believe that our balance sheet and the performance of our company assures that should we be found to owe the Government the amount in question, that we will be able to make that payment.

Mr. HORTON. Can either of you or both of you comment on the other question, not the deferment question, but the manufacture or the contract, the ability to perform? It was canceled. The indication is it's cost overruns, that you were late, so far nothing has been produced that's tangible that can be turned over to the Government. Can you comment, Mr. Lanese, on that briefly?

Mr. LANESE. In our annual report, we have a page where we address our dispute on the A-12 contract and we talk about what we believe to be the facts on that contract and the fact that we——

Mr. HORTON. Can you provide that for the record then? Mr. Chairman, I'd like to include that in the record at this point.

Mr. LANESE. Yes, sir, I can.

[The information from McDonnell Douglas annual report—1990 follows:]

contractor is entitled to receive payments for its contract costs and the proportionate share of its fee or earnings for the work done, subject to availability of funding.

MDC, as a large defense contractor, is subject to many audits, reviews and investigations by the U.S. Government of its negotiation and performance of, accounting for, and general practices relating to Government contracts. An indictment of a contractor may result in suspension from eligibility for award of any new Government contract, and a guilty plea or conviction may result in debarment from eligibility for awards. The Government may, in certain cases, also terminate existing contracts involved, recover damages, and impose other sanctions and penalties. Based upon presently known facts, MDC believes that it has not engaged in any criminal misconduct with respect to any of the matters currently known to be under investigation and that the ultimate resolution of these investigations will not have a material adverse effect on MDC's financial position.

On January 7, 1991, the Navy notified MDC and General Dynamics Corporation (the Team) that it was terminating for default the Team's fixed price incentive type contract for development and initial production of the A-12 aircraft. MDC and General Dynamics Corporation (GD) have reported different financial results for the program. For the quarter ended June 30, 1990, GD reported a $450 million pretax provision for loss on the full scale development and test portion and the first production option of the contract which included reversing $24 million of earnings it had previously recognized on the contract. At that time, MDC reported no loss on the contract (including the first production option) based on cost estimates that differ from those used by GD, the recognition of claims as future revenue, and the fact that it had not previously recognized earnings on the contract. In the second quarter, MDC in preparing its estimate of cost at completion of the full scale development and test portion of the contract used its current estimate for its portion of the work and used a GD estimate for GD's portion of the work. MDC's estimate took into account the planned reassignment or previously announced layoff of engineers and other direct employees when their services were estimated to be no longer required on the contract, cost savings attributed to its specific and overall cost cutting initiatives, see page 25, and reduced provision for procurement costs. These estimates reduced an earlier estimate of MDC's portion of its work, which was prepared in conjunction with GD, by approximately $390 million. It is MDC's understanding that GD's estimates gave greater weight to projection of trends and to historical data. MDC's recognition of estimated future revenues with respect to claims was based on extensive work of outside counsel and MDC program engineering, estimating and fiscal personnel in analyzing facts, law and estimates of damages. Based on the work and analysis it had accomplished, GD did not include in revenue any claims revenue as probable of recovery. MDC recognized contract claims for its portion of the work only to the extent of its projected loss on the program.

For the fourth quarter of 1990, GD announced an additional loss provision on the A-12 contract of $274 million. MDC has established a pretax provision of $350 million for loss on the contract. MDC and GD continued in the fourth quarter to utilize different estimates of costs and different consideration of claims recovery in preparation of financial results.

The Team intends to file a legal action to contest this default termination, assert its rights to convert the termination to one for "the convenience of the Government," and obtain a determination that it is entitled to specification, schedule and price adjustments and damages. See Contracts in Process and Inventories, page 39. The Department of the Navy has agreed to defer repayment of $1.352 billion alleged to be due from the Team as a result of the termination for default of the A-12 contract.

MDC's T45TS Training System and C-17 Airlifter programs are in the development stage under fixed price type contracts. Failure to satisfactorily resolve performance, contract specification, schedule and resulting cost issues related to these programs could have a material adverse effect on MDC's earnings from continuing operations. See Contracts in Process and Inventories, page 39.

Military spending by the U.S. Government has declined, and is likely to continue to decline as a result of improved relations with Eastern Bloc countries and efforts to reduce the federal deficit. On February 4, 1991, President Bush sent the fiscal year 1992-93 Department of Defense budget request to Congress. Adjusting for inflation, there was a real decline in defense budget authority for 1992 of 1% below 1991 and 12% below 1990. Of the four current Department of Defense major military aircraft programs that are proposed to remain in the budget beyond 1993, MDC will remain the prime contractor on three of them - the F/A-18, the C-17, and the T45TS. Funds were also requested for the Tomahawk missile, Advanced Cruise Missile, and Space Station. The Department of Defense increased its budget for research and development and included funds for such programs as the F/A-18E/F upgrades, the Longbow Apache, Advanced Tomahawk, and work related to the Strategic Defense Initiative. The budget request included funding for programs MDC is competing for including the LH helicopter and the Air Force's Advanced Tactical Fighter program. The Army is

Mr. HORTON. Mr. Putnam, how about you?

Mr. PUTNAM. I'm not sure I understood your question, Congressman.

Mr. HORTON. The question has to do with the ability of the companies to perform and the fact that you were behind on schedule, that there were cost overruns?

Mr. PUTNAM. The ability of the company to perform I do not believe was in dire jeopardy. The problem posed to our company would have been the demand of that large amount of cash at that particular time. It would have been very stressful.

The behind schedule and overrun situation, sir, are you talking about the A-12 there?

Mr. HORTON. Yes. Do you have any knowledge about that or not?

Mr. PUTNAM. I have very limited knowledge about the A-12.

Mr. HORTON. I'm not going to ask you to answer it then. Thank you.

Mr. CONYERS. Thank you very much.

Mr. Schiff.

Mr. SCHIFF. Thank you, Mr. Chairman. I'll be brief, gentlemen. I assume you know what those buzzers mean for us.

I have a question. If your two companies did apply for the deferment in this claim against you from the Department of Navy, is that right? You asked to defer payment?

Mr. LANESE. That's correct.

Mr. SCHIFF. Was part of the reason for asking concern about your own cash-flow problem if it had to be paid in cash immediately?

Mr. LANESE. From McDonnell Douglas' standpoint, the answer is yes. It's also the equities of the dispute that we had.

Mr. SCHIFF. I understand this was a dispute, but was at least part of the reason concern about the cash-flow situation if it had to be paid in cash?

Mr. DUESENBERG. That certainly was the case with GD.

Mr. SCHIFF. If that's the situation, and I can certainly understand it with that amount of a matter in dispute, have either or both of your companies made provisions for what will happen if you ultimately lose the dispute and you do have to pay $1.35 billion plus interest to the U.S. Government? Have you begun a planning system to prepare for the possibility of that eventuality, though I acknowledge the amount is in dispute? That means you could win, you could lose.

Mr. LANESE. From our standpoint, from McDonnell Douglas' standpoint, sir, our cash situation is really caused more than anything else by the introduction of a widebody airplane which requires a tremendous upfront cash requirement. That airplane is going into full production right now.

The problems we have with cash-flow today are dissipated by the production and sale of that airplane in 1992 greatly. Our cash position becomes a nonevent for us in 1992 based on the production of that airplane.

Mr. SCHIFF. So starting with McDonnell Douglas in 1992, if McDonnell Douglas loses this dispute you can then write a check for half of $1.35 billion and that's not a problem?

Mr. LANESE. I believe we can.

Mr. SCHIFF. Thank you. May I ask the same of General Dynamics?

Mr. PUTNAM. I expect that we could also, yes, sir.

Mr. SCHIFF. That answers my question on the contract. Let me ask one general matter. Very briefly, none of us wanted the problem with the A-12, the Government did not, the team did not, we know that. I wonder if very briefly each of the team members can tell us where they think we go from here? I don't mean in terms of a dispute as to why it was canceled, but how can we use the assets that were purchased through the A-12 existing contract to come back on line with the Navy's mission for the future? I wonder if I could get a brief answer from both contractors on that?

Mr. LANESE. I would say from McDonnell Douglas' standpoint, that despite some of the assertions that nothing was received for the amount spent, we think there was a lot received. There was a tremendous amount of design work and technical identification that took place.

The information that's been paid for has been given to the Department of Defense. There is still some information in the possession of McDonnell Douglas that deals with this unliquidated amount or the $1.3-plus billion.

It's our belief in terms of where we go from here that there is some valuable information there that should be shared and needs to be shared if you're going to be building another advanced airplane with stealth capability.

Mr. CONYERS. Excuse me, Mr. Schiff. Would you be willing to rejoin us? We're going to regroup after these several votes.

Mr. SCHIFF. That was my last question, Mr. Chairman.

Mr. CONYERS. You can come back anyway. We need a quorum for the committee.

If that's permissible, gentlemen, we do need to repair to the floor for recorded votes. Unfortunately we will take a recess. There are several votes. So this may be some 30 minutes. There are luncheon facilities here and we'll instruct you how you may be able to take a little break during this recess.

Then we will resume the hearing immediately after we've concluded the votes.

[Recess taken.]

Mr. CONYERS. The subcommittee will come to order.

We were hearing from our corporate witnesses and Mr. Schiff was concluding his questions and it wasn't clear that he had finished.

Mr. SCHIFF. I have just a little bit more, if I may continue?

Mr. CONYERS. Please continue, sir.

Mr. SCHIFF. I thank the Chair.

Let me turn to the General Dynamics representatives and repeat the question, and we all apologize for that interruption but we had to vote as you know.

I know there is a dispute, it's been amply stated, as to the reason for the cancellation of the A-12 contract and that dispute will have to be resolved at some point. My question is, from General Dynamics' point of view, how can we all make the most of what everyone agrees is a bad situation? How does General Dynamics feel that we can take whatever assets were produced from the investment that was made in the A-12 contract and use them for the benefit of the national mission which still remains?

Mr. PUTNAM. I find your question very challenging, sir, and I will try to be responsive, but I have to caution that I'm not used to dealing with matters of that sort of scope.

Let me first at least try to make a point that the contract did result in much, much useful and usable information. The difficulty, of course, is whether that will apply to a next generation aircraft. To make the most use of what occurred would mean that you would need a follow-on to that program. That would certainly, from my point of view, as a citizen, make some sense. It is a tragedy that so much human effort has been brought to an unexpected end and basically is in pieces.

There was a great deal of work done, much meaningful work. I read recently a report on the termination at our company that there were some 21,000 parts that were inventoried for purposes of establishing where it was that we were at the completion of the contract, or at the termination of the contract, and that their weight was in excess of 2 million pounds. I was struck by that amount of material that had been generated. We really were in the process of starting to produce the aircraft at the time of the termination.

I guess I think it might be instructive, helpful to the country if the committee were to pursue that. I'm somewhat at a loss to give a more definitive answer recognizing that to pick up the program and move it forward from where it was terminated is difficult and to use the pieces that are left over requires study and would require an understanding of where the Navy now wants to go with the new aircraft.

Mr. SCHIFF. In the opinion of both of the contractors, if it were the chairman's decision to do so, how could this subcommittee try to determine how much of the A-12 inventory that was put together under the A-12 contract remains useful in trying to put together a new solution to the Navy mission? What should we do? What can we do to try to make that evaluation to either representative?

Mr. LANESE. Sir, I would say that certainly the Department of Defense has a very key role to play in that decision. We delivered a tremendous amount of information, technical information, information on software, on design from an engineering standpoint. All that is of significant use if it's the intent of the Government to build an advanced aircraft with stealth capability. That information should not go to waste.

Certainly, maybe through this process, a vehicle will arise where you're able to coordinate and deal with that through the Department of Defense. They're really our conduit.

Mr. SCHIFF. Any addition on that from General Dynamics?

Mr. PUTNAM. No, sir. The question you pose is really a very technical question as to how, given the status at time of termination, how to best exploit that information and those documents.

I'd have to also caution that what has occurred is not only the development of a large body of data, but what has also occurred has been the development within the minds of our engineers—both of McDonnell Douglas, General Dynamics and the subcontractors to each of us—regarding the problems that were posed by the A-12 contract and the technology that was to be developed there. Those people, by and large, sir, are gone.

Mr. SCHIFF. One last question. The Navy's talking about basically starting from scratch on a new contract because they still wish a more advanced aircraft from the present A-6. Has the Navy sent out any specifications or otherwise given any indication of what its requirements are in the new contract to indicate whether what was invested in the A-12 would, in fact, be useful to apply to the new contract? Can that question be answered at the present time?

Mr. LANESE. From McDonnell Douglas' standpoint, I'm sorry, I cannot. I know they've asked us for interest in bidding on a new requirement.

Mr. SCHIFF. Any specifications yet for what to bid on?

Mr. LANESE. They may have discussed that with us, Congressman, but I'm not aware of that.

Mr. PUTNAM. The best answer I can give sir, is that I have heard discussions of what people believe would be in the document—or was in a document they had seen but I have not personally seen it and am not aware of it. The admiral's statement about the synopsis and the request for expressions of interest is probably factually the status that we have.

Mr. SCHIFF. Thank you very much, gentlemen. I thank the Chair.

Mr. CONYERS. Thank you, Mr. Schiff.

Mr. Chris Shays.

Mr. SHAYS. Thank you, Mr. Chairman.

Gentlemen, thank you for being here and thank you for tolerating the delay and also these long hearings.

May I just first get some housekeeping out of the way and I don't want to dwell a long time on this but I would like to just have a perspective. In 1990, what were your overall gross sales of each of your companies?

Mr. LANESE. For McDonnell Douglas, it was approximately $16 billion. I have the exact figures if you'd like.

Mr. SHAYS. No, approximately is fine.

Mr. LANESE. Approximately $16 billion.

Mr. PUTNAM. I'm advised it was around $10.3 billion, sir.

Mr. SHAYS. What did you declare as revenue profit?

Mr. LANESE. McDonnell Douglas' profit was slightly over $300 million of net income.

Mr. PUTNAM. I think we reported a loss in excess of $500 million, sir.

Mr. SHAYS. The final question in that regard, did you pay dividends in that year?

Mr. LANESE. Yes, sir, we did.

Mr. PUTNAM. Yes.

Mr. SHAYS. Even with a loss, you still paid dividends?

Mr. PUTNAM. Yes, sir.

Mr. SHAYS. I want to just verify whether you agree with some of the information that I have—I'll just run through it.

The Secretary of Defense, following completion of the MAR report to the Committee on Armed Services that the A-12 program was healthy, that the day before the Navy, Capt. Lawrence Elberfeld, Program Manager for the A-12, briefed Vice Adm. Richard Gintz, the Commander of the Navy Air Systems, that the program was in trouble, and that on May 31, the Navy exercised lot 1 option of the FSD contract for six aircraft at a fixed price of $1.2 billion and then finally, on June 1, the contractors advised the Navy that there would be a slip in the schedule for the first flight. Are those pretty much the way you remember at least those events, gentlemen, each of you?

Mr. LANESE. I remember the last two. The earlier ones, I do not. I was not cleared on the program at that point in time and I'm not knowledgeable.

Mr. PUTNAM. I have no personal knowledge of those dates or events, sir. They are consistent with my——

Mr. SHAYS. Let's just take the last two events. Basically, the Navy was expecting six planes for $1.2 billion, is that accurate?

Mr. LANESE. I believe that's accurate.

Mr. SHAYS. And you advised the Navy you couldn't perform according to the contract, is that correct?

Mr. LANESE. I don't ever remember McDonnell Douglas advising the Navy that it couldn't perform on the contract.

Mr. SHAYS. Did you advise the Navy and the Defense Department that you could not provide those six aircraft at the fixed price of $1.2 billion?

Mr. LANESE. I don't recall the discussions that were had.

Mr. SHAYS. Let me just cut through it then, see what's your answer and then I'll come back to you.

Mr. PUTNAM. I was not present for any such meetings; I cannot tell you, sir, what was said.

Mr. SHAYS. Is it not true that you all were supposed to provide six aircraft for $1.2 billion?

Mr. LANESE. I believe that's right.

Mr. SHAYS. What was the date that they were supposed to be provided?

Mr. LANESE. Again, I don't have those program details. I remember the six airplanes, I remember $1.2 billion, but I'm not aware of the specifics on the program.

Mr. SHAYS. You do not know when those six airplanes were due to the Navy? That's your testimony to this committee.

Mr. LANESE. My testimony to you is that I'm not on the program. My program people would have that knowledge. The chief financial officer of the company would not.

Mr. SHAYS. Let me just say this to you. You are coming here representing your company and I at least have to have some confidence that you know when you were supposed to produce these aircraft. If you want to give it within 3 or 4 months, fine, but when was your understanding that these planes were supposed to be produced?

Mr. LANESE. Since I'm testifying under oath, I would rather find out the facts and respond to you instead of trying to guess what the answer is.

Mr. SHAYS. Let me ask, did you believe they had to be produced in 1990?

Mr. LANESE. Again, sir, I can't answer that question without reviewing the facts.

Mr. SHAYS. Sir?

Mr. PUTNAM. Sir, I would have to have the contract and examine the contract to see what it says.

Mr. SHAYS. I find both your answers absurd. I would think even the men and women working in your plant know that you were supposed to produce six planes at some date and the fact you don't know when you were supposed to produce those planes, I find mindboggling. Is that your testimony, you don't know when you were supposed—under oath, gentlemen—you don't know when you were supposed to produce those planes, is that your statement to us, under oath?

Mr. LANESE. Congressman, under oath, I've just said to you that I'm not on the program.

Mr. SHAYS. That's not what I asked.

Mr. LANESE. I don't have the detailed information on the program.

Mr. SHAYS. That's not what I asked.

Mr. LANESE. The program people do. McDonnell Douglas knows what those dates are.

Mr. SHAYS. That's not what I asked.

Mr. LANESE. If you'd like that information, we certainly can get that for you.

Mr. SHAYS. No, this is what I want to ask you. Under oath, I want to ask you if you knew when the airplane was supposed to be produced, not whether you were a part of the program?

Mr. LANESE. Under oath, I would respond to you by saying I may have known that at one time, but I do not recollect that today here. I didn't come prepared to answer questions about when options were to be built on the program.

Mr. SHAYS. Sir?

Mr. PUTNAM. I do not know the delivery date of the aircraft, sir.

Mr. SHAYS. So under oath, I'm assuming that you never saw any documentation that described when these planes were supposed to be delivered?

Mr. LANESE. I'll respond again, Congressman, by saying I don't recall today. Those facts I may have had at my disposal at one point in time but that's been quite some time. That's been almost a year ago.

Mr. SHAYS. Let me ask you another question. You described to this committee that having to pay back the $1.3 billion would be viewed by the banks as a material adverse change, is that correct?

Mr. LANESE. There were some of the banks who said they would view that as a material adverse change.

Mr. SHAYS. Mr. Putnam, how would the banks have viewed it in your circumstance?

Mr. PUTNAM. I think they would have viewed it as a major adverse development and it would certainly have caused them to reconsider both the amount which they continued to try to provide loans on and the rate at which they would make such loans.

Mr. SHAYS. Let me ask you this. How did the banks view the cancellation of the contract, how did they view that based on the fact it was a cancellation on default? Did that not constitute a material adverse change?

Mr. LANESE. If it was their belief that it really is a contract that was canceled for default, that could have resulted in them assessing that as a material adverse change for the company.

Mr. SHAYS. So is it your testimony that the banks do not believe that this is a contract that will not ultimately be verified to be a cancellation based on default? Are you telling us the banks view it the same way you view it?

Mr. LANESE. The banks have heard the position of McDonnell Douglas and they know that we feel very strongly that we have a case and a dispute that we feel will vindicate our position and based on the representations that we've made to them, they at this point in time don't view that as a material adverse change.

Mr. SHAYS. Mr. Putnam.

Mr. PUTNAM. I don't feel I could answer a question as to what the bankers might have thought or do think about our situation, sir. I do not deal with bankers as a rule other than in connection with my own checking account, so I don't feel competent to answer, sir.

Mr. SHAYS. You're more than worried about your own checking account; you're here representing your company based on the whole point of deferral and the justification for deferral of the payment was the reaction of the banks in large measure and cash-flow. We're going to get to that in just a second.

I would like to know in each case how you have recorded the action of the Government in terms of a cancellation based on default in terms of your financial documents. Let me be more specific.

In terms of McDonnell Douglas, have you written off any of the contract or have you in fact put in your books that the Government owes you money?

Mr. LANESE. From McDonnell Douglas' standpoint, we closed the yearend and took a $350 million pretax loss related to the A-12 program.

Mr. SHAYS. Is it your testimony under oath that in fact then, not only in your books, you do not show in any case in your books that you are making additional claims on the Government but you actually have taken of that $1.3 billion, you've written off $300 million?

Mr. LANESE. What I'm saying is, for financial reporting purposes, McDonnell Douglas has taken a writeoff of $350 million that's thoroughly explained in our annual report.

Mr. SHAYS. What I'm trying to understand though is exactly what you're saying and you understand and I don't, and ultimately I'm the one who has to understand. Let me put it this way, the Government has claimed that collectively you both as contractors owe about $1.3 billion. It's my understanding it's your claim that you've spent more than the total amount of $2.6 billion that the Government has given you, is this correct?

Mr. LANESE. I believe that's correct.

Mr. SHAYS. Have you written off the amount that you have spent in addition to the $2.6 billion or have you written off some of the $1.3 billion that the Federal Government is claiming?

Mr. LANESE. Congressman, the two aren't related. For financial reporting purposes, there are very defined rules that we follow and those rules required us to one, get an estimate of what the overrun would have been had the program continued; two, to take a percentage of that based on our current position on that program; namely, how far complete the program was; three, we reflected in our financial condition some minimal, realizable value based on the claims that we would be submitting to the Government for relief.

Out of those three numbers, out of those three calculations, falls the $350 million loss I talked about earlier. I'm sorry it's not as simple as looking at what cash is owed to whom; there are very specific accounting rules that we follow to reach that.

By the way, it's unrelated to what we believe the ultimate recovery will be for McDonnell Douglas only because the accounting rules require that you be much more conservative than what you may believe future recovery to be, and we've tried to be so.

Mr. SHAYS. Frankly, it doesn't describe to me that you've been very conservative at all. You are making an assumption you're going to get this money. That's the way I view it.

Mr. Putnam, have you dealt with this issue the same way or have you dealt with it differently?

Mr. PUTNAM. We've dealt with it somewhat differently. The amounts of writeoffs I think, in our case, are larger, closer to $700 million we've recorded as writeoffs against the contract.

Mr. SHAYS. This is the crux of my interest. Both McDonnell Douglas Corporation and General Dynamics on February 5, 1991, requested a deferment after the project was canceled based on default, and it's a one page document which has already been discussed today in regard to the A-12 contract.

You said, "In accordance with the FAR 32.613, this will constitute a request by the contractor team for a deferment of repayment. The basis for the request is (a) immediate payment of the amount demanded is not practical and (b) the amount is in dispute." Were there any accompanying documents to this letter given to the Government? Was this pretty much a letter without an enclosure? I don't see enclosure stated on it.

Mr. LANESE. From McDonnell Douglas' standpoint, there was significant amount of data that was transferred prior to that document.

Mr. SHAYS. That's not what I asked.

Mr. LANESE. There was nothing attached to that document.

Mr. SHAYS. The answer to the question is there was nothing attached to this document?

Mr. LANESE. There was nothing attached to that document that I'm aware of.

Mr. SHAYS. This is the formal request, is that correct? Is that your understanding, Mr. Putnam?

Mr. PUTNAM. That is correct, sir.

Mr. SHAYS. Now, I want to know specifically what you gave the Government to back up that and I want to know where in this letter you referred to those documents?

Mr. LANESE. If I can speak for McDonnell Douglas first?

Mr. SHAYS. Yes.

Mr. LANESE. Congressman, I think it is important to understand that we had been working with the Department of Defense for an extended period of time prior to February 5. McDonnell Douglas' cash-flow has been tight throughout 1990.

Working closely with them, by that I mean we have supplied to the Government over a number of months key information regarding McDonnell Douglas' financial condition, so when February 5 came around, the Government was by no means unaware of where we stood.

Mr. SHAYS. Mr. Lanese, that's such a general response. We are talking about $1.3 billion and basically what the Government has done is it extended you a loan——

Mr. LANESE. That's not true.

Mr. SHAYS. Basically, that's what they have done.

Mr. LANESE. No, that's not true at all.

Mr. SHAYS. They have given you money——

Mr. LANESE. They haven't given us anything, sir.

Mr. SHAYS. You're interrupting me. You can finish. They have extended you money beyond what the Government believes you performed. I realize that's in dispute and that's clear, you've made it clear that you're disputing that amount, but you now have collectively as far as the Government is concerned, $1.3 billion at an eight point something interest rate, not compounded, it's simple interest rate, and there's no way you could get money like that at that interest rate that I know of. Now, what's your response to that, sir?

Mr. LANESE. My response to that is that it's not a loan. For you to assume it is a loan, you have to base it on the fact that this contract is in fact a cancellation for default and we don't believe the facts will support that.

Mr. SHAYS. Mr. Putnam.

Mr. PUTNAM. We would agree with Mr. Lanese.

Mr. SHAYS. What you have told me is that this was a one page letter that asks for deferment and you say you provided information about cash-flow. I want to know more specifically, sir, what you provided in the sense that is there any one document or two documents, was it verbal, was it in writing? There was reference to 10 to 20 pages by you; there was reference to a stack of papers by the Government. I want to know what we need to find to see this justification and I don't want it to be an oral one, I want to know what was in writing.

Mr. LANESE. May I clarify something first? The 10 to 20 pages represented the initial information that we submitted to the Department of Defense in support of our request for a deferment.

Mr. SHAYS. Let me just ask you this. When was that submitted to the Department and what's the title of that document?

Mr. LANESE. I am not sure of the title but it was a McDonnell Douglas financial review. It was marked "McDonnell Douglas Sensitive" and "Proprietary." It was sometime in early January, I would say mid-January probably. Counsel on my right says the 16th of January.

Congressman, from that, there was a tremendous amount of discussion because as I'm sure——

Mr. SHAYS. Can I just interrupt you a second, sir, and I'll let you answer. In that document, did you at that time ask for a deferral?

Mr. LANESE. We told the Department of Defense after the cancellation of the program on January 7 that we would be coming back with a request for a deferral.

Mr. SHAYS. Verbal?

Mr. LANESE. We did that verbally. Shall I go on?

Mr. SHAYS. Yes.

Mr. LANESE. After submitting the initial pieces of paper, we went through a lot of discussion explaining what the papers mean. Some of that information was public documents that you could find today in the annual report that we've submitted to the committee here. Some of the information, however, was very proprietary to McDonnell Douglas.

I would say if I were to summarize the kind of information that it was, it's the same information that we give our lenders. It's the same internal information that we use with our banks.

Once that information was passed out, initially there was a lot of discussion and a lot of followup that took place. I'm not aware of how much more paper was generated. The parts that I'm sensitive to are the parts related to McDonnell Douglas' competitive situation, it's forecasts, the kind of information we passed on of things that we would be doing that if exposed would compromise those future actions with either our customers, our suppliers or our competitors.

That information was a part of the overall package. It was certainly not the overall package though, Congressman.

Mr. PUTNAM. Congressman, from General Dynamics' standpoint, the letter which says that information had been furnished refers to information furnished on the 16th of January and given to the Navy at that meeting.

Mr. SHAYS. The 16th of January?

Mr. PUTNAM. The 16th of January, sir.

Mr. SHAYS. How many pages was that document?

Mr. PUTNAM. I think I answered earlier that I would estimate it was 20 to 30 pages. I think it would have been identified as information being furnished regarding the potential request for deferment. Again, a demand had not been made at that point but we certainly anticipated one, so I think we would have identified it that way. It had a cover sheet; the cover sheet did identify it as proprietary information or as containing proprietary information.

Mr. SHAYS. Gentlemen, I would make a request to you that you supply those documents, specifically your 10 to 20 page document, your 20 to 30 page document, directly to the committee and I would also respectfully request that you provide the backup material that you say gives added voice to those materials. Is that something you can do, sir?

Mr. LANESE. Sir, a fair amount of the backup that took place, took place with the involvement in the work of the Department of Defense. Specifically, one thing I mentioned earlier was once we submitted the data that we did, the DOD requested a DCAA review of that documentation and they did a very thorough review.

The papers that were generated from that process we're not privy to. Those papers went to the Department of Defense.

Mr. SHAYS. Well, do you have any objection to supplying the 10 to 20 page document to this committee?

Mr. LANESE. I have no objections to supplying any of the public information that's in that. I do have an objection to supplying information on——

Mr. SHAYS. Let's be specific. You do object to providing that document is what you're telling me? You would edit it, is that what you're saying?

Mr. LANESE. In its entirety, I do, yes, sir. Again, the reason why I do is because that document contains projections and future actions that McDonnell Douglas will be taking to improve its financial position, and if disclosed, would compromise us with our customers, our suppliers and our competitors here in the United States and abroad. For that reason, it's very sensitive.

There is commercial airline information in there that we would be very sensitive to having disclosed.

Mr. SHAYS. If I might just react, it seems to me that the public is entitled to some information and they certainly were entitled, it seems to me, before June, they were entitled to know that you wouldn't be able to perform the contract. It seems to me that there are some things even the public is entitled to.

Mr. Putnam, do you have any objection to providing the 20 to 30 page document?

Mr. PUTNAM. I would have to ask advice of counsel on that point, sir. The information that we would consider sensitive are forecasts that we do not normally make available because they could aid our competitors and it would work to our disadvantage in the international marketplace. Other than that, certainly we would have no objection and I would have to ask counsel his opinion.

Mr. DUESENBERG. I'll comment on that. Generally, Congressman, as I recall, the data that was provided on January 16, I really don't see any problem about producing it to this committee, except for one situation. There are projections in that data and from an SEC point of view, it would be unfortunate if that somehow leaked or were disclosed because our company, like most corporations, does not make public projections.

Most of the material that we provided to the Navy as I recall is historical and I just don't have any problem with that; I don't anticipate that I'd have any difficulty with our CFO in talking to him about it. I think the general answer to you is we would make it available. If we have a difficulty about it, we'd address that.

Mr. CONYERS. Would the gentleman yield?

Mr. SHAYS. Yes.

Mr. CONYERS. I'd like to make it clear to both the corporation representatives and their counsel that we have files full of sensitive, proprietary, and top secret information. This is not a case of first instance where the material is extremely sensitive. We're not depreciating the importance and the value that you place on the information that you provided without anticipating that it might come to this pass.

What I want to try to do is give you as much comfort as I can that your material will be treated with the same sensitivity that we treat all other like information that of necessity in these kinds of oversight problems flow through the committee.

What we get down to and the heart of this matter—and Mr. Shays has been probing it as effectively as he can—is what are the materials upon which this deferment was based. Some were public and some were not public.

We understand and have been made perfectly clear that these materials would be damaging were they to enter into the public domain. This committee has no record of leaks or information dissemination and I want to tell you that we want to have you fully check the law on this matter. This is not a case of first instance.

I think that you will quickly realize that as delicate as this position is to you, we would quite frankly be violating our obligation to try to pass over this in some kind of way. I'm trying to speak directly to you about this, but there would be no point in having hearings of this nature if this problem were dealt with in any other way but that the materials would ultimately repose in the committee and go back to you.

I thank the gentleman for permitting me that interruption.

Mr. SHAYS. Thank you, Mr. Chairman. I appreciate your comments.

Let me just conclude by saying as a new Member of Congress, I find it pretty unbelievable that a request of deferment of $1.3 billion would be noted on one page with no cross reference to documents supplied and I will pursue with all the vigor I have in obtaining the documents that you seem so unwilling to provide us because ultimately we do need to see those documents.

It may in fact substantiate your claims and it may not. We have to know where the screwups were and our job is to do our best to make sure they don't occur in the future. Obviously, we've spent $2.6 billion, we have all these parts around and you have some knowledge base, but the bottom line is we don't have a plane put together and we're starting, it seems to me, from ground zero.

I will just conclude my comments, and I don't usually do this, but I want to give you gentlemen one last chance on one issue and that's how I started off. You both are very distinguished individuals in your company. You're here to testify on the A-12 and you have both said to me that neither of you have any recollection of when you were supposed to produce six planes.

That is so hard for me to believe. Obviously, you're under oath and I have to believe you, but I just have to tell you that of all the hearings I've ever attended whether it's these hearings or HUD hearings, I've never found a statement harder for me to accept than that one.

I'm going to once again just ask you if either of you gentlemen knew when you were supposed to produce the six planes?

Mr. LANESE. Congressman, we produce hundreds of airplanes a year, I would find it incredible if a senior officer of any corporation producing the kind of airplanes that we produce would know when he's going to produce six airplanes.

Mr. SHAYS. Is that your answer to me?

Mr. LANESE. Yes, sir, it is.

Mr. SHAYS. You're here to testify about a particular project and I assume this was an important project to you. Let me ask you this, do you know when you were supposed to produce the first plane?

Mr. LANESE. I know when the first plane was to have flown, yes, sir, I do.

Mr. SHAYS. When was that?

Mr. LANESE. It was supposed to have flown in June.

Mr. SHAYS. June of what?

Mr. LANESE. Excuse me. Is that information unclassified? I'm not sure if the information is unclassified on that Congressman, I'm sorry.

Mr. CONYERS. If the gentleman will yield. It's not only not classified, but it's been discussed here this morning, not to mention yesterday at the Armed Services Committee hearing. It's probably in the newspaper as well.

Mr. LANESE. The date has moved quite a bit but it was my understanding it was first to fly in June 1991. That was my understanding.

Mr. SHAYS. As the alternate, a deferred date or was that the time it was originally supposed to fly? Feel free to ask one of your other gentlemen. Is there someone in your company that can tell me what the company knows?

Mr. LANESE. It was June 1990, I apologize, not 1991.

Mr. SHAYS. June 1990.

Mr. Putnam, did you know when the six were to fly?

Mr. PUTNAM. No, sir, I did not. I have never laid eyes on the contract, sir.

Mr. SHAYS. But basically in June 1990, the first plane was not only to have been built but to have flown and you told the Navy then that you couldn't produce the contract, does that meet the——

Mr. LANESE. Sir, we never told the Navy we couldn't produce the contract. I'm sorry, I've never heard that.

Mr. SHAYS. In other words, you never told the Navy that you wouldn't be able to get that plane flying on schedule?

Mr. LANESE. We never told the Navy we couldn't build the airplane.

Mr. SHAYS. That's not what I asked. Obviously some day you can build the airplane. Didn't you tell the Navy you wouldn't be able to meet the schedule?

Mr. LANESE. The schedule on the airplane slipped, that's correct.

Mr. SHAYS. What's correct?

Mr. LANESE. That the schedule on the airplane slipped.

Mr. SHAYS. And you would not be able to meet that deadline, correct?

Mr. LANESE. Pardon me?

Mr. SHAYS. And when did you tell the Navy that?

Mr. LANESE. Sometime prior to the first flight.

Mr. SHAYS. No, no. It seems to me you told them about the day before that you wouldn't be able to. When did you tell them?

Mr. LANESE. Congressman, I don't know who was told and when they were told. Those are certainly facts, if you'd like those facts, I could find out what those facts are.

Mr. SHAYS. I guess I'll conclude, Mr. Chairman. I just would say to you that what I find interesting is that basically there was an assumption on the part of the public that the program was right on track and then when it became known, and it became known to the embarrassment of the Secretary after he made a statement it was right on track, a few days later and then we have record that you tell the Navy practically very shortly before it was to fly, that you hadn't even put the plane together. The whole thing is beyond absurdity to me and we're going to pursue it to the end.

Thank you.

Mr. CONYERS. Thank you very much.

Gentlemen, we thank you for your testimony, counsel's presence and helpfulness. As we conclude this hearing, let me just point out that it is clear that the Department of Defense from our point of view has bailed out the two largest defense contractors. What isn't clear is the basis for that decision.

We've heard nothing here today that can answer for the documents that have not been forthcoming. It's not clear yet that the Government has learned the lessons identified in the Navy's own official report, the Beach report, which clearly states that the failures in the A-12 program resulted "from a plain lack of objectivity at the contractor team level and wholly inadequate oversight by General Dynamics and McDonnell Douglas corporate management."

At another point, the report states that "The contractor request for progress payments were not properly reviewed to assess their validity, and required analysis supporting critical estimates used to determine contract physical progress not performed."

The report concludes that "The failure of the military managers to comprehend and pass bad news up the civilian chain of command, represents an abiding cultural problem for which it can be anticipated to occur again in the same or similar form."

We here are concerned that the cultural problem has not been cured and that the problem is occurring again in the deferral agreement. As a matter of fact, other defense contractors are now rising up to take advantage of this new situation.

We intend to vigorously pursue the possession of the documents now held by yourselves and the Department of Defense bearing on the deferral decision and as you've heard with our agreement between Defense Department counsel, we will pursue and resolve this matter rather early on.

If it's not resolved by Monday, then we will proceed with the process that will enable us to secure possession of the documents. I'm convinced that the Department of Defense understands this commitment that the members of this committee and myself have and that the oversight function of this committee cannot be obstructed particularly in a matter that regards billions of dollars of taxpayers' money.

Neither you nor the Department of Defense has any monopoly on proprietary or sensitive information, so I will expect your fullest cooperation in this matter and appreciate your presence here today. Thank you very much.

The subcommittee stands adjourned.

[Whereupon, at 3:10 p.m., the subcommittee adjourned, to reconvene subject to the call of the Chair.]

OVERSIGHT HEARING ON THE A-12 NAVY AIRCRAFT

WEDNESDAY, JULY 24, 1991

House of Representatives,
Legislation and National Security Subcommittee
of the Committee on Government Operations,
Washington, DC.

The subcommittee met, pursuant to notice, at 10 a.m., in room 2154, Rayburn House Office Building, Hon. John Conyers, Jr. (chairman of the subcommittee) presiding.

Members present: Representatives John Conyers, Jr., Glenn English, Frank Horton, Christopher Shays, and Steven Schiff.

Also present: Representative Andy Ireland.

Subcommittee staff present: Robert J. Kurz, deputy staff director; Eric M. Thorson, professional staff member; Cheryl G. Matcho, clerk; and James L. George, minority professional staff.

Full committee staff present: Julian Epstein, staff director; and Donald W. Upson, minority staff director.

Mr. Conyers. The Subcommittee on Legislation and National Security of Government Operations will come to order.

Today we continue the investigation into the cancellation of the Navy A-12 attack aircraft and the subsequent deferment of $1.3 billion of funds due the Government.

There are four basic issues before the committee:

First, was there an adequate analysis performed by the Department of Defense before their officials gave these two large defense contractors the largest deferral of debt ever granted?

Two, did the Department of Defense officials mislead Congress as to the nature of their analysis, and does the Department have any constitutional basis for its continued refusal to release relevant documents?

Three, is the Department of Defense granting McDonnell Douglas most-favored-contractor status through a series of sweetheart deals involving deferrals, loans, unusual progress payments, and advanced payments on contracts?

And finally, how many other deferrals have been granted by Defense and how many more are there going to be in the future?

At the first hearing, the committee had to fight for relevant documents held by the Department of Defense. We were assured that the Department had performed a very good analysis before granting the deferment, one that they were proud of. We were told that it was essential to grant this deferment, or else one or more of these contractors could have declared bankruptcy right at that point, and we would have never been repaid.

However, we found that there was no analysis performed. The contracting officer in charge of the analysis told the committee investigative staff that it was more of a review than an analysis. We discovered that this review lasted all of 1 week, from the time the contractor requested the deferral on January 24 to the time the recommendation was made for the deferral on January 30.

This review consisted almost entirely of information provided by McDonnell Douglas without any independent verification of this information, for example, by checking with the company's major creditor banks, a very basic procedure. And this review did not follow the minimum requirements established by law, specifically 32 CFR, section 163.

We found that there was virtually no analysis of General Dynamics, the other partner. General Dynamics was granted a deferral simply because of their team agreement, and in the April hearing, their officials testified that they never considered declaring bankruptcy with or without a deferment.

We found that McDonnell Douglas explicitly told a Department of Defense official during her review that they would not go bankrupt.

Far from bankruptcy, the two contractors are enjoying rising stock prices, are paying incredible bonuses to their executives, and a number of other things that don't suggest to me that they are in any trouble at all. One of them is so flush with funds that it is looking to buy other companies.

Then we found something really extraordinary. At the same time McDonnell Douglas was looking for $1 billion deferment on the A-12 program, it was also requesting a loan from the Department of Defense for another billion dollars.

Much of the information provided to the committee after the April hearing was not in reference to the deferment, but to this remarkable loan application by McDonnell Douglas. This loan request has been kept secret from the public, but no more.

Because of its importance, I am making it available to the public, the letter from the chief executive officer of McDonnell Douglas to the Under Secretary of Defense. The people who have to pay for these billion-dollar deals at least have a right to know what is being negotiated in their name.

In another document, the committee is releasing today, it appears that some $770 million may have been, was, who knows, funneled to McDonnell Douglas, as well as information, possibly critical, to the negotiations then under way on the C-17 aircraft program. We will ask for an explanation of this extraordinary action.

And we will be looking at other deferments.

Although the law provides that deferments are for small and potentially weak contractors, we found that last year DOD granted deferments to Lockheed and Delco Electronics. Both are involved in defective pricing cases, which doesn't ring very well. Neither seems small or financially weak, and one is a wholly owned subsidiary of the General Motors Corp.

And to top everything off, the GAO has reviewed the last 10 years of deferments. They could find no records whatsoever for deferments granted before 3 years ago. So the committee's investigation has some important goals.

We want to ensure that the money deferred by the Department of Defense may, hopefully, be returned to the Treasury. Maybe, if we dare, soon returned to the Treasury.

We also want to expose this pattern of practice, this process of care and feeding of the big contractors in military procurement, clearly at the expense of our citizenry and others, not to mention other competing contractors.

And finally, we are going to find a way to stop this backroom, secret dealing by which the Pentagon frequently does business. If these extraordinary efforts by the Department of Defense are as noble as they would have us believe, then let's make sure that the deals are done out in the public where we can see what is being done with tax dollars.

I would like now to recognize the ranking member of this committee, Frank Horton, the gentleman from New York.

Mr. HORTON. Thank you, Mr. Chairman.

Mr. Chairman, I would like to commend you for continuing our hearing surrounding the cancellation of the Navy A-12 airplane program. Although the topic of today's hearing is the deferment issue, I hope we do not forget that the cancellation of the A-12 has set back Navy plans for a new attack aircraft at least a decade, meaning it will have to rely on the old A-6.

The real tragedy may be that existing rules and normal procedures were simply ignored. As we learned during our last hearing the problem was improper oversight procedures were not followed by those responsible for the program. Then, when it came time to consider the deferment, it appears again proper and normal accounting procedures were once more simply ignored. A $1.3 billion deferment was given with little more than a cursory review of old financial reports rather than proper and thorough analysis.

The more the staff looked into the deferment issue, the worse it gets. Apparently, there are no records prior to 1988, which you documented in your statement. In other words, if you were defense contractor and owe the Government some money, all you have to do is apply for a deferment, stall for about 3 years, and it will be lost in the system.

I would like to repeat the warning I gave in April. Every time I meet a general or an admiral, they complain about congressional micromanagement. But without congressional oversight, the Government would be losing billions of dollars. The actual amount is unknown, since there are no adequate records.

Mr. Chairman, that must be corrected, and that is not unnecessary micromanagement, but essential oversight. And that is what our responsibility is on the subcommittee. We are looking out for the taxpayer and watching the shrinking defense dollars.

So I am happy that you are having this hearing. I am sure you are going to get some valuable information today.

Mr. CONYERS. Thank you, Mr. Horton.

The Chair recognizes the gentleman from Connecticut.

Mr. SHAYS. Thank you, Mr. Chairman. I want to thank you and the staffs on both sides who, I think, have done a superb job of preparing us for this hearing. I have to say that the longer I serve on this committee, the more I feel that the Department of Defense, DOD, and contractors who do business with DOD are one and the same. It seems to me, as I look at the evidence that we have here—some of which, amazingly, will not be made public—that the more I look at information like this, it is almost like the motto of the Department of Defense is, we take care of our contractors. And I just can't help but ask the question, at whose expense?

We see a deferral of $1.3 billion without much reserve, which I view as an overpayment. And then we have seen documents that show a real effort on the part of the Department of Defense to provide McDonnell Douglas with over $700 million.

On the surface, very candidly, it looks like the Department of Defense and McDonnell Douglas have conspired to transfer billions of dollars to McDonnell Douglas; to have it done without people being made aware of it, and then when we see evidence of this, to claim that the public does not have a right to know. They are now seeking to prevent this committee from making this information public.

The losers are the taxpayers, and very candidly, I wonder why the SEC has not stepped in to consider whether the Government and McDonnell Douglas have not, in fact, conspired to keep this valuable information away from investors who have the right to know about the investments they make.

And so I see this as not the final step in the hearing process, but the beginning; and ultimately, I think, the public will be made aware of what they need to be made aware of, in spite of the reluctance of the Department of Defense to have this be known.

Mr. CONYERS. I thank the gentleman very much.

Before we begin, I think it is only fair that the Chair makes a comment about the release of alleged trade secrets or proprietary information. Following our last hearing on the A-12 program, we obtained Department of Defense documents concerning the A-12 deferral agreement and requests by McDonnell Douglas for other financial assistance. One of these documents, a January 24, 1991, letter from McDonnell Douglas Chairman John McDonnell to the Department of Defense requests an advance payment pool of $1 billion.

In correspondence to the subcommittee and the Department of Defense, McDonnell Douglas has asserted that this letter contains trade secrets and proprietary information that are protected from public release by a law, 18 U.S.C. 1905. The Department of Defense has taken the position that it will honor the company's assertion.

Now, 18 U.S.C. 1095 is a criminal statute that generally prohibits Government employees from disclosing trade secrets or confidential statistical data that have been provided by a corporation. By its terms, section 1905 does not apply to the Congress, but only to an officer or employee of the United States or any department or agency.

The general counsel of the House has confirmed that this provision of law applies only to the executive branch, not to Members of Congress acting in their official capacity. At this hearing, acting in my official capacity as chairman, I have full authority to release this information.

In addition, in conducting this hearing, members are engaged in core legislative activities that are fully protected by the speech or debate clause of the Constitution as recognized by the Supreme Court in the 1972 case of *Gravel* v. *United States*.

As a matter of law, the chairman and the subcommittee and all its members are thus fully authorized to release and to discuss publicly matters that relate to or contain trade secrets or proprietary information.

Moreover, the January 1991 McDonnell letter does not, in fact, contain any trade secrets or proprietary information. Sensitive information is shielded to prevent a company from obtaining the secrets of its competitors and unfairly gaining an advantage in the marketplace.

Nothing in the McDonnell letter would or could confirm such an unfair advantage. There is no litmus test that defines trade secrets or proprietary information, particularly in the area of financial data. Indeed, some details of a corporation's financial positions are already matters of public record and are filed with the Securities and Exchange Commission and other official bodies. In particular, detailed financial forecasts or projections are not generally made public.

The January 1991 McDonnell letter contains no detailed financial forecasts or projections for the company. This letter contains only the most general statements about the company's financial position and the availability of commercial credit. Even when coupled with the request for an advance payment pool of a billion dollars, the letter's contents constitute neither trade secrets nor proprietary information.

In repeated discussions with our staff, representatives of McDonnell Douglas have been unable to identify any proprietary data or trade secrets in the letter, although it asserts that the company's marking of the letter as proprietary precludes its disclosure. Not so.

The Department of Defense general counsel also could not identify any proprietary data or trade secrets in the letter. The mere use of a proprietary stamp does not convert a potentially embarrassing document into a protected trade secret. That protection is a very narrow one, which does not apply to the January 1991 McDonnell letter.

When anyone seeks a billion-dollar loan from the United States Government, the American people have a right to know about it, and as their elected representatives, we have a duty to ensure that such transactions are not hidden under a veil of unwarranted secrecy.

So I would like now to proceed with the hearing. We have got the Honorable Frank Conahan before us from GAO, no stranger. He has been before the committee innumerable times and occasions as Assistant Comptroller General for National Security and International Affairs at the U.S. General Accounting Office.

With him is, of course, Paul Math, Director of Research Development, Acquisition and Procurement.

Thank you very much, gentlemen, for joining us. If you will stand and raise your right hand, please.

Do you solemnly swear the testimony you are about to give will be the truth, the whole truth, and nothing but the truth, so help you God?

Thank you very much. Please be seated.

Your statement will be incorporated in its entirety in the record, without objection, as with all of the other witnesses.

Welcome, Mr. Conahan.

STATEMENT OF FRANK C. CONAHAN, ASSISTANT COMPTROLLER GENERAL, U.S. GENERAL ACCOUNTING OFFICE, ACCOMPANIED BY PAUL F. MATH, DIRECTOR OF RESEARCH, DEVELOPMENT, ACQUISITION AND PROCUREMENT ISSUES

Mr. CONAHAN. Thank you, Mr. Chairman.

You asked us essentially to comment on three matters. You asked us to evaluate: One, the analysis performed before making the deferment decision; two, the data used in making that decision; and three, the reasonableness of the deferment decision.

First, I will say that the DOD analysis was not documented, as you might expect that it would be. The DOD officials that we spoke with throughout this evaluation say they see its analysis as consisting of a deliberative process of meetings and a January 31, 1991, briefing to the Service's Acquisition Executives and Comptrollers, and that this supported their decision.

Mr. Chairman and members of the committee, I would have expected to find better documents associated with this exercise. I think that the Department would have some difficulty, and of course, had some difficulty in demonstrating that it is properly exercising its fiduciary responsibilities.

I will talk about the substance and merit of the case a little later on, but I think this is an important matter that we need to think about as we go through this series of hearings.

I don't have, really, much more to say about that. Let me talk about the data that were available for DOD's analysis, and DOD's deliberative process, as we saw it in going through our own analysis.

As you mentioned, because McDonnell Douglas's financial condition was believed to be weaker than General Dynamics, DOD limited its attention to McDonnell Douglas. What I would like to do is cite a number of events and information over the period from the summer of 1990 until the decision was made to give an indication of the kind of deliberative process that was undertaken, and the kind of information that was available.

Beginning in August 1990, the administrative contracting officer at the corporation alerted DOD officials to McDonnell Douglas's weakened financial condition. That same office, in August and later in September, described a series of actions McDonnell Douglas had taken to conserve cash, improve credit arrangements, and strengthen its financial position. Memos indicated the McDonnell Douglas debt had been downgraded.

The Defense Contract Audit Agency, in September, stated in its report that the then current financial capability of McDonnell Douglas was weak when compared with industry standards.

Beginning about that time, there were numerous meetings within the Department of Defense concerning McDonnell Douglas's financial condition. The Air Force at that time was doing analysis of the C-17 program. They were taking a look at McDonnell Douglas's cash-flow position. That analysis and that information was presented to the people who ultimately were involved in the decision to take the deferment action.

On January 16, 1991, McDonnell Douglas provided financial information to the Navy. Later on, or about the same time, McDonnell Douglas gave the corporate contracting officer its debt forecast. It showed McDonnell Douglas would be in a negative cash-flow position in 1991.

Finally, on January 24, in connection with this letter you have up on the board, Mr. Chairman, requesting an advance of $1 billion, the CEO submitted a financial package. In late January, additional information was requested and received.

Finally, the Director for Defense Procurement briefed the Service Acquisition Executives and the Comptrollers on January 31, and the tentative conclusions reached by the Director at that time were that McDonnell Douglas' bankruptcy would not be in DOD's best interests. McDonnell Douglas could not afford to repay the A-12 debt, McDonnell Douglas needed additional short-term financing, and McDonnell Douglas's financial problems would be a continuing concern.

As I said at the outset, I think that the Department had—will continue to have difficulty in demonstrating that it met its fiduciary responsibilities with respect to this transaction, because of the way it went about this whole matter and the absence of documentation.

But in our own analysis, we found a great deal of pertinent information, and in the final analysis, based on that information, I don't think we can conclude that the Department's decision was unreasonable. And I would like to cite some of the reasons for that.

And it starts, again going back to the fall timeframe, with the DCAA September 1990 audit report, which contained the financial status indicators suggesting that McDonnell Douglas was in a weakened financial position. It showed the declining debt ratios, and they were declining.

We subsequently saw negative cash-flow information, and some pretty good projections. Whether you use McDonnell Douglas's data or whether you use data that was modified by the Department of Defense, I think you can clearly see negative cash-flow positions going out into 1991.

There were representations on the part of McDonnell Douglas that its banks would have difficulty in continuing to deal with it. We don't have direct verification of that, but inasmuch as Standard & Poors and Moody's had downgraded McDonnell's position twice during that period of time, that is further indication.

There is more information that came out in late January on the company's negative cash-flow. We saw, indeed, that the company had undertaken a number of initiatives to respond to its weakened financial condition. It had initiated cost reduction initiatives and cash conservation initiatives. These were in response to its own assessment.

And then, finally, as I mentioned earlier in connection with the analysis associated with the C-17, we found that the Government had available to it additional information that showed the financial condition of the company.

There were a few other considerations that we thought were pertinent, that various folks in the Department took into account, and one was that the company was responsible for developing and producing a number of weapons systems, and if the company went under, it would adversely affect performance there; that the loss of this contractor could adversely affect the United States defense industrial base overall. It is an important contractor.

And then, finally, the Persian Gulf war was ongoing at that time and the Department was relying on the continued support of that company. Then there are the financial situations with respect to the appeal itself. The contractor team disputed the amount owed, and filed its appeal; and if the court rules in favor of the team, it will not have to repay the deferred amount. That was a consideration that's covered in the regulation on these kinds of decisions.

That concludes my summary, Mr. Chairman. We will be willing to take any questions that you may have.

[The prepared statement of Mr. Conahan follows:]

United States General Accounting Office

Testimony

For Release
on Delivery
Expected at
10:00 a.m. EDT
Wednesday,
July 24, 1991

Deferment Actions Associated
With the A-12 Aircraft

Statement of
Frank C. Conahan, Assistant Comptroller General
National Security and International Affairs
  Division

Before the
Legislation and National Security
  Subcommittee
Committee on Government Operations
House of Representatives

GAO/T-NSIAD-91-50

Mr. Chairman and Members of the Subcommittee:

We are pleased to appear before the Legislation and National Security Subcommittee of the House Committee on Government Operations. Our testimony today is in response to your request to us at your hearing on April 11, 1991. That hearing addressed the Navy's default termination of the A-12 contract on January 7, 1991, and the subsequent agreement on February 5, 1991, to defer repayment of $1.35 billion by the contractor team of McDonnell Douglas and General Dynamics until litigation over the termination is resolved or a negotiated settlement is reached.

At the hearing, Department of Defense (DOD) officials used the term "analysis" in describing their activities leading to the decision to grant the deferment. For example, the Director of Defense Procurement stated that a thorough analysis had been performed before making the deferment decision. You asked us to evaluate the analysis performed, data used, and the reasonableness of the deferment decision regardless of the kind of analysis DOD had before it when it made the deferment decision.

BACKGROUND

On January 7, 1991, the Navy terminated the A-12 full-scale development contract for default. On February 5, 1991, it issued a demand letter to the team of contractors for repayment of $1.35 billion in progress payments for which no completed items had been accepted by the government. On the same day, at the team's request, the Navy--with DOD approval--agreed to defer the repayment until litigation over the termination is resolved in court or a negotiated settlement is reached.

According to Federal Acquisition Regulation section 32.613, the government may defer the collection of debts it is owed. Deferments pending the disposition of an appeal may be granted to small businesses and financially weak contractors with a

reasonable balance of the need for government security against loss
and of undue hardship on the contractor. The regulation also
provides that if the contractor has appealed the debt under the
procedures of the disputes clause of the contract, the information
supplied by the contractor with its request for deferment may be
limited to an explanation of the contractor's financial condition.
On the other hand, if there is no appeal pending or action filed
under the disputes clause of the contract, the following
information about the contractor should be submitted with the
request for deferment:

-- its financial condition,

-- its contract backlog,

--its projected cash receipts and requirements,

--the feasibility of immediate payment of the debt, and

--the probable effect on the contractor's operations of immediate
  payment in full.

This information, once supplied, is to be promptly reviewed to
determine whether it is adequate to grant a deferment. If the
information is inadequate, the government may request the
contractor to furnish the needed information. Although the
existence of a contractor appeal of the debt does not of itself
require the government to suspend or delay collection action,
consideration is to be given to whether deferment of the debt
collection is advisable to avoid possible over-collection.

In its February 5, 1991, demand letter, the Navy advised the A-12's
team of contractors that it could submit a request for deferment of
collection if immediate payment was not practical or if the amount
was disputed. On the same day, February 5, the team requested the

deferral of payment, stating that immediate payment of the demanded amount was not practical and the amount was disputed. The team also stated that while it had not yet filed a notice of appeal, it intended to do so.[1] The Navy and the team signed the deferral agreement on February 5, 1991.

According to the Navy contracting officer, the team had advised the government before it issued its demand letter that the issuance of such a letter and the resulting reaction of the credit markets would cause financial hardship. Therefore, coordinated action was taken to execute the demand letter, the request for deferment, and the deferment agreement on the same day.

The deferral agreement provides that the government will take no action to enforce collection pending (1) a decision by the Armed Services Board of Contract Appeals or the Claims Court on the team's appeal or (2) a negotiated settlement between the government and the team. The deferral agreement also provides for the payment of interest at the time of repayment. The interest rate is established by the Secretary of the Treasury, as provided in section 12 of the Contracts Disputes Act. The rate as of February 5, 1991, was 8-3/8 percent, and will be reviewed every 6 months. The agreement will remain in full force until it is reviewed on December 1, 1992, and annually thereafter.

Because McDonnell Douglas's financial condition was known to be weaker than General Dynamics, DOD limited it efforts to McDonnell Douglas. The data available for DOD's consideration was almost exclusively on McDonnell Douglas's financial condition. Because we were asked to review the information considered by DOD, we limited

---

[1] On June 7, 1991, the team filed a 78-page complaint with the U.S. Claims Court. The team's appeal requests that debt of $1.35 billion be reduced to zero and that the Court increase the contract target price by an additional $1.4 billion. The team is also requesting recovery of termination costs which are not yet determined.

our review to the information on McDonnell Douglas and did not
review information on General Dynamics. As indicated at the
hearings, DOD did not consider alternatives to granting a full
deferment to both contractors.

RESULTS IN BRIEF

There is some evidence that DOD officials did follow a
deliberative process in deciding to grant a deferment. However,
documentation showing what was discussed during this process is not
available. There is also no documentation available that indicates
why data was used in a particular manner, nor is there a formal
document or written decision paper prepared supporting the
deferment decision.

According to DOD officials, DOD's deferment decision was based on
information from the Defense Contract Audit Agency (DCAA) and the
government's Corporate Administrative Contracting Officer (CACO)
indicating that McDonnell Douglas was in a weak financial condition
and on numerous discussions between services and DOD officials. In
addition, the financial data package provided by McDonnell Douglas
on January 24, 1991, and referred to at the April hearings,
accompanied its request for significant advance payments in
addition to the deferment. Once the information was provided, DOD
focused much of its attention on the request for advance payments.

Although DOD did not prepare a documented analysis of McDonnell
Douglas's financial data, we believe that the decision to grant the
deferment appears reasonable. Although we did not perform a
financial analysis, a variety of factors indicate that McDonnell
Douglas was in a financially weak condition and could not
immediately repay the amount demanded.

DOD "ANALYSIS" UNDOCUMENTED

During hearings on April 9 and 11, 1991, DOD witnesses stated that they had thoroughly analyzed what would have happened if a deferment was not granted. The DOD officials told us that the deliberative process of meetings and a January 31, 1991, briefing to the services' acquisition executives and comptrollers supported their decision. The DOD witnesses believe that an analysis was performed but agree that it was not formalized through documentation and that the majority of the analysis for the financial package submitted by McDonnell Douglas was focused on the request for advance payments.

DATA AVAILABLE FOR DOD'S "ANALYSIS"

DOD believed that General Dynamics could repay its share of the debt, but that if the government demanded immediate repayment, General Dynamics would be less capable of supporting current operations. DOD officials stated that both contractors are jointly and severally liable for the entire amount of $1.35 billion. Even if one contractor was able to pay its share, it would still be liable for the remaining amount if the other contractor could not pay its share. Consequently, because McDonnell Douglas's financial condition was believed to be weaker than that of General Dynamics, DOD limited its attention to McDonnell Douglas and did not consider any alternatives but to grant the deferment to both companies. DOD personnel told us that they based the deferment decision on early information indicating that McDonnell Douglas was in a weak financial condition and on discussions at numerous meetings on the need for a deferment.

Early Information Alerted DOD to Potential Problems

Beginning in August 1990, the government's CACO alerted DOD officials to McDonnell Douglas's weakened financial condition. At that time, the CACO believed that McDonnell Douglas had adequate credit to sustain current operations. The CACO also reported to DOD officials on the actions the contractor was taking to improve its operations. CACO memos dated August 20, 1990, and September 4, 1990, described a series of actions McDonnell Douglas had taken to conserve cash, improve credit arrangements, and strengthen its financial position. These memos indicated that McDonnell Douglas's debt had been downgraded in May 1990; it was put on "credit watch" in June 1990 by Moody's and Standard & Poor's credit rating services; and the company's debt was again downgraded in July 1990 by Moody's Investor Service. This early information set the stage for DOD's favorable consideration of the deferment.

DCAA in its September 13, 1990, audit report stated that, in its opinion, the then-current financial capability of McDonnell Douglas was weak when compared with industry standards. However, DCAA did not believe that continued performance on government contracts was endangered. The audit report was prepared in response to a request from the CACO to determine whether potentially adverse financial conditions existed that could affect performance on government contracts. DCAA reviewed McDonnell Douglas's financial statements, cash flow projections, and other documentation. DCAA also computed ratios that are generally accepted as indicators of a firm's financial condition. DCAA recommended that the CACO make arrangements for monthly financial briefings to examine McDonnell Douglas's financial condition.

DOD's principal analyst-- the Director for Cost, Pricing, and Finance, Office of the Deputy Assistant Secretary of Defense (Procurement)--told us that it was generally known that McDonnell Douglas was already in a weak financial condition before the termination and that this awareness came from the early DCAA audits and the CACO memoranda mentioned above. Thus, DOD officials believed that a deferment would be required because McDonnell Douglas could not repay its share of the amount demanded.

Financial Condition Addressed in Meetings and Briefings

DOD personnel told us that there were numerous meetings concerning McDonnell Douglas's financial condition beginning in the fall of 1990. Some of these meetings involved Air Force status reports to Office of the Secretary of Defense personnel on the C-17 aircraft program. In addition, the DOD principal analyst held discussions with the Navy and had numerous telephone conversations with the CACO. The CACO confirmed that he had numerous conversations with the principal analyst and that he was convinced that granting of a deferment was necessary.

The Deputy Chief of Staff for Financial Management and Comptroller, Air Force Systems Command, confirmed that during the briefings on the status of the C-17 aircraft program, McDonnell Douglas's cash flow data was presented. DOD officials responsible for the A-12 deferment were present at these briefings. The Deputy Chief explained that he compared McDonnell Douglas's monthly debt forecasts to actual monthly debt and found that the forecasts were within plus or minus five percent. He said that his analysis was limited to the corporate cash flow and was not an analysis of McDonnell Douglas's overall financial condition and that his effort was intended to improve efficiency on the C-17 program.

Financial Data Submitted With Request For Deferral

On January 16, 1991, McDonnell Douglas met with the Navy contracting officer and gave the Navy the following documents:

-- a draft letter requesting a deferral and indicating that the company anticipated that the deferral would take place in January 1991,

-- a draft deferment agreement referring to the same January 1991 date, and

-- a financial data package.

We confirmed with Navy officials that this data was given to them. Concerning the January 1991 date, the Navy officials said that the contractors wanted the deferment as soon as possible.

McDonnell Douglas also gave the CACO a copy of its January 11, 1991, debt forecast on January 22, 1991. This forecast showed that McDonnell Douglas would be in a negative cash flow position by April 1991. The CACO sent a memorandum to the Defense Logistics Agency headquarters the next day, January 23, 1991, alerting officials to this information and stating that an infusion of cash would be necessary. The CACO assumed that McDonnell Douglas could not issue new debt instruments or obtain a new bank loan and had insufficient cash. The CACO considered having the debt forecast audited by DCAA, but McDonnell Douglas told the CACO that its debt forecast was a repetitive document routinely used by corporate management. The CACO therefore decided to accept the forecast without audit.

Additional Financial Assistance Requested

A day later, on January 24, 1991, the Chief Executive Officer of McDonnell Douglas met with the Under Secretary of Defense for Acquisition and presented a letter requesting advance payments for a number of DOD programs. This was in addition to the request for deferral on the A-12 program. The Chief Executive Officer also presented a financial data package similar to the package presented to the Navy on January 16, 1991.

The DOD principal analyst stated that McDonnell Douglas's January 24, 1991, financial data package was intended to support its

request for significant advance payments, not the deferment.
Therefore, after January 24, 1991, DOD focused its attention on the
request for advance payments.

According to DOD officials after January 24, 1991, DOD was not
making a single decision focusing only on the granting of a
deferment, but was also being asked to consider providing
additional financial assistance to McDonnell Douglas. In a January
28, 1991, memorandum the Under Secretary for Acquisition stipulated
those actions to be taken by the military services before he would
brief the Deputy Secretary of Defense. The services, for example,
were to provide their perspectives on the near- and long-term
requirements for continued performance by McDonnell Douglas and on
the probable impact if the corporation should go into Chapter 11
bankruptcy. Other officials were directed to document McDonnell
Douglas's financial needs, determine which programs should be used
as sources for advance payments, and determine the legality of any
recommended option.

Banks' Concerns Over Possible Denial of Deferment

At the April hearings, DOD's Director of Defense Procurement said
that McDonnell Douglas had told her that its banks could view DOD's
denial of the deferment as a material adverse change and withdraw
their lines of credit. In a January 29, 1991, memo to her,
McDonnell Douglas's Senior Vice President for Finance provided a
letter from McDonnell Douglas's Treasurer, which stated that
certain of key banks were concerned that the termination of the A-
12 might have resulted in a material adverse change in McDonnell
Douglas' financial condition. If the banks invoked the material
adverse change provisions in revolving credit agreements, the
company could not borrow any additional amounts under those
agreements.

We asked the McDonnell Douglas's Senior Vice President for Finance whether there was any documentation from the banks regarding the withdrawal of their lines of credit. He told us that the agent bank had told him verbally that three member banks had expressed their concern. He said the three banks were persuaded to wait before they took action.

Additional Financial Information Provided

On January 25, 1991, DOD's principal analyst asked McDonnell Douglas to respond to 22 questions. McDonnell Douglas responded in writing on January 26 and 29, 1991. Answering these questions involved providing additional information on a variety of subjects dealing with the company's financial condition, including federal income tax liabilities, its dividend policy, commercial sales projections, and liabilities and debts to subcontractors. The information was to provide data not contained in the financial data package McDonnell Douglas provided on January 24, 1991.

The Director for Defense Procurement briefed the services' acquisition executives and comptrollers on January 31, 1991. The tentative conclusions shown in the briefing charts were the following:

-- McDonnell Douglas bankruptcy would not be in DOD's best interest;

-- McDonnell Douglas could not afford to repay the A-12 debt,

-- McDonnell Douglas needed additional short-term financing, and

-- McDonnell Douglas's financial problems would be a continuing concern.

In addition, the Director presented the financial data McDonnell Douglas had provided on January 24, 1991, unchanged but reformatted. This was the briefing the DOD witnesses were referring to at the April 11 hearing.

Financial Review Continued After the Deferment Decision

As indicated earlier, McDonnell Douglas requested advance payments on January 24, 1991. On February 7, 1991, 2 days after the deferment agreement was signed, the CACO, McDonnell Douglas officials, and personnel from the services and the Office of the Secretary of Defense met to review the financial data submitted by McDonnell Douglas. The Director of Defense Procurement told McDonnell Douglas officials that if the advance payments were approved, they would have to explain how any remaining cash shortfall would be resolved.

In materials prepared on February 4, for a meeting between the Under Secretary of Defense for Acquisition and McDonnell Douglas, there is evidence that DOD wanted a better understanding of McDonnell Douglas's cash flow needs and further assurance that additional payments would solve the company's problems. DOD did not request a DCAA audit of the data submitted by McDonnell Douglas until February 12, 1991, after the deferment decision was made. The purpose of the audit was to determine if cash flow projections were consistent with the assumptions made by McDonnell Douglas and to comment on the accuracy of previous cash flow projections.

A decision on additional advance payments was set forth in a March 20, 1991, letter addressed to the Chief Executive Officer of McDonnell Douglas and signed by the Under Secretary for Acquisition. The letter suggested four areas in which the company could take action to improve its cash flow. On April 1, 1991, during a visit to McDonnell Douglas's corporate headquarters in St.

Louis by the Under Secretary of Defense for Acquisition and the Director of Defense Procurement, McDonnell Douglas withdrew its request.

REASONABLENESS OF DOD DEFERMENT DECISION

There is no documented analysis demonstrating that DOD made a detailed evaluation of McDonnell Douglas's data before making its deferment decision, but it did have a great deal of pertinent information. We believe that the decision to grant the deferment was reasonable for the following reasons.

-- The DCAA September 13, 1990, audit report contained financial status indicators suggesting that McDonnell Douglas was in a weak financial position, even though contract performance was not endangered. DCAA calculated a number of ratios that showed a trend of declining financial well-being. For example, the ratio of total debt to net worth increased from 38 cents of debt for every dollar of net worth in 1986 to 92 cents of debt for every dollar of net worth in 1990.

-- McDonnell Douglas's data, which was not subjected to any verification, shows that it would be in a negative cash flow position during 1991. This is consistent with McDonnell Douglas's projection of a negative cash flow from operations during calendar year 1991 as published in the corporation's annual report to the stockholders for calendar year 1990.

-- McDonnell Douglas told DOD that its financial condition made obtaining additional credit from its banks or the securities market unlikely. Furthermore, McDonnell Douglas's debt rating had been down graded by Standard & Poors and Moody's Investment Service twice.

-- The government's CACO in a January 23, 1991, memorandum expressed concern about McDonnell Douglas's negative cash flow position. The CACO suggested that the contractor would have to take drastic action to remedy its cash flow problem. The data that is the basis for the CACO's memorandum was not subjected to independent verification.

-- McDonnell Douglas was already taking a variety of actions to improve its weakened financial condition. It had instituted a cost reduction and cash conservation effort with a goal of saving between $700 million and $1 billion. It sold some assets and identified other assets for possible sale.

-- McDonnell Douglas's annual report stated that the continuing negative cash flow from operations was primarily the result of increased investment in its commercial aircraft work. In addition to the cash needed to support the increase in commercial work, McDonnell Douglas is experiencing difficulties in performing concurrently on major government fixed-price development contracts. According to the Air Force, McDonnell Douglas could experience a loss on the Air Force C-17 aircraft program and additional losses on the Navy's T-45 aircraft program.

-- The McDonnell Douglas Senior Vice President For Finance summarized the company's financial position when he testified under oath that to have paid the government the disputed amount would have been extremely difficult, seriously strained the company's financial capability, and jeopardized continued performance of other government contracts.

-- McDonnell Douglas is responsible for a variety of major weapon systems that could have been and may well still be adversely affected if it is unable to continue performing.

167

-- The loss of a major defense contractor like McDonnell Douglas could adversely affect the U. S. defense industrial base.

-- The Persian Gulf War was ongoing when the deferment decision was made, and DOD was concerned that McDonnell Douglas's continued support of the war effort would be interrupted.

Finally, the contractor team disputed the amount owed and has filed its appeal with the Claims Court to convert the termination for default to a termination for convenience. If the court rules in favor of the team, it will not have to repay the deferred amount.

IMPLICATIONS OF MCDONNELL DOUGLAS'S FINANCIAL PROBLEMS

The short- and longer-term implications of McDonnell Douglas's financial problems on government programs require DOD's and the Congress's continuing attention for several years.

DOD did not deny McDonnell Douglas's request for advance payments; rather, McDonnell Douglas withdrew its request. If McDonnell Douglas encounters further financial difficulties, it could renew its request for financial assistance. McDonnell Douglas is also experiencing cost problems on the T-45 aircraft program and the C-17 aircraft program.

T-45 Navy Aircraft Program

In its T-45 aircraft program, McDonnell Douglas is currently working off a $45 million overpayment of progress payments. When the overpayment was identified, the Navy suspended further progress payments until McDonnell Douglas made up the difference with continued work on the contract. Furthermore, McDonnell Douglas is engaged in a dispute with its principal subcontractors, British Aerospace and Rolls Royce, over the costs of work performed and the

amount paid for such work. The parties in dispute are awaiting the
results of audits performed by the British government's audit
office. This T-45 contract is resulting in a negative cash flow.

C-17 Air Force Aircraft Program

McDonnell Douglas could lose substantial amounts on the C-17
aircraft program. In addition, we were told there were still
unresolved problems with this program. For example, the first
flight milestone in June 1991 was not met and scheduled delivery of
the first production aircraft in December 1991 may not be met.
Because of these and other performance shortcomings, an Air Force
official told us that serious consideration is being given to
modifying the C-17 contract.

Mr. Chairman, that concludes our prepared remarks. We will be
happy to answer any questions.

(396939)

Mr. CONYERS. I don't have many questions.

I am very troubled. I had a difficult time with your statement. You gave us a lot of advice about the war and the nature of the contracting industry, which apparently you took into account. But how was it generally known and how could it be stated that over $1 billion, a loan of over $1 billion, because they believed that something was generally known—in other words, how much independent investigation did you get into?

You are supposed to be dealing with the facts. Did you verify anything about the Department of Defense or McDonnell Douglas, what they said regarding the availability of credit or the change in the cash-flow due to the A-12 cancellation, or the suspected cash-flow required by the $1 billion IRS debt, or any other statement?

I mean, how did you conduct your investigation? What we have is that GAO—you are told by DOD, who is told by McDonnell Douglas, who is told by their banks, that it might affect their credit line. And how do we get some independent confirmation in here?

Mr. CONAHAN. Insofar as the independent confirmation on the part of the banks, I mentioned in my opening summary remarks that we did not do that.

However, insofar as the other indicators are concerned, we did spend a good bit of time with the DCAA people and the Administrative Contracting Officer people, trying to see how they went about doing their analysis. They had been out there for a long period of time, and if you take a look at their reports over time, they are done on a consistent basis.

And we rely on other audit organizations. We do this as part of our methodology, and we think it is quite appropriate. We think so long as they are doing a good job that we can rely on their information.

Mr. CONYERS. So you didn't find anything unusual about the literally secret nature of the way some of these transactions were taken care of?

Mr. CONAHAN. Oh, I think, like you and Mr. Horton and Mr. Shays, that there was a veil over what took place right here. And I do not believe this is the way it should be done. It should be done much more openly than it was.

But you have to separate the two things—No. 1, what indeed was done and how it was done. As I said at the outset——

Mr. CONYERS. There may be a connection, Mr. Conahan, for why it was done secretly as opposed to being done publicly. Normally, there is some reason that these things go on beyond the knowledge of all the appropriate parties. That is was disturbs us here. We have contradictions and conflicts in dates and documents that are really quite disturbing, over and above what has actually happened. And it suggests that there are problems.

If we negotiated in the Government in this manner, GAO would be outraged. You would be the lead agency in Government telling us we can't do business this way. And that is what we are here to examine, and that is what we are saying, at these and previous hearings.

Mr. CONAHAN. I appreciate that, Mr. Chairman, and insofar as the manner in which this was done, I quite agree with you. As a matter of fact, this document you have up on the board, we have had that in our possession and have been discussing that with the Department of Defense in terms of the need to disclose it.

I am very happy to see you were able to do that. I think it is important that it gets out. There is a lot more information that carries that very same stamp on it, and I don't really believe it is proprietary in nature. I don't think it is all that sensitive.

But we do have difficulty, as Government employees, in releasing that information. I am happy to see there is a way we can get that out.

Mr. CONYERS. Thank you:
Mr. Horton.

Mr. HORTON. Mr. Chairman, I do have some questions, but Mr. Ireland has to get back. Maybe I should defer to him.

Mr. CONYERS. Yes, let me recognize Andy Ireland, the gentleman from Florida, distinguished leader on the Armed Services Committee, former member of Government Operations.

Mr. IRELAND. Thank you, Mr. Chairman and ranking member. I appreciate it. As you both know, we have a hearing going on this moment about the A-12, and we did yesterday in our House Armed Services Investigation Subcommittee.

I would only like to make three points before I go back over there, because all of you on this committee have been an integral part of fleshing out what is going on here, and—which is a serious, at-least-$3-billion problem for this country.

I would say these three things. You have as a witness Mr. Donald Yockey, probably little noticed, but of great importance, Mr. Yockey recently, in a memorandum to Comptroller O'Keefe, outlined the need for the services to show full funding for major weapons systems in the out years. That sounds like a very innocuous statement, but it goes to the very real heart of the front loading operation that has historically gone on within the military services and the Pentagon on their budgets. And Mr. O'Keefe, I believe, deserves a great deal of credit for calling attention to that, in making that change.

In addition, of course, you will be talking to Mrs. Spector. I think we have all seen what analysis took place of the overall figures—in my judgment, wholly inadequate—and I think the GAO's comments and such hold that out. One of the great inadequacies was the fact that absolutely no analysis was made to give decisionmakers an idea of whether a course of deferment or nondeferment, nondeferment leading perhaps to bankruptcy, was the best course of action—absolutely no analysis made, whatsoever, about that.

And the last thing is an update that I will tell you—Congressman Mavroules made this announcement in our meeting just now—an integral part of the A-12 investigation yesterday, after our subcommittee took testimony that conflicted significantly with Program Manager Elberfeld's testimony to us that in previous times Captain Elberfeld met with the Secretary of the Navy yesterday and requested that his planned promotion to admiral be withdrawn and submitted his application for retirement, which was accepted.

And I think that that is an indication that accountability is on the march, and I would only point out that things of the nature that you are talking about here, and we are talking about in the

House Armed Services, indicate that despite roadblocks of Captain Elberfeld, a considerable amount of this information—warning signals, if you will—went to senior managers, senior managers should have at least seen that the kind of work put out by Mrs. Spector was an inadequate analysis.

Senior managers did get warnings that the project was behind schedule and over budget. They ignored them, and I think that is important—not as important as it was for Captain Elberfeld to take the move that he did. It is also important to realize that others that are in senior management should have at least said, gee, these warning signals are out here, this analysis is inadequate, maybe we had better look for it. We have a right to expect that from senior people at the Secretary of the Navy's level.

And I would thank you for your attention and also thank you again for your willingness to let me participate from time to time.

Mr. CONYERS. Your presence here underscores the cooperation that is going on between you and Mr. Mavroules's committee and ours. I was, in fact, invited to join your committee hearings. You are holding 3 days of hearings on this subject—yesterday, today, and tomorrow.

We are holding one, but we are working very closely together. I acknowledge that on the record.

Mr. IRELAND. I thank the gentleman for yielding. Thank you.

Mr. HORTON. I want to join with the chairman in thanking Mr. Ireland for his coming to our hearing. We appreciate your assistance and help. And I agree with the chairman that we are working very closely with the Armed Services Committee on this very vital and important subject.

Mr. IRELAND. Thank you.

Mr. CONYERS. Thank you very much.

Mr. Shays.

Mr. HORTON. I was going to ask a question.

Mr. CONYERS. Excuse me. All right.

Mr. HORTON. I want to ask a couple of questions by way of background. I would like to have the General Accounting Office's interpretation of the Federal Acquisition Regulations, FAR, with regard to deferments. Is it limited to small companies or financially weak companies? What is the deferment basis under FAR regulations?

Mr. CONAHAN. Mr. Horton, I think there are some internal inconsistencies in that regulation, but in direct response to your question, no, I do not believe that it is limited to small businesses or finally weak contractors.

I will just read what it says. "Deferments"—well, these are the categories from which deferments can be made—"Deferments pending disposition of appeal may be granted to small business concerns and financially weak contractors." So that is one provision; that is provision E. Now provision D says that "Deferments can be made to avoid possible overcollection," and that is kind of interesting, because the chairman, in his opening statement, referred to deferments to Delco, and the deferment to Delco, which was a fairly sizable deferment—not on the order of what we are talking about here—was made for that particular reason.

Another one that we are investigating for this subcommittee is one to Lockheed, and that provision was also cited for justification for that.

There is another provision in here that says, if the contractor is unable to pay at once in full, or the contractor's operations under the national defense contracts would be seriously impaired. So there are a whole series of justifications that the FAR seems to provide for. So I don't think we can have it an either-or in terms of small business or financially weak companies.

Mr. HORTON. Do you think the deferments given to these two companies, General Dynamics and McDonnell Douglas, are within the deferment FAR regulations, within their scope?

Mr. CONAHAN. Yes, I think within the scope of this, if we all agree that those firms are financially weak contractors.

Mr. HORTON. I haven't agreed to that conclusion. I want to get to that in a minute. I am trying to establish the basis on which the General Accounting Office feels that FAR permits deferment and whether or not it is in your view and of this action whether these deferments were within the scope of the FAR regulations.

Mr. CONAHAN. Yes, sir. We cited a number of events and facts which we believe lead to the conclusion that these companies were in a financially weakened position.

Mr. HORTON. I want to get to that in just a minute.

Mr. CONAHAN. But that is the basis.

Mr. HORTON. You are putting it on the basis of the financially weak corporations; is that what you are saying?

Mr. CONAHAN. That is correct.

Mr. HORTON. Any other basis?

Mr. CONAHAN. Well, we had—I think that there was some question that the contractors' operations could be impaired, and we said that, as well, because there are a number of defense programs that these contractors were responsible for.

Mr. HORTON. Do you think we need more clarification with regard to these regulations and also with regard to analyses that lead up to these deferments?

Mr. CONAHAN. I think, in view of the discussion that we are having here today, both would be helpful. I think we have to go about it carefully. The words here are "financially weak contractors." I suppose, if we had some elaboration on what that meant, we could have better agreement on whether that condition was met. That is one thing.

Second, if we had some standards for the kind of analysis that was required, financial analysis required to support deferment, then we could be closer to agreement as to whether those standards were met.

Mr. HORTON. I understood from your testimony earlier and in your statement, that in the analysis process, the military, the Department of Defense, did not have any documentation. And you were critical of their analysis of the financial stability of these two companies; is that correct?

Mr. CONAHAN. No, I didn't say that they didn't have any documentation. As a matter of fact, there is an——

Mr. HORTON. What did you say?

Mr. CONAHAN. There are an awful lot of documents, and it took us quite a bit of time to ferret that documentation out. It is not available in one place over in the Department of Defense. We had to go out and find it at the contractor's location, and at other locations.

Now, when you bring——

Mr. HORTON. That is not what I am asking you. I am asking you about the Department of Defense. If you had to go out to the contractor to get information, that is one thing. What makes you think they went out and got it?

I thought you were critical of their analysis procedures.

Mr. CONAHAN. I was critical of their procedures, because I think——

Mr. HORTON. Tell me what it is you were concerned about with regard to the Department of Defense deferment.

Mr. CONAHAN. I suppose the way I see that is that if—given a deferment on the order of magnitude of $1.3 billion, I would expect to go in and find that the Department had brought together in one place all of the information that supported that decision; that they said here is the financial condition tracked over time of this company, that we think that it can only get to this point so far as cashflow is concerned, you can only get to this point in terms of retained earnings, in terms of the other financial categories.

Once it is at that point, that permits us to conclude it meets the criteria of regulation that it is in a weakened financial condition.

Mr. HORTON. But you found no such study, no such analysis; is that correct?

Mr. CONAHAN. No, I didn't say "analysis." There was no document that brought that all together.

Some of that analysis might have been done. I expect some of that analysis was done.

Mr. HORTON. There is no documentation that it was. You are just guessing now, aren't you?

Mr. CONAHAN. I am guessing that the analysis was done, yes.

Mr. HORTON. Why do you guess? I mean, you checked them, didn't you? Didn't you go to the Department of Defense? What good is your analysis if you didn't check them?

Mr. CONAHAN. They told us they made this analysis. We are talking about two things.

Is the information available? As I say, if you did for the administrative——

Mr. HORTON. Mr. Conahan, look. In your statement, you just told me a few minutes ago that there was documentation. In your statement on page 4—"Results in Brief" is the paragraph—"There is some evidence that DOD officials did follow a deliberative process. However, documentation showing this process is not available.

"There is also no documentation available that indicates why data was used in a particular manner, nor is there a formal document or written decision paper prepared supporting the deferment decision."

That is what you said in your testimony.

Mr. CONAHAN. Well, in my oral comments, I changed it a bit. I said——

Mr. HORTON. Well, that is nice.

Mr. CONAHAN. There are some cases that you find that documentation, but overall—and that is the key—overall that information is not brought together.

Mr. HORTON. I want to ask him a couple more questions.

Now, both of these companies, General Dynamics and McDonnell Douglas, according to information, Aviation Week and Space Technology indicates that both these companies are doing very well. As a matter of fact, their stock is up, and they appear to be financially on sound footing.

Now, you indicated, after you gave us this information with regard to the lack of documentation and the other with regard to the Department of Defense making their decision, you then told us that you found information that made it justifiable that they gave this deferment. I am curious about that.

On what basis are you, the General Accounting Office, finding that this deferment was justifiable or reasonable?

Mr. CONAHAN. I cited in my statement, Mr. Horton, a series of reports done by the Defense Contract Audit Agency, information that was submitted by McDonnell Douglas and analyzed by the Department of Defense. I cited the ratings that were given by Standard & Poor's and Moody's. I cited additional DCAA and Administrative Contracting Officer analysis. I cited the analysis that was done in connection with the C-17 program and the T-45 program, which was also used in connection with the analysis in connection with this deferment, and other information.

All that brought together at the time the decision was made, in our opinion, would not permit us to say that what the Department concluded was unreasonable. I think perhaps that a lot of people would have made that same decision, based on that information.

Insofar as the current situation——

Mr. HORTON. Again, you are guessing.

Mr. CONAHAN. Well, no. That is our conclusion, based on that information; and it is a lot of information. It is a fair amount of information.

Mr. HORTON. But you went out to the companies and got that information from them, didn't you?

Mr. CONAHAN. From the Defense Contract Audit Agency and the Government's Administrative Contracting Officer.

For example, I have a DCAA report dated April—April 5, 1991, and the overall conclusion is that McDonnell Douglas is in an unfavorable financial condition, which would adversely affect its ability to perform Government contracts.

Mr. HORTON. When was this?

Mr. CONAHAN. April 5, 1991.

Mr. HORTON. April 5, 1991. And July 1991, according to this market focus, do you have any information about the status of both these companies at the present time?

Mr. CONAHAN. I have a report from the CACO—I don't have the audit report with me, but I have a notation that says the CACO report dated July 16, 1991, says essentially the same thing I just read to you that was in the April 5 report.

Mr. HORTON. This is, of course, just from a magazine, and this is what they report. But they say McDonnell Douglas will likely post earnings of $1.75 to $2 versus $1.49 a year ago.

Mr. CONAHAN. I don't have that information. I have the DCAA report here.

Mr. HORTON. I think it would be helpful if you got the up-to-date information and gave this committee your analysis of what their status is as of now. We are talking about July 1991, and your analysis was what date, the early one?

Mr. CONAHAN. This one right here was April 1991.

Mr. HORTON. So at that time it appears as though they are in trouble, and according to this, it would appear they are not in financial trouble.

Now, what was the amount of the waivers?

Mr. CONAHAN. The amount of the waiver?

Mr. HORTON. Right, that was given to these two companies.

Mr. CONAHAN. The deferral, $1.35 billion.

Mr. HORTON. Was that for both companies?

Mr. CONAHAN. Yes, sir.

Mr. HORTON. Was there also an additional loan to either one of these companies?

Mr. CONAHAN. There was a request for a $1 billion loan by McDonnell Douglas.

Mr. HORTON. Did they get that?

Mr. CONAHAN. To my knowledge, no, sir. That request was withdrawn in the early part of April.

Mr. HORTON. What is your analysis of General Dynamics's financial condition?

Mr. CONAHAN. We have not looked at General Dynamics at all.

Mr. HORTON. You said they were in better financial shape.

Mr. CONAHAN. I said that the Department of Defense said they were in better financial shape.

Mr. HORTON. You don't know that?

Mr. CONAHAN. No, sir, I don't know that.

Mr. HORTON. Then why would you lump these two together? Shouldn't they be separated?

Mr. CONAHAN. The arrangements of this procurement were that the two companies were jointly and severally responsible for financial liability. The Department determined that General Dynamics possibly could have paid its share, but that it didn't think it could pay both, and therefore, that the analysis had to be done to see what McDonnell Douglas would look like.

And that is what we are talking about here today.

Mr. HORTON. Thank you, Mr. Chairman.

Mr. CONYERS. Thank you very much.

The gentleman from Connecticut, Mr. Shays.

Mr. SHAYS. Thank you, Mr. Chairman.

Mr. Conahan, if we can't trust you, we can't trust anybody; and you have given answers that simply defy logic to me. You basically say, they didn't do the analysis, you have no documentation that they did the analysis, but if you go through a lot of papers, there can be some justification for what they did.

And you were asked questions like, did they get $1 billion, and you basically said, in their advance payment; and you said, they withdrew it, and, to my knowledge, they didn't.

The question is, you have no knowledge; isn't that true? You don't know if they did or didn't perform the analysis.

Mr. CONAHAN. I am fairly certain they didn't get this $1 billion right here.

Mr. SHAYS. This billion. They may have gotten another billion. Do you have any documentation that they may have gotten advance payments of over $700 million? Have you seen any documentation that would give you the idea that maybe they did?

Mr. CONAHAN. On which program?

Mr. SHAYS. Well, you tell me, sir.

Mr. CONAHAN. Well, I think——

Mr. SHAYS. Let's not play games. The reason I say that is, they can ask for a billion dollars here and then withdraw it, and then get $750 million somewhere else. And now they don't need the advance billion here, because they got it in another program.

Mr. CONAHAN. Let me see if I can shed some light on that. This document——

Mr. SHAYS. I am not interested. I am interested in you answering my question.

This is the question I asked. The knowledge—you have no knowledge that they got a billion-dollar advance payment. That is correct, isn't it?

Mr. CONAHAN. That is correct.

Mr. SHAYS. You do not have any knowledge that they didn't?

Mr. CONAHAN. They did not.

Mr. SHAYS. The point I am trying to make is, if you have done an investigation, and you can tell us and be confident they didn't, that is fine. But if you haven't looked at all the facts, please don't tell us that you don't think they did, if you don't know.

Mr. CONAHAN. Let me answer that question. I need to answer that question. They certainly did not get this $1 billion right here.

The question on the $700 million advance payment stems from a discussion of the C-17 program. And this document that I was talking about up here talks about the C-17 program and it talks about how possibly during the first 6 months or so of 1991, $700 million could be made available on the C-17 program.

Now, if you take a look at most of that, some of those events did not occur, so that some of that $700 million could not have gone out to McDonnell Douglas.

Now let us take a look at the facts concerning the progress payments on the C-17 program.

Mr. SHAYS. I am not interested in that right now. I am asking you the questions, and if you want to bring it up later, that's fine. The only question I asked you was, is it not true that they got advance payments, some advance payments, whether it was this billion, that they got payments somewhere else. Is that not true?

Mr. CONAHAN. We have not done that work. We were not called upon to do that work.

Mr. SHAYS. So you don't know if they got advance payments anywhere?

Mr. CONAHAN. No, sir.

Mr. SHAYS. Your testimony is, in all the documents you have seen, you are telling this committee that you have no documentation that they received any advance payments?

Mr. CONAHAN. Beyond the normal progress payments that they would receive on a program.

Mr. SHAYS. That is your testimony to us?

Mr. CONAHAN. And as a matter of fact, right now they are getting flexible progress payments on some of it; and until very recently and as of today, they are getting either 100 percent or close to that in progress payments on the C-17 program.

Mr. SHAYS. Have you been investigating the C-17 program?

Mr. CONAHAN. Yes, sir.

Mr. SHAYS. Are you satisfied with how it is going?

Mr. CONAHAN. No, sir.

Mr. SHAYS. It has got a lot of problems, doesn't it?

Let me back up a second. We have an A-12 program for research and development that was to cost $4.7 billion, $4.8 billion. Am I fairly accurate here, that's what the program was to cost?

Mr. CONAHAN. Yes. The target price on the full-scale development contract was $4.4, and the ceiling price was $4.8.

Mr. SHAYS. So between $4.4 and $4.8.

That program was canceled after an expenditure of what, $2.7 billion?

Mr. CONAHAN. Yes, sir.

Mr. SHAYS. Of which it is our feeling that $1.35 was a deferred payment, in other words, a payment above and beyond what the Government feels it should have made for the program; is that correct?

Mr. CONAHAN. Yes, sir.

Mr. SHAYS. Is it not true that the only thing we got for this was six design packages, that no plane has been assembled?

Mr. CONAHAN. Yes, sir, that is correct.

Mr. SHAYS. So we have parts and design packages; that is it?

Mr. CONAHAN. That is correct.

Mr. SHAYS. And we—Mr. Cheney, canceled this program, where we have now spent $2.7 billion and have given a deferment of $1.35; and now we are canceling that program, and we are going to go to the A.X., and is it not true we are looking at $12 billion for research and development, approximately?

Mr. CONAHAN. We have seen that estimate from the Department of Defense.

Mr. SHAYS. And we will have a 10-year delay now in the process of building this plane, so that is the general, broad picture.

Now, what I just find absolutely intriguing is that you have your testimony, when you are pressed for an answer, you say, well, I said something different in my oral testimony in response to Mr.— to my ranking member Mr. Horton's questions. Which do you want us to listen to, what you say publicly or what is in your document?

Mr. CONAHAN. Insofar as the analysis was done, perhaps the written statement is too broad.

What I want to say is that we did find some analysis, but overall, we didn't find the kind of analysis that should be done.

Mr. SHAYS. Let me say this to you. There was no formal analysis done, correct?

Mr. CONAHAN. There was no formal document capturing all of the analysis that was done.

Mr. SHAYS. So you can't tell us whether there was a formal analysis done, because you have not seen one, correct?

Mr. CONAHAN. Correct.

Mr. SHAYS. Now, if you had not seen one, why do you jump to the conclusion that one was done?

Mr. CONAHAN. I didn't jump to that conclusion. I presented a series of information, data, and events that did occur that led us to the conclusion that we took.

Mr. SHAYS. Now, you are the General Accounting Office, correct? You have a job to protect the taxpayers? You have the job of protecting and working for Congress; in our work, is this the way it is supposed to happen?

Mr. CONAHAN. No, I think not. And I think I said that at the outset.

Mr. SHAYS. No, you said this is what they did, and we are satisfied that they did an analysis.

Mr. CONAHAN. I didn't say that.

Mr. SHAYS. I want to know, did they do one or didn't they?

Mr. CONAHAN. You are going to have to ask them. They did some analysis——

Mr. SHAYS. I am asking you.

Mr. CONAHAN. I don't know the full extent of analysis. The only way I can tell is by asking them and trying to verify what they tell us, and looking at the documentation.

Mr. SHAYS. The problem with you asking them, when they can't show you any formal analysis, is that you become part of the conspiracy, rather than being on the outside, looking in; you are a player now in this mess.

We have got to put you into that pile, because you are covering up, in my judgment, what they have done, because you have made assumptions that you have no right to make.

Mr. CONAHAN. I thought I accurately reported what took place there. We cannot find documents for the full extent of analysis that they did. We can see some analysis.

Mr. SHAYS. If you cannot find documentation, then how do you know that the decision was a reasonable decision to provide for deferment?

Mr. CONAHAN. We put together a body of information, and when we analyze that body of information, we came to the conclusion that we could not say that their decision was unreasonable.

Mr. SHAYS. That is an interesting term. You can't say it is reasonable and you can't say it is unreasonable?

Mr. CONAHAN. I think if I were sitting in their shoes, with the information I had available to me, to include all of the matters I cited in my statement, I would say it was a reasonable decision to make.

Mr. SHAYS. Is it not a fact that the reason why McDonnell Douglas is in a financial problem is not because of their Government contracts but because they have invested so much in the McDonnell Douglas-11 and that the commercial side has a financial cash-flow problem?

Mr. CONAHAN. I don't have those numbers before me, but, in general, yes.

Mr. SHAYS. So on their defense side they are getting paid for projects, and so on. Maybe there are cost overruns. But where they have their problems is on the commercial side?

Mr. CONAHAN. They have problems on both defense and commercial sides.

Mr. SHAYS. Have they not put a plethora of money into the McDonnell Douglas-11, and is it not true they have not had a return for that?

Mr. CONAHAN. I don't have the numbers, but the answer is yes.

Mr. SHAYS. You are telling me you have made an analysis and said it was reasonable that they did what they did and yet this was a major component of that decision.

All I can say to you, Mr. Chairman, and to our witnesses, is that he has come before us on many occasions, and I have felt very comfortable with his testimony. But, sir, your testimony today I find close to shocking, and I feel that way because you have, basically, made the comment they did not do an analysis, a formal analysis, but now you, I guess, have done the analysis and you are comfortable that they made the right decision. And there is something left out in between. And we are trying to find out what is left out in between.

And I just look forward to the next witnesses.

Mr. CONYERS. I thank the gentleman from Connecticut.

I recognize the gentleman from New Mexico, Mr. Schiff.

Mr. SCHIFF. Thank you, Mr. Chairman.

Mr. Conahan, thank you for your testimony. I just have a couple of things to ask about.

One, I would like to go back a step and just talk about the deferment idea as a concept. If the Navy had not granted the deferment in its claim against McDonnell Douglas, against General Dynamics, what would the Navy have done then to recover this money?

Mr. CONAHAN. The Navy did make a claim for the money but then agreed that, simultaneous with the claim, that it would defer it.

Mr. SCHIFF. And if they had not done that, that is, if they had made the claim and not agreed to the deferment, what, exactly, would the Government do to get the money ahead of a judgment in its favor in court?

Mr. CONAHAN. Well, I would expect that the contractors would have immediately gone to court, as they did 6 months later.

Mr. SCHIFF. To prevent the money from coming directly back to the Navy at that point?

Mr. CONAHAN. Right.

Mr. SCHIFF. Here I am not as concerned about this incident as to how it is supposed to work. Is the Government supposed to stop payments on other contracts to recover the money if it makes a claim and doesn't give a deferment?

Here is what I am getting at. In most cases that I know of, if not all, if anyone asserts a claim against another party, that party doesn't have to pay money if there is a judgment against them. So I am kind of curious about how the Government gets money without a judgment if it doesn't get a deferment. Can you help me with that?

Mr. CONAHAN. Let me ask Mr. Math to give you the details on that.

Mr. MATH. It is my understanding that one of the ways that you can recover that money is through offsets on other existing Government contracts that have been entered into with that corporation. According to section 32.611 of the FAR, a disbursing officer who has contractor invoices for payment on hand shall make an appropriate offset if the disbursing officer is the official responsible for collection of a contract debt or is notified of the debt. Section 32.612 of the regulation requires offset 30 days after issuance of a demand letter if payment is not completed and deferment is not requested. Under offset procedures, payment on other contracts is withheld until the debt or claim is satisfied.

Mr. SCHIFF. But that could jeopardize, from the Government's point of view, those other contracts, if it makes the contractor unable to perform, and that was largely a concern here.

Mr. MATH. It definitely could have an affect on the other contracts, yes, sir.

Mr. SCHIFF. Let me talk about this particular deferment. If I understand you correctly, Mr. Conahan, you are saying that there is not full documentation of the Navy doing the analysis it said it made, but whether that documentation can be found or not, doesn't mean the Navy didn't do the analysis. Do I have that about right?

Mr. CONAHAN. Yes, sir. That is how we tried to characterize it.

Mr. SCHIFF. However, at least you would have expected to find some document in one place that would have gone through all that analysis, that normally is what we would have expected with an amount of this magnitude in consideration.

Mr. CONAHAN. That was the point that we were trying to make at the outset. I think there are two parts to this.

One, the merits of the case itself, and then, also, the responsibility of the Department of Defense to be able to demonstrate to the Congress and the American people that they did, indeed, discharge their responsibilities before they made their decision.

And it is that latter point that we find lacking.

Mr. SCHIFF. So, at least in part, the analysis documentation is not adequate, in your judgment?

Mr. CONAHAN. That is correct.

Mr. SCHIFF. Now, when you talk about the bottom line, then, having sifted through the documentation that you can find, either documentation of analysis or underlying information on behalf of the GAO, do you have a conclusion as to whether the deferment was properly granted by the Navy under the FAR regulations in this incident?

Mr. CONAHAN. Based on everything we have seen, it was properly granted under the regulations.

Mr. SCHIFF. One final thing I would like to ask. We had a brief hearing, as you know, on the A-12 contract, and there are hearings going on in the Armed Services Committee, and I don't want to go over all of that. There has been a great deal of discussion already as to how we got to this point and the various points of view.

What I would like is, from the work that you and your agency have done, what is the best way for us to go? Is there a way we can make use of the investment that the taxpayers already made of over $2 billion, which has resulted, although not in an assembled airplane yet, but in design and number of parts. And I understand quite a number of parts if we were to go look at it.

Or do you think we need to just start from scratch and say, sorry about that. It didn't work. And it needs to be a ground zero?

Mr. CONAHAN. I think the Navy has a responsibility to determine what, if anything, is applicable to other programs or future programs. We know that they are doing some of that work right now. We ourselves have been asked to monitor what the Navy and the Department of Defense are doing in that regard.

So I do believe there are current responsibilities to determine what is the best disposition of the work that has been done to date.

Mr. SCHIFF. Thank you, Mr. Chairman.

Mr. CONYERS. Thank you, Mr. Schiff.

The gentleman from Oklahoma, Mr. English.

Mr. ENGLISH. Thank you very much, Mr. Chairman.

Mr. Conahan, you were sworn this morning. You are under oath, is that correct?

Mr. CONAHAN. Yes, sir.

Mr. ENGLISH. Were you given access to all documents relating to this matter, as far as you know?

Mr. CONAHAN. No, not as far as I know. There is one document we have identified that we do not have in hand, although one of our evaluators did see it. It is a memorandum that went to the Deputy Secretary through the Service Secretaries which indicated their concurrence in the deferment action that was taken.

Mr. ENGLISH. Why were you not given access to that document?

Mr. CONAHAN. The deliberative process was cited as a basis for not handing it over to the General Accounting Office.

Mr. ENGLISH. Would you explain that further?

Mr. CONAHAN. I have difficulty in explaining that, as I have for a long period of time. They take the position that it is predecisional, and they only need to give to the General Accounting Office decisional information. We disagree with that, but that is where we stand at the moment on that.

I believe we have the same case here with the committee, that that document has been withheld from this committee.

Mr. ENGLISH. So we don't have all the information available to us?

Mr. CONAHAN. That is at least one that we don't have.

Mr. ENGLISH. With regard to the letters that the—the documents that are before us that are displayed, the letter, the statements for an advanced payment pool arrangement. What is an advanced payment pool arrangement?

Mr. CONAHAN. I don't have any information beyond what I see right there, but as I understand it, in order to take care of their current cash requirements, they wanted the Department of Defense to deposit the billion dollars into its bank account to use to meet current requirements. Advance payments are advances of money, made by the Government to a contractor for the purpose of financing performance under a contract or contracts. They are expected to be liquidated from payments due to the contractor incident to performance of contracts. Under section 232.471 of the DOD FAR supplement, an advance payment pool arrangement is an instrument for conveniently financing the performance of more than one contractor held by a contractor.

Mr. ENGLISH. Is that a loan? Is that what that is?

Mr. CONAHAN. I see that as a loan.

Mr. ENGLISH. Then why is it described as an advanced payment pool arrangement?

Mr. CONAHAN. I can only look at the words as you have, Mr. English. I have no idea why that is.

Mr. ENGLISH. Is that—do you think that is just kind of a gussied up way to get around the fact that we need a loan?

Mr. MATH. As we understand it, that is what the Federal regulations call it, an advanced pool.

Mr. ENGLISH. Is that, in effect, a loan?

Mr. MATH. As we said——

Mr. ENGLISH. Is that what the purpose is under Federal regulations?

Mr. MATH. It is a loan, as Mr. Conahan stated. Yes, sir.

Mr. ENGLISH. So this is just—who drew up this regulation? Is this a DOD regulation?

Mr. MATH. It is a Federal regulation.

Mr. ENGLISH. Federal regulation? Who drew it up? Where did it come from?

Mr. CONAHAN. There are some statutory bases for it, I believe. I would like to put that forward for the record, if I can. Advance payment pools are provided for in section 232.471 of the DOD FAR supplement [DFARS], which is developed and issued by the DOD.

Mr. ENGLISH. That is what I am curious about, as I said. If it is a loan, why can't we call it a loan? I don't understand if this is—if this was the intent as far as Federal regulations are concerned, then if that is what its purpose is I think we should call it a loan.

If it has some other purpose and it is being used here to achieve some other end, in other words to make a loan when, in fact, this is not supposed to be a loan, then that is what I was curious about.

Mr. CONAHAN. Well, it is clear that it was to be used to meet current cash requirements.

Mr. ENGLISH. The information that you have at hand, all the information that you have at hand and conclusions that the General Accounting Office has drawn with regard to this matter, have you provided us today with every bit of information that was provided to you? And have you then testified before this committee providing us with each and every conclusion that the experts in the General Accounting Office have come to in examination of this information?

Mr. CONAHAN. No, I see this as an interim report. We have an effort ongoing. We certainly haven't provided you with all the information. There are stacks of information. As a matter of fact, we talked earlier about the difficulty in reporting some of this information in an open hearing like this because it is classified as proprietary or business sensitive.

Mr. ENGLISH. Who makes the determination on whether, in fact, something is actually proprietary or business sensitive?

Mr. CONAHAN. In the first instance, the company designates it as proprietary or business sensitive, but there are discussions that occur after that. I have had some difficulties with this one in determining who had the final say on this. We learned earlier that certainly those provisions do not apply to the Congress, and, therefore, we are able to get this kind of information out.

The statute is fairly clear when it comes to the penalties for release of information so designated by a Government employee, but it is not all that clear as to who has the final determination for determining that it is indeed proprietary.

Mr. ENGLISH. You mean if I was the head of a company and this month's order for coffee for the coffee room, if I want to classify that and say that is proprietary information, then that information could not be released by the General Accounting Office?

Mr. CONAHAN. I don't think that that would hold up.

Mr. ENGLISH. Then who is going to make the decision?

Mr. CONAHAN. That decision generally comes out as a result of discussions between the company and the Government recipient.

Mr. ENGLISH. As far as I am concerned, it is proprietary. What basis of law do you have for discarding that——

Mr. CONAHAN. I don't have anything beyond the rules of reasonableness. And in that case I would contend that that is not very reasonable, and I don't know how your position otherwise would be sustained.

Mr. ENGLISH. You are saying that information in material that has been withheld, that you are not discussing, then in your judgment that is legitimately proprietary?

Mr. CONAHAN. Some of it I do not believe is proprietary.

Mr. ENGLISH. Why have you not provided us with that, then?

Mr. CONAHAN. The committee has the same information that we have. We are not discussing here in a public forum today is all I am saying.

Mr. ENGLISH. Would you identify for us the information you are withholding?

Mr. CONAHAN. I would have to go back to the office and get the information and go through it. Can I do that?

Mr. ENGLISH. I would appreciate it if you would so identify the information that you are withholding.

Have you been requested by anyone to withhold information from this committee?

Mr. CONAHAN. No, sir. And I am not withholding information from this committee.

Mr. ENGLISH. Other than that that has been labeled as proprietary by the company?

Mr. CONAHAN. Let me give you an example. I was having an awful lot of difficulty in deciding what I was going to do with this. On this particular letter, we decided as an institution last night that we would have released this. And we told the Department of Defense and the contractors that we would have released this if we were the ones that were called upon to release it.

Now, that was our decision.

Mr. ENGLISH. Now that you have agreed that it should be released and it, obviously, is released, would you review that and tell us exactly what this means? What do we see? What does that note from Eleanor that she is thanking somebody so much for—Herb, I guess—so much for, and what is the attachment? What does all that mean?

Mr. CONAHAN. Mr. English, that is not what we are talking about in terms of being released. Because that was not designated as proprietary. I was talking about this letter over here from McDonnell Douglas.

Mr. ENGLISH. We have talked a little bit about that. I raised the question of what is a loan and what is an advanced pool arrangement. And I guess it is the same thing.

Now, go to the second display. What is it we are seeing there? What does that mean?

Mr. CONAHAN. We are talking about the C-17 aircraft. Mrs. Spector is saying to McDonnell Douglas, when we get together on Thursday, I guess it is, I would like you to be prepared to discuss the following information. And she sets forth up front the assumptions with respect to the contract.

No. 1 says, use $7.1 billion for the estimate to completion cost for the full-scale engineering development contract, and for lots one and two of that aircraft.

I might say that the DOD——

Mr. ENGLISH. Maybe before you do that, would you read for us, then, the handwritten word?

Mr. CONAHAN. "Attached are the assumptions we would like you to use in a revised cash-flow analysis. Please have it for us when you come in Thursday. Call us if you have any questions."

Mr. ENGLISH. Why would we do something like that?

Mr. CONAHAN. McDonnell Douglas had submitted some cash-flow information, and I think Mrs. Spector wanted to see what that cash-flow would look like concerning the C-17, using different assumptions.

Mr. ENGLISH. How would you make different assumptions?

Mr. MATH. We were told by the Department of Defense that——

Mr. ENGLISH. Let me cut through this very quickly. I guess I assume what we are after or what you would legitimately be looking for are reasonable, responsible, solid, assumptions, if you are making assumptions. Now, we have got the Department of Defense coming back to McDonnell Douglas in this case and saying, we want you to make these assumptions.

Mr. MATH. We were told by the Department of Defense, you are absolutely correct. McDonnell Douglas came in with certain assumptions with regard to the cash-flow. They took a look at them, and they felt that their assumptions were liberal.

I will just start with the top one where it says 7.13, whatever that figure is up there. That was, at that time the Department of Defense's estimate at completion. McDonnell Douglas had something that was substantially less. They had 6 billion or something around that number for their figure on the estimate at completion.

Mr. ENGLISH. Now, just a minute. Who is the one that has got to perform in this case?

Mr. MATH. Who is the one that has to perform? Well, the contractor has to perform.

Mr. ENGLISH. In this case, McDonnell Douglas?

Mr. MATH. They also have to provide realistic estimates. As we found in the A-12, the contractor did not provide realistic estimates at completion. This is what they are saying as well. McDonnell came in with their estimate at completion and DOD didn't think it was accurate, and they said, for your assumptions, use this figure.

Mr. ENGLISH. On what basis did DOD base their assumption?

Mr. MATH. They based their assumption on the information that was, as I understand it, gathered from the defense plant representatives who were physically located in the contractor's plant, who were observing the construction of the C-17 aircraft.

Mr. ENGLISH. The second assumption was, assume two aircraft will be delivered during calendar year 1991—T-1 in June and T-2 in December. Was the T-1 delivered in June?

Mr. MATH. My understanding is it was not.

Mr. ENGLISH. It was not?

Mr. MATH. It was not. This was an assumption that was made back in January.

Mr. ENGLISH. This was the last day of January? What—that is 5 months ago, 5 months before the T-1 was to be delivered?

Mr. MATH. To my understanding. Yes, sir.

Mr. ENGLISH. You mean the plant representatives for the Department of Defense at McDonnell Douglas didn't know that the T-1 wasn't going to be delivered in June, back in the end of January?

Mr. MATH. Apparently.

Mr. CONAHAN. That was their best estimate at the time.

Mr. ENGLISH. Has the T-1 been delivered since then?

Mr. CONAHAN. No, sir. I don't believe it has been delivered.

Mr. ENGLISH. You mean it is 30 days later now?

Mr. CONAHAN. Oh, yes, sir. I think it is December.

Mr. ENGLISH. The T-1?

Mr. CONAHAN. The first airplane to fly will be December of this year.

Mr. ENGLISH. So they are 6 months off on that?

Mr. CONAHAN. I believe so.

Mr. ENGLISH. And 5 months before that, they didn't know?

Mr. CONAHAN. This program had substantial schedule delays right from the very beginning.

Mr. ENGLISH. Is the P-2 going to be delivered in December?

Mr. CONAHAN. I don't have that information.

Mr. ENGLISH. You don't have any idea? Mr. Math, do you know whether the P-2 will be delivered in December?

Mr. MATH. I don't have that, either.

Mr. ENGLISH. OK.

Now we go down, and we are assuming that lot three negotiations will be completed by the end of February 1991. Why would we make that assumption? Why would you assume that the negotiations are going to be completed by the end of February 1991? That is 30 days away.

Mr. CONAHAN. I can't really get to the assumption here. I can tell you that lot three negotiations were completed on March 3——

Mr. ENGLISH. It is pretty close, isn't it?

Mr. CONAHAN [continuing]. 1991.

Mr. ENGLISH. During this time—I want to make sure I understand things—during this time, do we have a situation where McDonnell Douglas and the Department of Defense were in negotiations, is that correct?

Mr. CONAHAN. Yes, sir.

Mr. ENGLISH. And we have here the Department of Defense saying, we are going to complete negotiations by the end, in the next 30 days? Is that right?

Mr. CONAHAN. That was their best estimate, according to this document, at the time.

Mr. ENGLISH. Well, if I was in negotiations with somebody, and they told me, hey, I have got to get up and go home by the end of March so I have got to have it wrapped up, I would understand that would give me something of an edge going into negotiations.

Mr. CONAHAN. I think that one of the things that we have been concerned about over time are the optimistic statements with respect to both schedule and cost that you see on the part of both contractors as well as the Department.

Mr. ENGLISH. The question I asked you is, if I tell you, hey, I have got to get up and go home by 5 p.m. today, so while we are sitting here trying to reach an understanding I have got to leave, are you going to have an advantage in negotiations with me if you know that I have got to leave at 5 p.m. and I have got to have something agreed to by 5 p.m. today?

Mr. CONAHAN. I think under your scenario, certainly.

Mr. ENGLISH. Isn't that the scenario we have got right here? We are telling you to assume the negotiations are going to be completed by the end of February, 30 days away from then.

Mr. CONAHAN. I suppose it could be construed like that.

Mr. ENGLISH. How else would you construe it?

Mr. CONAHAN. I am not going to construe it. I am going to let the author——

Mr. ENGLISH. That is what we pay you for. We pay you to construe, and we pay you to reach conclusions. I mean, we can sit here and read this. We don't need you if that is the case. We expect you to provide us with your best informed sense of what the situation is.

And, you know, as I said, it seems pretty simple to me, if somebody is telling me, I want to complete negotiations in 30 days, period, I have just been handed a pretty good bit of leverage in this negotiation.

Now we are also telling you that we are going to assume that we are adding an additional $338 million to the existing lot three long lead document to cover termination of liability incurred until the signed contract is executed. What are they doing, giving $338 million more while we are in negotiations?

Mr. CONAHAN. What they are saying, as I understand it, is that if the contract for the long lead items is terminated that they are setting aside $338 million to cover termination costs.

Mr. ENGLISH. Is that normally something that is negotiated?

Mr. CONAHAN. Yes. The termination costs are negotiated.

Mr. ENGLISH. So, in effect, what we are saying, hey, we are in negotiations, and I have got to get up, and I have got to have this thing finished here in 30 days. And, by the way, even though we are negotiating about it, I am going to give you an additional $338 million?

Mr. CONAHAN. I don't think that I would want to make that number available.

Mr. ENGLISH. That would't be very wise, would it, Mr. Conahan?

Mr. CONAHAN. I don't think I would at this point.

Mr. ENGLISH. That kind of puts you at a disadvantage? That is kind of throwing in your hand?

Mr. CONAHAN. Yes.

Mr. MATH. If I could add one thing. It is not an advance of money. It is a contingent liability. So it is not a loan per se.

Mr. ENGLISH. It is a benefit, isn't it?

Mr. MATH. It is a contingency if the contract is terminated. Then they will get that money, yes.

Mr. ENGLISH. Isn't that what we call sweetening the pot?

Mr. MATH. It is called a contingent liability. It is contingent on something happening, the termination of the contract.

Mr. ENGLISH. Do they always provide this kind of provision in a contract?

Mr. MATH. I don't know about always, but it is not uncommon.

Mr. ENGLISH. Is that something that is negotiated or is that something granted going in, that we are going to give you this?

Mr. MATH. It is negotiated.

Mr. ENGLISH. Then why in the world would you give it away?

Mr. MATH. Because it is my understanding, again, as Mr. Conahan said, we will hear it from the next witness, but it is my understanding that this was to develop a cash-flow analysis as part of the discussion as to whether they were going to provide the $1 billion advance.

Mr. ENGLISH. Let me tell you how it appears to me, and you tell me whether I am wrong. It is my understanding that we have the United States Government through the Department of Defense negotiating with a vendor. They are negotiating to get the best possible price they can for the taxpayer. That is what they are negotiating, supposedly. We are trying to acquire something, in this case an airplane, and we are trying to get it at the cheapest possible price.

Now what we have here is, we have the United States Government through the Department of Defense saying, gosh, we have got to have this wrapped up in 30 days, so we have only got 30 days to strike this kind of a deal. And, by the way, even though I know we are negotiating over this, I am just going to throw this in, $338 million we are just going to pitch in the pot. That is what it is, isn't it?

Mr. MATH. I don't know where the exact figure——

Mr. ENGLISH. A $338 million benefit is pitched into the pot?

Mr. MATH. For contingent liability, yes, sir. Subject to negotiation, as I understand.

Mr. ENGLISH. Let me also say, on completion of lot three negotiations, assume an additional $52 million will be added to existing lot four long lead documents. So we are going to throw in another $52 million benefit, just pitched into the pot. That is what we are telling you when we tell you to assume that, isn't that right?

Mr. MATH. I don't know what McDonnell Douglas had in their pot in terms of their cash-flow is what I am saying. I don't have that——

Mr. ENGLISH. It looks to me like you are sure dealing them a lot of cards.

Mr. MATH. All I am saying is, what we were told is that these were what they felt were the more realistic assumptions to be considered in a cash-flow analysis.

Mr. ENGLISH. I will tell you, in my part of the country, Mr. Math—I am from western Oklahoma—they go through and read this. It looks like dealing the cards underneath the table. That is the way it looks to folks out in my part of the country. This looks like a pretty sweet deal. It is one of those things you can't miss. This is not tough negotiations on behalf of the taxpayer. This is what you call stacking the deck.

And that is what I think troubled this committee a good deal. I have got to say, with my colleagues, I am concerned about the reluctance of the General Accounting Office to really get in and dig on this one. It seems like there is a lot of dancing around going on over at GAO on this issue, and, quite frankly, that is a disappointment. I would hope that you all would not take anybody's word for anything and get in there and dig out the facts.

Mr. CONAHAN. Mr. English, Mr. Chairman, I would like to make a comment on that.

Mr. ENGLISH. Sure.

Mr. CONAHAN. We are here today to testify on the deferment action. This piece of paper that we have been going over right here really does not relate in a direct way to the deferment action. And so, therefore, I see this as something outside of what our work to date has been called upon to do.

Now I quite agree with you, we are aware of this sort of stuff, and I have the same concerns that you have on this, and, as a matter of fact, this information was used as part of the decision—of the analysis in the final days on this thing. But this does relate to this matter right here, rather than to some of the earlier things we were talking about.

Mr. ENGLISH. Let me read you your own testimony, then. Let's read the testimony here. On page 9 it says, "DOD was not making a single decision focusing only on the granting of deferment but was also being asked to consider providing additional financial assistance to McDonnell Douglas."

This is part of an overall approach to McDonnell Douglas. It is my understanding that your responsibility is to follow the trail wherever it goes. This is certainly part of the trail.

Mr. CONAHAN. No, I quite agree with you. What I am talking about is, in terms of the slice of this as to whether it makes contractual sense in negotiations to do this. That is the only point I was trying to make.

Mr. ENGLISH. And this was from the documents produced to you by DOD, right?

Mr. CONAHAN. Right.

Mr. ENGLISH. So I don't think you could say this was outside the realm of what GAO was supposed to be looking at.

Mr. CONAHAN. I guess what you could say was outside the realm was the specific intent of these individual items in terms of taking a look at future cash-flow.

Mr. ENGLISH. Wouldn't you say that this little document here, those little provisions I have been talking about, those little benefits of $338 million on one item and $52 million on the other, don't you think that kind of smells to high heaven?

Mr. CONAHAN. As you go through it the way you did, this certainly seems to give McDonnell Douglas an awful lot right up front, yes.

Mr. ENGLISH. So my characterization that it smells to high heaven is correct. Would you agree with that?

Mr. CONAHAN. Why don't you let me stay with my characterization?

Mr. ENGLISH. My folks from Oklahoma that are watching this like straight talk, Mr. Conahan.

Thank you, Mr. Chairman.

Mr. CONYERS. This was supposed to be a short first witness, but this testimony has tried the patience of the members of this subcommittee, and I want to just close it down. And I know my friend from Connecticut wants to comment on this as well.

But look at the Code of Federal Regulations 163.27, "Financial Information and Analyis," and what the Department of Defense is to use as a standard in examining these financial analyses is, "The sensitivity of financial information and analysis and the scope, depth and detail of analysis of the financial capability of contractors for contracting finance purposes must vary reasonably with circumstances of particular cases. The obtaining of information relevant to financial capability and the analysis and proper evaluation of that data are of particular importance where the contractor is on any current list indicating current or past contract defaults or delinquencies."

Is there any study that you came across to show that DOD complied with that provision in the Code of Federal Regulations in the course of your analysis?

Mr. MATH. We did not. No, Mr. Chairman, we did not come across the documented analysis you are talking about.

Mr. CONYERS. Well, is it not correct that this subcommittee staff provided it to GAO over a week and a half ago, this information itself?

Mr. MATH. Mr. Chairman, it is my understanding that this financial analysis is applicable to the analysis made prior to awarding a contract to a contractor. And, according to my understanding, not to the particular situation at hand.

Mr. CONYERS. In other words, and, in fact, a loan of $1.35 billion doesn't kick in these same examinations and requirements?

Mr. MATH. That is my understanding.

Mr. CONYERS. In other words, the information we sent you was irrelevant to this hearing because it doesn't fit the definition of a deferral?

Mr. CONAHAN. One of the definitions, Mr. Chairman, as we have talked many times, is that these FAR provisions right here are sometimes difficult to relate. I am told by counsel that this relates to the awarding of a contract but does not specifically relate to the kind of a situation we have here in deferment.

Mr. CONYERS. 163.13, "Scope of Subpart. This subpart sets forth policies applicable to guaranteed loans, advance payments and progress payments."

Mr. CONAHAN. I cannot dispute what I just heard you read.

Mr. CONYERS. And we are working along together. We are giving you the clue on that.

Mr. CONAHAN. Would you read that again, Mr. Chairman?

Mr. CONYERS. Sure. "This subpart sets forth basic policies applicable to guaranteed loans, advance payments and progress payments."

Look, now, if you are going to take these regulations and slice them into parts where we have got 1.3 billion deferral and say that that doesn't fit into any of these definitions, it is true, we will go back and rewrite it. But it is strange to have this kind of argumentation coming from the General Accounting Office.

Mr. CONAHAN. You will permit us to take a look at that and get back to you?

Mr. CONYERS. Be my guest.

[The information follows:]

The Defense Acquisition Regulation (DAR) was superseded by the Federal Acquisition Regulation (FAR) system and does not apply to contracts entered into after 1984, such as the contract for the A-12. Part 163 of Title 32 of the Code of Federal Regulations is part of DAR and therefore does not apply to the A-12 deferment decision.

The current DoD FAR Supplement (48 CFR Chapter 2) contains provisions at section 232.173 concerning financial information and analysis that are very similar to those in section 163.27 of the DAR. Based on our reading of these provisions, however, they do not appear to apply beyond the agency's assessment of a firm's financial status in connection with the awarding and financing of a contract. Specifically, there is no indication that the financial information and analysis provisions were intended to apply to agency decisions related to deferments. In this regard, we note that the DoD FAR Supplement lacks a provision comparable to section 163.115 of the DAR, which explicitly provided that the financial information and analysis standards of DAR 163.27 and 163.28 were to be used as guidance in processing deferment requests. Similarly, the DOD FAR Supplement does not have a provision similar to DAR 163.112, which provided that deferment requests pending the outcome of appeals should be freely granted in order to minimize the possibility of overcollection.

In any event, DFARS section 232.173 merely requires DoD personnel to use their judgment in determining the extent of financial information described in DFARS section 232.174 that may be needed in any particular case. In this case, DoD had received much of the information and data described in section 232.174 such as income statements, orders on hand, cash forecasts, and credit ratings, prior to making its deferment decision.

Mr. CONYERS. Let me ask Chris Shays to close this down.

Mr. SHAYS. Thank you, Mr. Chairman. I have decided that this is just a very bizarre part of our hearing, and I am calming down here. I am new here, and I have to learn that the system works this way.

You were asked by Mr. Schiff whether regulations were followed. And I wrote down, "The deferment was properly granted under the regulations." That is what you said. And we sent you some regulations. You have said they don't apply because counsel said they don't apply. Then the chairman reads you an example of how it would seem to apply.

But let's forget the regulations we sent you. You made a very strong statement. Tell me what regulations you are following.

Mr. CONAHAN. This was FAR section 32.613(e).

Mr. SHAYS. OK.

Mr. CONAHAN. Which says that, "Deferments pending disposition of appeal may be granted to small business concerns and financially weak contractors with a reasonable balance of the need for government security against loss and undue hardship on the contractor."

Mr. SHAYS. We are not disputing whether they have a right to apply for a deferment. We want to know a little more than that.

You are the second in command of the GAO. Is that the basis to your making the comment that they followed all the regulations?

Mr. CONAHAN. The question that we had earlier was this regulation right here.

Mr. SHAYS. You were asked a question. You said, deferment was properly granted under the regulations.

Mr. CONAHAN. Well, under the deferment regulations.

Mr. SHAYS. Is that the total part of it?

Mr. CONYERS. No.

Mr. SHAYS. Let me just—for your own protection and our own knowledge—you were asked whether the regulations were properly followed. You carry a lot of weight. And the company will use you as a defense. Is it your testimony before this committee that all the regulations were properly followed by the Navy, the Department of Defense, and the contractor?

Mr. CONAHAN. Oh, certainly not.

Mr. SHAYS. Oh, certainly not. Could you expand?

Mr. CONAHAN. I couldn't make that statement.

Mr. SHAYS. Thank you. But you did earlier. You said deferment was properly granted under the regulations.

Mr. CONAHAN. I thought we were talking about the deferment regulations, this section of the FAR.

Mr. SHAYS. What am I to assume as a new Congressman here when someone in your status comes and says to us, the deferment was properly granted under the regulations? You didn't provide any qualification. You just made that statement. Is that a true statement?

Mr. CONAHAN. No. I think that we were talking in the context of this regulation at that time. Now when you broaden it to cover all regulations, my statement is that I am in no position to assure you that they complied with all the regulations. There are a multitude of regulations.

Mr. SHAYS. Let's not play games here.

Mr. CONAHAN. I am not.

Mr. SHAYS. You are playing a game. I just can't let it drop here. The inference was that the regulations were followed, dealing with the deferment. Is it your testimony that that is the total, complete limit to the regulation governing deferment? Is that your statement before us?

Mr. CONAHAN. I am saying this, sir. That the FAR has a section in here on deferment of collection. And it goes for about a page and a half. And my testimony is that based on the work that we have done to date that they have complied with this section right here.

Mr. SHAYS. Which merely says they have a right to apply, correct?

Mr. CONAHAN. Well, it says that they may be granted.

Mr. SHAYS. They may be granted, but are you saying there is no process that governs these regulations, no process they have to follow? They can be granted, we just allow a department to grant someone a deferment with no process? You know, I just—I will take your testimony in a very limited way, now that the chairman has rightfully questioned you.

Mr. MATH. Can I just add one thing, Mr. Shays? The regulations we were talking about in terms of financial analysis, to my understanding, do not apply to the deferment. It applies to the granting of a contract.

Mr. SHAYS. What does apply? Is that the total? You were speaking on behalf of the GAO and you are saying, with all your expertise, that that is the total limit and regulation that governs deferment?

Mr. MATH. With regards to the deferment, the regulation that Mr. Conahan cited is the regulation that is applicable.

Mr. SHAYS. These apply if you are one of these, and that is it?

Mr. MATH. For the granting of the deferment, yes, sir.

Mr. CONAHAN. I think this whole hearing has to do with whether there was justification for it.

Mr. SHAYS. No. The hearing has to focus on whether there was a process followed. We are not going to go after the fact and say, were they justified. We are going to decide whether a process was followed because we are not talking about $1,300. We are not talking about $10,300. We are not talking about $100,300,000. We are talking about $1.3 billion.

And I do not believe that this Government would allow for such an open-ended process. But you seem to be endorsing it. Because you are saying that was the regulation and they followed it, and no other regulation governs deferments. That is your testimony. And I find that pretty shocking. And hard to believe. I do. I find it hard to believe.

Mr. MATH. And that includes the process, yes, sir.

Mr. SHAYS. That includes the process as well. That is your testimony. OK. Thank you.

Mr. CONYERS. We will have to change the law and also work with GAO more closely on that.

Mr. SHAYS. Mr. Chairman, I just don't feel that we should let the GAO off as easily as we are or the company to say that that is the only limit that governs this. And so I am just not going to all of a sudden say, well, somehow we now have to change the regulation.

Mr. CONAHAN. Can I make a comment on that, please? We said from the outset that we did not see that and we were not able to determine that the Department of Defense made the kind of analysis that we thought would be reasonable to support the decision that was taken, one.

Two, we said that that was not brought together in any one place. We said we went out to see what we could find about what they had beforehand. And we looked to the Department of Defense and the Department of the Navy and a number of defense agencies such as the Defense Contract Audit Agency and so on.

Now, there are processes and there are regulations associated with all of the various bits and pieces of all that sort of stuff. Indeed, when you are talking about whether or not you can rely on a DCAA report, you have to take into account both the standards, the principles and regulations that apply to the conduct of an audit by DCAA.

And we test those standards out. And in some cases we find that they are done very well, and in others that they are not done very well.

So coming back to your statement right there, in terms of the totality of this transaction, we have to look at regulations as they apply to DCAA, as to the responsibilities of the contracting officer and to the responsibilities of the procurement people and so on down the line. And I think that they all have to be taken into account.

Mr. SHAYS. And under that basis, the regulations were not followed.

Mr. CONAHAN. That is correct. I can't make the statement that all those were followed, although I have to say I did not look at compliance across the board.

Mr. SHAYS. Basically, you are saying some regulations were followed and some were not. That is your testimony, really, isn't it?

Mr. CONAHAN. That—but I can't give you a global statement because I can't say we looked for compliance with all applicable regulations.

Mr. SHAYS. Then you are qualifying that the deferment was properly granted under the regulations—you are qualifying that statement?

Mr. CONAHAN. Yes.

Mr. SHAYS. Thank you.

Mr. HORTON. I would like to go back for a minute. When I was asking you questions earlier, you did indicate that you were concerned about the process and that they didn't have the documents and all the other information which you thought they should have in order to make that deferment.

I also asked you with regard to the basis for the deferment, which is basically $1.35 billion for these two companies, and you indicated to me that your understanding or your analysis of the basis for that deferment was a financially weak company, is that correct?

Mr. CONAHAN. Yes, sir.

Mr. HORTON. That, basically, is what your statement was.

Mr. CONAHAN. That is correct.

Mr. HORTON. You did not find documentation or sufficient information from the Department of Defense upon which to find that they had gone through that type of process, but then you found additional information which you said, at least in your opinion, made it a reasonable decision for that loan. Is that correct?

Mr. CONAHAN. That is correct. Yes, sir.

Mr. HORTON. Now, one of these companies, nobody has ever questioned it, and you indicated General Dynamics was not—I think your language was that they were not as bad off as McDonnell was. Is that basically what you——

Mr. CONAHAN. I reported the Department of Defense made that statement.

Mr. HORTON. And both these companies shared in the deferment of $1.35 billion, is that correct?

Mr. CONAHAN. Yes, sir.

Mr. HORTON. I still think when you talk about just a few months' difference from the data that you looked at, that is, the General Accounting Office and the information which apparently is true, that both these companies are very solid in July 1991, that it would be important for this committee to have your analysis of that situation as of July of this year.

In other words, what is the financial status of those two companies as of now? Can you get that information?

Mr. CONAHAN. I would be happy to make that reconciliation for you, yes, sir.

[The information follows:]

As to the McDonnell Douglas Corp. (MDC), the Corporate Administrative Contracting Officier's (CACO) report of July 16, 1991, states "MDC is still in financial distress". The CACO pointed out that while MDC has been able to defer costs and increase deliveries giving some the impression that the corporation has returned to financial health, he believes these measures are only temporary and the underlying causes of financial distress remain. The DCAA in an April 5, 1991, memorandum to the CACO stated that the results of their audit indicated that MDC is in an unfavorable financial condition which could adversely effect its ability to perform government contracts.

As to the General Dynamics Corp. (GD), DOD believed GD could have paid its share of the debt, but not the entire $1.352 billion. The DCAA issued a report on GD's financial capability on May 13, 1991. DCAA concluded that the chance of financial jeopardy is remote and contract performance is not likely to be endangered in the near term. In addition, the DCAA determined that GD is: (1) not in violation of loan convenants; (2) able to meet upcoming debt payments; (3) able to raise required funds; and (4) currently rated by Moody's Investment Services and Standard and Poor's Corporation as an investment grade quality debt issue. DCAA recommended that the contractor's quarterly financial statements be monitored since the contractor is experiencing an erosion in earnings coupled with the uncertainties facing the defense industry.

Mr. HORTON. I think that would be very helpful for us in the understanding. I think you also ought to indicate what has changed so substantially in that brief period of time. What you were looking at was dated what?

Mr. CONAHAN. April 1991.

Mr. HORTON. We are talking about April and July?

Mr. MATH. And July. There is information from the Corporate Administrative Contracting Officer that—in his document dated July—that the concern with the financial health of McDonnell Douglas is the same now as it was before. And we are talking about cash-flow. In other words, the ability to pay the required $676 million or whatever that figure is.

So we are talking about cash-flow and ability to pay. And that was the original reason for the deferment.

Mr. HORTON. Thank you.

Mr. CONYERS. Thank you very much, gentlemen. So much for a short hearing with GAO this morning.

Mr. Conahan, you are the No. 4 man in GAO. You know we have an oversight hearing on GAO coming up this fall.

Mr. CONAHAN. Yes, sir, I do.

Mr. CONYERS. I thank you very much.

We now would like to turn to our final panel of witnesses here, Hon. Donald J. Yockey, Under Secretary of Defense for Acquisition, then we have the Honorable Robert McCormack, Assistant Secretary of the Navy for Financial Management, and Mrs. Eleanor R. Spector, Director of Defense Procurement, Department of Defense.

We welcome you on behalf of the subcommittee. We ask you to please stand and raise your right hand.

[Witnesses sworn.]

Mr. CONYERS. Thank you very much. Please be seated. We have your statement. Before you begin, Mr. Secretary, you must know that we have been asking for all the documents related to the deferral decision, and either you or your Department have been refusing to provide us with the so-called decision memorandum.

This committee has been seeking to work cooperatively with you for a fair amount of time. We wrote you on April 19, then on June 13. I want to indicate to you personally and publicly that we need and want this document.

This is a demand request. The law is very clear, 5 U.S.C. section 2954 requires the cooperation of your Department with this committee in the exercise of its oversight responsibilities.

In addition, the doctrine of executive privilege shields only personal consultations with the President of the United States by his immediate advisors. Third, as both case law and a November 4, 1982, memorandum from President Reagan recognize, an assertion of executive privilege requires the direct approval of the President.

The Department therefore has not met any of these conditions with reference to your memorandum, and so, as we have indicated in our last letter to you, as of June 13 we are making a final effort to resolve these problems. We have pointed out as clearly as we can that if the President decides to invoke executive privilege, the Department head shall advise the requesting congressional body that the claim of executive privilege is being made with the specific approval of the President.

So we have negotiated and written letters. We are now talking in person, and it is my responsibility to advise you that we have received none of the prerequisites to invoke executive privilege.

So I am notifying you that as of next Monday, this subcommittee will be prepared, if this matter is not resolved, to take whatever legal action that we are empowered to take to secure the documents in question.

With that——

Mr. ENGLISH. Would the chairman yield? Does that mean we are going to subpoena the documents?

Mr. CONYERS. It means we will take the subject matter under consideration.

Mr. ENGLISH. I appreciate the chairman.

Mr. CONYERS. You are welcome. With that friendly discussion, we welcome you to the witness table and invite your discussion on this matter and any others related to this subject.

STATEMENT OF DONALD J. YOCKEY, UNDER SECRETARY OF DEFENSE (ACQUISITION), ACCOMPANIED BY DENNIS TROSCH, ASSISTANT GENERAL COUNSEL (LOGISTICS); ROBERT C. McCORMACK, ASSISTANT SECRETARY OF THE NAVY (FINANCIAL MANAGEMENT); AND ELEANOR R. SPECTOR, DIRECTOR OF DEFENSE PROCUREMENT, DEPARTMENT OF DEFENSE

Mr. YOCKEY. Well, thank you, Mr. Chairman.

I will certainly convey those remarks to the general counsel of the Department of Defense.

I have with me today Mrs. Eleanor Spector, our Director of Defense Procurement and Mr. Robert McCormack, our Assistant Secretary of the Navy for Financial Management. The subcommittee previously heard the testimony of Mrs. Spector on the deferment of the A-12 debt and related issues.

Since this is the first hearing on the deferment decision that Mr. McCormack has participated in, I would like to take just a moment to give you a brief summary of his background.

Mr. McCormack has a master's degree in business administration with a concentration in finance from the graduate school of business, University of Chicago.

He spent 19 years in the investment banking industry, specializing in corporate finance matters before coming to the Department in 1987.

He became very familiar with the financial condition of McDonnell Douglas, beginning in July 1990, which is based on his reviews of publicly available financial data and discussions with the corporation's chairman and chief financial officer.

We have provided the subcommittee and the General Accounting Office with the background information on our deferment. I hope that your review of the deferment decision, as well as the review completed by the General Accounting Office, has led you to the same conclusion that the Department reached; namely, that the deferment was appropriate and in conformance with applicable regulations.

The fundamental question remains the same, was our decision reasonable and supportable? We continue to believe that any review of the financial data available to the Department at the time in question will clearly show that the contractors did not have the money available to repay the $1.35 billion debt and that they could not readily obtain it.

McDonnell Douglas, in particular, had cash-flow problems, and we believe that demanding repayment could have resulted in lending institutions limiting or withdrawing sources of credit, thereby exacerbating the problems that McDonnell Douglas had.

The Department could not lose sight of the fact that if bankruptcy did occur, it could have allowed McDonnell Douglas to reject several large ongoing Department of Defense contracts that are in a loss position. The total amount of the losses on those contracts exceeded McDonnell Douglas' share of the deferred A-12 debt.

If the Department had been forced to renegotiate those contracts in a bankruptcy environment to eliminate the losses being incurred by McDonnell Douglas, the Department could have ended up paying more than we would have received through immediate repayment of the A-12 debt.

If we insisted on immediate repayment, we faced the likelihood that we would not receive the money and that we would also set in motion a series of actions that would have ended up costing the taxpayer even more money.

We believe that it was more prudent and more likely that the Department would ultimately recover the $1.35 billion owed it if a deferment were granted. As to the criticism that the analysis was not extensive enough, we believe it was more than sufficient to support the decision.

The Department had been performing an ongoing review of the overall financial condition of McDonnell Douglas for almost 6 months prior to the deferment, primarily due to the losses on the C-17 and the T-45 programs. Thus the financial data supplied in support of the request for deferment should not be considered as standing alone. Rather, it was part of all the information we were receiving on McDonnell Douglas' financial condition, and the Department clearly had an ongoing familiarity with the company's financial situation.

GAO has just stated that we may not have done what we should have regarding collection of the data in one place or in compiling one document in support of our analysis, yet GAO came to the same conclusion that our decision was, in fact, reasonable based on the same data that we used.

I listened very carefully to Mr. Conahan, and he described what GAO relied on. All of it was supplied by the Department of Defense. The bottom line remains the same; that this deferment was reasonable and supported by the facts of the situation.

Thank you, Mr. Chairman. The other witnesses and I are available to answer your questions.

[The prepared statement of Mr. Yockey follows:]

STATEMENT

of

HON. DONALD J. YOCKEY

UNDER SECRETARY OF DEFENSE (ACQUISITION)

On

DEFERMENT OF REPAYMENT OF A-12 DEBT

Before The

SUBCOMMITTEE ON LEGISLATION AND NATIONAL SECURITY

of The

COMMITTEE ON GOVERNMENT OPERATIONS

U.S. HOUSE OF REPRESENTATIVES

JULY 24, 1991

For Official Use Only Until Released By The Subcommittee

GOOD MORNING, MR. CHAIRMAN AND MEMBERS OF THE SUBCOMMITTEE.

I HAVE WITH ME TODAY MRS. ELEANOR SPECTOR, DIRECTOR OF DEFENSE PROCUREMENT, AND MR. ROBERT MCCORMACK, ASSISTANT SECRETARY OF THE NAVY FOR FINANCIAL MANAGEMENT. THIS SUBCOMMITTEE PREVIOUSLY HEARD THE TESTIMONY OF MRS. SPECTOR ON THE DEFERMENT OF THE A-12 DEBT AND RELATED ISSUES. SINCE THIS IS THE FIRST HEARING ON THE DEFERMENT DECISION THAT MR. MCCORMACK HAS PARTICIPATED IN, I WOULD LIKE TO PROVIDE YOU A BRIEF SUMMARY OF HIS BACKGROUND.

MR. MCCORMACK HAS A MASTER'S DEGREE IN BUSINESS ADMINISTRATION WITH A CONCENTRATION IN FINANCE FROM THE GRADUATE SCHOOL OF BUSINESS, UNIVERSITY OF CHICAGO. HE SPENT 19 YEARS IN THE INVESTMENT BANKING INDUSTRY SPECIALIZING IN CORPORATE FINANCE MATTERS BEFORE COMING TO THE DEPARTMENT IN 1987. HE BECAME VERY FAMILIAR WITH THE FINANCIAL CONDITION OF MCDONNELL DOUGLAS BEGINNING IN JULY 1990 BASED ON HIS REVIEWS OF PUBLICLY AVAILABLE FINANCIAL DATA AND DISCUSSIONS WITH THE CORPORATION'S CHAIRMAN AND CHIEF FINANCIAL OFFICER.

WE HAVE PROVIDED THE SUBCOMMITTEE AND THE GENERAL ACCOUNTING OFFICE WITH THE BACKGROUND INFORMATION ON THE DEFERMENT. I HOPE THAT YOUR REVIEW OF THE DEFERMENT DECISION, AS WELL AS THE REVIEW COMPLETED BY THE GENERAL ACCOUNTING OFFICE, HAS LED YOU TO THE SAME

CONCLUSION THAT THE DEPARTMENT REACHED -- NAMELY, THAT THE DEFERMENT WAS APPROPRIATE AND IN CONFORMANCE WITH APPLICABLE REGULATIONS.

THE FUNDAMENTAL QUESTION REMAINS THE SAME: WAS OUR DECISION REASONABLE AND SUPPORTABLE? WE CONTINUE TO BELIEVE THAT ANY REVIEW OF THE FINANCIAL DATA AVAILABLE TO THE DEPARTMENT AT THE TIME IN QUESTION WILL CLEARLY SHOW THAT THE CONTRACTORS DID NOT HAVE THE MONEY AVAILABLE TO REPAY THE $1.35 BILLION DEBT, AND THAT THEY COULD NOT READILY OBTAIN IT. MCDONNELL DOUGLAS IN PARTICULAR HAD CASH FLOW PROBLEMS. WE BELIEVE THAT DEMANDING REPAYMENT COULD HAVE RESULTED IN LENDING INSTITUTIONS LIMITING OR WITHDRAWING SOURCES OF CREDIT, THEREBY EXACERBATING THESE PROBLEMS.

THE DEPARTMENT COULD NOT LOSE SIGHT OF THE FACT THAT, IF BANKRUPTCY HAD OCCURRED, IT WOULD HAVE ALLOWED MCDONNELL DOUGLAS TO REJECT SEVERAL LARGE ONGOING DOD CONTRACTS THAT ARE IN A LOSS POSITION. THE TOTAL AMOUNT OF THE LOSSES ON THOSE CONTRACTS EXCEEDED MCDONNELL DOUGLAS'S SHARE OF THE DEFERRED A-12 DEBT. IF THE DEPARTMENT HAD BEEN FORCED TO RENEGOTIATE THOSE CONTRACTS IN A BANKRUPTCY ENVIRONMENT TO ELIMINATE THE LOSSES BEING INCURRED BY MCDONNELL DOUGLAS, THE DEPARTMENT COULD HAVE ENDED UP PAYING MORE THAN WHAT WE WOULD HAVE RECEIVED THROUGH IMMEDIATE REPAYMENT OF THE A-12 DEBT. IF WE INSISTED ON IMMEDIATE REPAYMENT, WE FACED THE LIKELIHOOD THAT WE WOULD NOT RECEIVE THE MONEY, AND THAT WE WOULD

ALSO SET IN MOTION A SERIES OF ACTIONS THAT WOULD HAVE ENDED UP COSTING THE TAXPAYERS EVEN MORE MONEY. WE BELIEVED THAT IT WAS MORE LIKELY THAT THE DEPARTMENT WOULD ULTIMATELY RECOVER THE $1.35 BILLION OWED TO IT IF A DEFERMENT WERE GRANTED.

AS TO THE CRITICISM THAT THE ANALYSIS WAS NOT EXTENSIVE ENOUGH, WE BELIEVE IT WAS MORE THAN SUFFICIENT TO SUPPORT THE DECISION. THE DEPARTMENT HAD BEEN PERFORMING AN ONGOING REVIEW OF THE OVERALL FINANCIAL CONDITION OF MCDONNELL DOUGLAS FOR ALMOST SIX MONTHS PRIOR TO THE DEFERMENT DECISION, PRIMARILY DUE TO THE LOSSES ON THE C-17 AND T-45 PROGRAMS. THUS, THE FINANCIAL DATA SUPPLIED IN SUPPORT OF THE REQUEST FOR DEFERMENT SHOULD NOT BE CONSIDERED AS STANDING ALONE. RATHER, IT WAS PART OF ALL THE INFORMATION WE WERE RECEIVING ON MCDONNELL DOUGLAS' FINANCIAL CONDITION, AND THE DEPARTMENT CLEARLY HAD AN ONGOING FAMILIARITY WITH THE COMPANY'S FINANCIAL SITUATION.

THE BOTTOM LINE REMAINS THAT THIS DEFERMENT WAS REASONABLE AND SUPPORTED BY THE FACTS OF THE SITUATION.

THANK YOU MR. CHAIRMAN. THE OTHER WITNESSES AND I ARE AVAILABLE TO ANSWER YOUR QUESTIONS.

Mr. CONYERS. Thank you very much, sir.

Let me ask the Assistant Secretary of the Navy two questions, what is the general position of the Department of the Navy with reference to deferment?

Mr. MCCORMACK. The Department of the Navy is in agreement with the decision to defer payment to McDonnell Douglas and to General Dynamics.

Mr. CONYERS. That isn't the question. The question is, what is the general position of the Department of Navy regarding deferments in general?

Mr. MCCORMACK. The Department of the Navy's policy on deferments is to look at them on a case-by-case basis and to make a determination, recommendation based on the facts in a particular case.

There is no general overall policy that we do this or we don't. It depends on the circumstances at the time.

Mr. CONYERS. Well, have you ever given a deferment before?

Mr. MCCORMACK. No, I have not.

Mr. CONYERS. Have any of your predecessors ever done that?

Well, I can tell you. I have checked the record. The Navy in general doesn't give deferments, and that is what has been told GAO by the Navy. Let me ask you, you signed the deferment agreement on behalf of the Government.

Will you describe for this committee the circumstances surrounding the request for you to do that?

Mr. MCCORMACK. The circumstances regarding that particular issue began on February—on January 7 with the termination, cancellation of the A-12 contract. We were approached by McDonnell Douglas between that time and the time the deferment was granted when they presented us with data that supported their position that they did not have the financial resources to meet that obligation at that time.

I agreed with that assessment, and after extensive work with the Office of the Secretary of Defense, the Air Force and the Navy, primarily, with the Army participating somewhat, we reached a decision that it was in the best interests of the Government and the Department of Defense to grant the deferment.

As the deferment was related to a Navy program, I was the appropriate official who executed that agreement.

Mr. CONYERS. Did you make the decision?

Mr. MCCORMACK. Did I make the decision to execute that agreement?

Mr. CONYERS. Did you make the decision that there would be a deferment agreement?

Mr. MCCORMACK. The decision with respect to the deferment agreement was arrived after an analysis of the impact the request would have on the total business operations of McDonnell Douglas, how it would affect the Department of Defense and related contracts.

Mr. CONYERS. Who made the deferment agreement, the deferment decision?

Mr. MCCORMACK. The deferment decision was made based on a recommendation, which I agreed with.

Mr. CONYERS. I know that, the record shows that, but let's save time here. This isn't a trial. Didn't it go to the gentleman's sitting to your right, and didn't it go to the lady sitting to his right?

It went upstairs to Secretary Yockey and Mrs. Spector, did it not?

Mr. YOCKEY. If it is acceptable to you, Mr. Chairman, I believe I can answer that question.

Mr. CONYERS. Well, I know you can, but I also think that the Assistant Secretary of the Navy can, too.

Mr. MCCORMACK. The decision was based on an analysis that was done jointly by the Office of the Secretary of Defense, the Navy, and the Air Force. The recommendation——

Mr. CONYERS. Right. It went upstairs, didn't it?

Mr. MCCORMACK. A recommendation was made to Mr. Yockey, who in turn made a recommendation to Mr. Atwood, the Deputy Secretary of Defense.

Mr. CONYERS. Well, what about Mrs. Spector? You don't mean you cut out the procurement person in the Department of Defense?

Mr. MCCORMACK. As I think you are aware, Mrs. Spector works for Mr. Yockey, so I don't think you can conclude that she was cut out of anything. She was a participant in this process.

Mr. CONYERS. That brings us right back to my question, and everybody here is—you know, you are holding the Nation in suspense. Who made the decision that there would be a deferment?

Mr. MCCORMACK. I think we are answering the question.

Mr. CONYERS. If you don't know, you are perfectly at liberty to say so.

Mr. MCCORMACK. I think I have described what the process was to you, Mr. Chairman.

Mr. CONYERS. OK. Well, then we can assume that you—do you understand the question?

Mr. MCCORMACK. Certainly I understand the question.

Mr. CONYERS. You do? OK. You have understood that you have been nonresponsive, that you haven't told us who? Are you refusing to answer the question?

Mr. MCCORMACK. I think I have answered the question.

Mr. CONYERS. I see. OK. Well, then, what is the answer as to who made the decision for a deferment?

Just let me know because I haven't heard it yet.

Mr. MCCORMACK. The Navy made the decision to grant the deferment based on a recommendation to Mr. Yockey which he concurred with, and it was reviewed by the Deputy Secretary of Defense.

Mr. CONYERS. Well, that takes care of that. Thank you very much, Mr. McCormack. You have been as helpful as I am sure that you could be. You also are reminded that you are under oath and that you have not responded to this question that has been put to you at least three times.

Now, let me turn to the Director of Defense Procurement. At this table we don't need people answering for other people. When I ask somebody the question, that is the person that I want the response from, not from somebody that knows the answer that wants to answer for them.

Now, Mrs. Spector, you have heard the GAO testify that there was no documented analysis or there was very little. In our own review of these documents, we found nothing that could even pass for an official analysis involving this amount of money, and this apparently seems to conflict with your testimony in April, and we ask you to identify for the committee the analysis performed by the Department of Defense of McDonnell Douglas and General Dynamics.

Mrs. SPECTOR. We received cash-flow information from the contractors month by month and by program. We saw that McDonnell Douglas's cash-flow was negative in many of the months. We then got their available bank financing and what their available loans were and determined it was insufficient to cover the cash-flow short fall.

We had the cash-flow information verified by our corporate Administration Contracting Officer [ACO]. They had been using the data—the company had been using it—and the ACO stated it was usable by us for the purpose for which we were using it.

We then predicted what might happen if we didn't defer and if we demanded the money. Our concerns were that McDonnell Douglas' banks might default or might not continue their credit, and if that were to happen, there was a possibility that the company might go into bankruptcy, and in addition might not continue to perform two very large contracts where the loss exceeded the amounts they owed us.

So our ultimate concern at the conclusion of our analysis was, if we did not defer, we might never get repaid the amount owed because the company would have gone into bankruptcy.

Mr. CONYERS. I understand the reasons, but I asked you for the analysis. Do you have the analysis?

Mrs. SPECTOR. The analysis consists of our reviews of all of the documents that we provided, the same documents we provided you and to GAO. The GAO reached the same conclusion we did, based on the same documents.

Mr. CONYERS. We don't need you to interpret. We have had GAO before us for 2 hours.

Let me just ask you this: You say there was an analysis?

Mrs. SPECTOR. There was.

Mr. CONYERS. OK. Can we have it for this committee?

Mrs. SPECTOR. Sir, I have said several times, there is not a document.

Mr. CONYERS. There is no single document?

Mrs. SPECTOR. There is a view graph presentation that comes closest to it that was presented on January 31, 1991. We have provided that to you.

Mr. CONYERS. All right. And that is what—that is your response to my request for the analysis?

Mrs. SPECTOR. You have been told there is no other existing single document that pulls together all of our analysis other than that which is a set of conclusions and reasons for the conclusions. That is all that exists.

There is extensive documentation. There is not one single document that summarizes it all in one place.

Mr. CONYERS. That is what I wanted to hear. Now, you have said that the data is adequate and that you have done a very thorough analysis. Is that a statement to which you still stand?

Mrs. SPECTOR. Yes, sir.

Mr. CONYERS. OK. You have also said that the analysis was done in your office and that you participated in it. Is that correct?

Mrs. SPECTOR. Yes, sir.

Mr. CONYERS. But the analysis that you have presented to us are slides, and then you say that there is supporting data that goes all over the place, and that consists of the analysis.

Mrs. SPECTOR. To quote Mr. Conahan, there are stacks of documents that we reviewed, including publicly available official data, including data from the contractors, and data from our own Defense Contract Audit Agency.

There is an abundance of data available that we analyzed to determine that these companies could not have afforded to repay a $1.3 billion debt, yes.

Mr. CONYERS. Well, here is GAO. There is some evidence that the Department of Defense officials do follow a deliberative process in deciding to grant a deferment. However, documentation showing what was discussed during this process is not available.

There is also no documentation available that indicates why data was used in a particular manner nor is there a formal document or a written decision paper prepared supporting the deferment decision.

In other words, in your own language, you said you reviewed other documents and that that constituted your analysis.

Mrs. SPECTOR. We did an extensive review of financial data that existed. There is not a single summary of all of that, but we do have all the financial data that supported our analysis, that drove us to our conclusion, which was the correct conclusion.

Mr. CONYERS. Well, that is your opinion. That is why we are here.

Mrs. SPECTOR. Yes, it is, and GAO's opinion.

Mr. CONYERS. And we respect it. Well, it isn't GAO's—well, I won't argue with you about GAO's opinion. Let me quote a part of the regulation that I think has some effect on your conduct in this matter, 163.27(a), "the obtaining of information relevant to financial capability and the analysis and proper evaluation of that data are of particular importance where the contractor is on any current list indicating current or past contract defaults or delinquencies or there are any known facts or circumstances which support reasonable doubts as to the contractor's financial capability."

Do you agree that that is a relevant part of the regulation that you are working with?

Mrs. SPECTOR. Not to deferment, it is not relevant, no.

Mr. CONYERS. It is irrelevant?

Mrs. SPECTOR. It is not relevant to the deferment decision is my understanding.

Mr. CONYERS. All right. OK. This same regulation makes a reference to particular requirements when there is a Federal tax deficiency, including an independent verification with the Internal Revenue Service. Was any independent verification made with the IRS as to the amount of taxes due from McDonnell Douglas Corp.?

Mrs. SPECTOR. No, it was not. Again, I am not familiar with what you are reading from, but it is not my understanding that that is relevant to the deferment decision process for which the rules are laid out in Federal Acquisition Regulation, and we followed them explicitly.

Mr. CONYERS. So it would make no difference to you whether they had a——

Mr. SHAYS. Excuse me, Mr. Chairman.

You said the rules are laid out explicitly on the regulations governing deferment, explicitly?

Mrs. SPECTOR. In the FAR, in the Federal Acquisition Regulation, the rules are laid out, and we followed them.

Mr. SHAYS. While the chairman asks you questions, I would love to have you make reference to where so we can look at those rules that were explicitly followed.

Mrs. SPECTOR. I am reading—I am looking at 32–613, Deferment of Collection.

Mr. SHAYS. Slow down. Slow down, please. Thirty-two.

Mrs. SPECTOR. 32.613, Deferment of Collection in the FAR.

Mr. SHAYS. These are the rules that were followed explicitly by you?

Mrs. SPECTOR. Yes, sir.

Mr. SHAYS. OK. Thank you, Mr. Chairman.

Mr. CONYERS. Well, we are reading how to perform an analysis, from what I am quoting. The other is when and how to give a deferment.

Now, since the tax deficiency question is not relevant, do you happen to know as a matter of fact the current tax liability of McDonnell Douglas to the United States of America?

Mrs. SPECTOR. No, I don't.

Mr. CONYERS. Do you think you ought to?

Mrs. SPECTOR. We did look into a calculation of what McDonnell Douglas was showing in its cash-flow for taxes owed the Government. We did review that as part of the cash-flow analysis. I don't recall the precise amount that was in for owed taxes. I recall that there was some indication from DCAA that repayment to IRS was not timed properly, and we did ask McDonnell to change the timing in the cash-flow forecast or we changed it ourselves.

Mr. CONYERS. Let me help you here. Suppose I told you that they owed the United States of America $1 billion in unpaid taxes. Would that stimulate your recollection?

Mrs. SPECTOR. I am sorry, I don't recall the amount. Only the timing of repayment of taxes that they did owe was discussed.

Mr. CONYERS. And that is because it is, in your view, neither required by the law nor relevant to this transaction, the deferment?

Mrs. SPECTOR. The data that we reviewed on the deferment was on McDonnell cash-flow. To the extent that their cash-flow was affected by when they would repay taxes that they owed, we were concerned with it. We were not concerned beyond that on the tax issue, as regards the deferment.

Mr. CONYERS. Well, did you know how much stock the IRS holds in the McDonnell Douglas helicopter firm?

Mrs. SPECTOR. I am sorry, I missed the last part of your question. McDonnell Douglas——

Mr. CONYERS. Do you know what IRS' position is in the stock of McDonnell Douglas Helicopter Inc.?

Mrs. SPECTOR. I don't understand.

Mr. CONYERS. Do you know what the Internal Revenue Service's position is on the stock that is held in the McDonnell Douglas Helicopter firm?

Mrs. SPECTOR. No, sir, I do not.

Mr. CONYERS. OK, would you feel that you should know that they hold a lien on all of the stock, 100 percent of it?

Mrs. SPECTOR. It is not directly relevant to the decision that we made.

Mr. CONYERS. OK. So, in other words, if this company was, as in certain parts of it, under liens by the IRS for taxes, it would have nothing—it would not play a role in your determining whether there would be a deferment?

Mrs. SPECTOR. The fact that they owe substantial amounts of money would be relevant to our analysis in that they don't have cash to repay a very large debt of this sort, and presumably have had similar negotiations with the IRS, of which I was not directly aware.

Mr. CONYERS. Well, then that would be relevant, wouldn't it?

I mean, how could you make this decision if, incidentally, you need to know what their tax position is, but yet you didn't make that determination here?

Mrs. SPECTOR. Sir, the evidence that we had was convincing that they could not repay the debt. We did not need additional evidence that they were unable to repay the debt.

Mr. CONYERS. So you never contacted the IRS?

Mrs. SPECTOR. No, sir, we did not.

Mr. CONYERS. And you didn't know that their helicopter company had a lien against it by the IRS?

Mrs. SPECTOR. No, I did not.

Mr. CONYERS. Did you perform an analysis of the change in cash-flow due to the cancellation of the A-12 program?

Mrs. SPECTOR. Our cash-flow included the impact of the cancellation of the A-12 program.

Mr. CONYERS. The answer is yes?

Mrs. SPECTOR. The answer is yes.

Mr. CONYERS. OK. And you stated in your presentation on January 30 that earnings for the fourth quarter of 1990 will not result from profits on operations but will relate to a "pension accounting gimmick."

Do you recall?

Mrs. SPECTOR. Yes, I recall.

Mr. CONYERS. What did you mean by a pension accounting gimmick?

Mrs. SPECTOR. Sir, this data is data that I consider to be proprietary and that I am forbidden by law from discussing it in open hearing, as I see it. I do not wish to discuss that information, though I will be glad to talk to you about it privately and give you all the answers you want.

There is information in that presentation which McDonnell considers proprietary and which I believe I have to protect. Information of the nature that you are reading now is in that category, I would say.

Mr. CONYERS. You mean you can't describe to me what you—you are the one that raised it.

Mrs. SPECTOR. Yes, I did.

Mr. CONYERS. I am asking you to describe your characterization of a pension accounting gimmick. Is that proprietary that you can't define that?

Mrs. SPECTOR. The information in that briefing is proprietary.

Mr. CONYERS. I didn't ask you for the information.

Mrs. SPECTOR. That information is proprietary, I believe.

Mr. CONYERS. Well, what about its publication in the annual report? Is that proprietary?

Mrs. SPECTOR. What is published in annual reports is not proprietary. What is in the briefing that I provided I consider to be proprietary.

Mr. CONYERS. But it is already in an annual report. I can't—well, we will get a copy of the annual report and read it back to you. Everybody that wants to get that information has got it.

The company couldn't possibly be claiming that is proprietary. It is published publicly. but I am not even asking for that. I just wanted to know what you meant by a pension accounting gimmick. I am not asking you for any information inside the report, a public report.

Mrs. SPECTOR. Sir, I consider the information you are asking for to be proprietary and to be damaging to McDonnell Douglas, and I do not wish to discuss it in this open forum.

Mr. CONYERS. OK. Let me ask you about the analysis that was done of McDonnell Douglas in connection with the billion-dollar loan request, which some analysis was done of the corporation after the deferment agreement was signed.

Is that true?

Mrs. SPECTOR. Yes.

Mr. CONYERS. Why was that?

Mrs. SPECTOR. The concern was that granting the deferment did not provide any cash to McDonnell. That money was already spent. There was concern that McDonnell might need additional cash, and we were looking at whether the Government would provide additional cash to McDonnell Douglas.

Mr. CONYERS. Well, the analysis, then, was done in support of a request by McDonnell Douglas for a bilion-dollar loan in the form of advanced progress payments.

Is that right?

Mrs. SPECTOR. They asked for advanced payments, which is somewhat different from a loan. We were doing additional analyses to look at, not advanced payments, but unusual progress payments, which is a different thing, and to decide whether we would provide unusual progress payments to the company.

Mr. CONYERS. Thank you.

What action has been taken by the Department of Defense in order to help solve the cash-flow problems of McDonnell Douglas?

Mrs. SPECTOR. We have not taken any additional action since the deferment to solve the cash-flow problems of McDonnell Douglas.

Mr. CONYERS. OK. Now, without going into specific numbers, which we have avoided in respect to the request by McDonnell Douglas, the cash requirement summaries showed a significant difference from the January 11, 1991, submission by MDC and your own presentation on January 30.

Who caused that change, you or MDC?

Mrs. SPECTOR. Sir, I am reluctant to discuss this information in an open forum on McDonnell Douglas's cash-flow, specifics of which I believe are proprietary information. I have very good explanations for everything you are asking. I promise you that I do. I will be glad to talk to you in your office or at a closed hearing.

This information is sensitive, proprietary information.

Mr. CONYERS. Wait a minute. We are not asking you to describe the proprietary information. I just said the question I asked is who caused the change. We know there was a change. Now, the question is, was it you or MDC?

Mrs. SPECTOR. There was information provided to me by McDonnell that I had verified by DCAA that caused a change in some of the numbers that I used from the numbers McDonnell had provided.

McDonnell gave me written indication of the changes, and I presented the numbers that I saw as the most realistic ones at that time.

Mr. CONYERS. OK. So to avoid any discussions of what you claim is proprietary, the change was caused by McDonnell Douglas?

Mrs. SPECTOR. No, the change was caused by my analysis of information I had received from McDonnell Douglas, that I had verified by DCAA orally.

Mr. CONYERS. Well, is it true that those changes accelerated the cash-flow crisis from April to January, thereby making the deferment and the request for $1 billion even more urgent?

Mrs. SPECTOR. Sir, the cash-flow crisis never manifested to the extent that we thought that it might. McDonnell took some draconian measures to improve its position, and the cash-flow crisis that we thought might occur did not occur, so——

Mr. CONYERS. OK, that is not the question. Isn't it true that those changes accelerated the cash-flow crisis from April to January, thus making the deferment and the request for $1 billion more urgent?

Mrs. SPECTOR. It had nothing to do with the deferment. It has to do with our consideration of whether to provide unusual progress payments. It did not make the deferment more urgent.

Mr. CONYERS. Let me just ask the question, and you respond. We will get all the other information you want us to know. We will get it into the record, but this question is, isn't it true that those changes that you say you initiated were accelerated—that accelerated the cash-flow crisis of McDonnell Douglas from April to January, thus made the deferment and the request for $1 billion more urgent?

Mrs. SPECTOR. No.

Mr. CONYERS. It does not?

Mrs. SPECTOR. No.

Mr. CONYERS. Isn't it true that the McDonnell Douglas Corp. requested the deferment to be completed prior to the close of business February 4, 1991? And to precede the company announcement of earnings and the dividend of $150 million on February 5, 1991?

Mrs. SPECTOR. Sir, we are getting into areas that are concerning the financial status of the contractor that I would rather not discuss in an open hearing.

Mr. CONYERS. This is private information?

Mrs. SPECTOR. I believe that it is, yes.

Mr. CONYERS. The committee doesn't need to know this?

Mrs. SPECTOR. The committee knows it and the committee has it, so does GAO. They have all the information that we have, with one document excepted, and you know it and you have it. The committee has it. I don't feel free to discuss it in an open hearing.

Mr. CONYERS. Well, isn't it true that the McDonnell Douglas Corp. sent the Department a draft of the deferment agreement that was just about the same as the one that was signed?

Mrs. SPECTOR. It was not the same as the one that was signed. They did send us a draft.

Mr. CONYERS. Well, you have the draft, and you have the deferment agreement, so what were the differences?

Mrs. SPECTOR. I believe, Mr. McCormack might be better able to address that. I did not negotiate the deferment agreement, sir. It was done by the Navy. I am not familiar——

Mr. CONYERS. Well, weren't the terms the same?

Mrs. SPECTOR. Sir, I don't recall. The Navy negotiated that agreement. I have seen them, but I don't know them by heart. I believe there were extensive differences between the two documents, but I am speaking from memory. I did not negotiate that document.

Mr. CONYERS. Will you, for the record, submit to us after you make an analysis what those differences were?

Mrs. SPECTOR. Sir, I believe that is more appropriately addressed to the Navy. That was their document and their negotiation, not mine.

Mr. CONYERS. Wait a minute. I am just asking you if you would do it, please.

Mrs. SPECTOR. Yes, I will do it.

[The information follows:]

INSERT FOR THE RECORD					
HOUSE / SENATE	APPROPRIATIONS COMMITTEE	HOUSE / SENATE	ARMED SERVICES COMMITTEE	HOUSE / SENATE	OTHER: Govt Operations
HEARING DATE July 24, 1991	TRANSCRIPT PAGE NO. 110	LINE NO. 2583		INSERT NO.	

Analysis of Deferment Agreement

The following is an analysis of the differences between the draft deferment agreement submitted by General Dynamics and McDonnell Douglas to the Navy for initial consideration, and the final negotiated agreement.

The draft deferment agreement addresses most of the minimum requirements for a deferment agreement set forth in Federal Acquisition Regulation (FAR) 32.613. It includes:

(1) Acknowledgment of the Government's allegation of indebtedness;

(2) A requirement that the contractors diligently pursue their appeal or suit, and that the Government take no action to collect while the appeal or suit is pending, or until a negotiated settlement is reached;

(3) A requirement that, if and when payment is made, the contractors pay interest on the amount due, at the Treasury rate;

(4) An agreement that each contractor will separately submit whatever periodic financial data the Government deems pertinent;

(5) An option for contractor prepayment of all or partial amounts;

(6) A requirement for immediate payment in full, plus interest, if the contractors are adjudicated bankrupt, or liquidation proceedings are commenced, prior to final disposition;

(7) A statement that if the contractors fail to diligently pursue their appeal or suit, and the Government does not exercise its right to immediate repayment, the Government's forbearance shall not be construed as a waiver of the Government's right to immediate collection; and

(8) A requirement that the contractors pay the debt in full, plus interest, after the court issues a final decision or a settlement is negotiated. The draft precluded collection action until after appeals were exhausted. The final agreement did not permit appeals; the debt is due and payable upon decision of the Board or Claims Court.

All of these provisions were included, in some fashion, in the final negotiated deferment agreement. However, the final agreement included several additional provisions:

(1) Representations that the contractors have shown that, absent a deferment, one or both would be placed in a financial condition that would endanger essential defense programs; and, in acknowledging their joint and several liability, DoD has determined it would not be in the Government's best interests to have either contractor in a financial condition that endangers essential defense programs

(2) A statement that the statute of limitations for collection of debts will be suspended while awaiting a court decision;

(3) A statement that any prepayments shall be without prejudice to the contractors' rights under their appeal, and that prepayments and related interest will be adjusted if necessary;

(4) A requirement that the contractors provide access to records and property the Government deems pertinent, including access to records regarding the contractors' commercial business;

(5) A requirement that the contractors and their respective successors-in-interest agree to maintain sufficient assets or available credit to pay the Government the full amount of the debt. The contractors further agree to provide sufficient documentation to establish their compliance with this provision;

(6) A provision that nothing in the deferment agreement shall be construed as a limitation, or waiver of any right, remedy, or defense that either the contractors or the Government could otherwise advance in any legal action;

(7) A provision that payment of the principal, plus interest, is due within 30 days of a court decision or a negotiated settlement (although proposed by the contractors in their draft agreement, there is no provision to extend the deferment should the contractors appeal a court decision);

(8) A statement that the agreement applies to the contractors and their successors-in-interest jointly and severally; and

(9) An agreement that the deferment remains in effect until reviewed on December 1, 1992, and annually thereafter. The Government may, at that time and at its sole discretion, terminate the deferment if either of the contractors has failed to diligently pursue their appeal or suit; or there is a substantial change in either contractors' financial condition such that deferment is no longer in the best interest of the Government.

The provision requiring review in December 1992 and annually thereafter is not required by FAR 32.613. The Government's unilateral right to terminate at that time, even if the contractors' appeal or suit is still pending, constitutes an additional protection of the Government's interests.

Mr. CONYERS. Thank you very much. Now, Mr. McCormack, the Navy is supposed to know the difference between the two, could you assist us on this question, sir.

Mr. MCCORMACK. We will give you a comparison of that, Mr. Chairman. As I recall, the primary difference was protective covenants with respect to protecting the Government's interest, as well as calling for a review of the financial condition of McDonnell Douglas in December 1992.

Mr. CONYERS. OK. Well let me thank you very much for the responses that you have given me so far.

Mr. Horton, the gentleman from New York.

Mr. HORTON. Thank you, Mr. Chairman.

I would just like to get a couple of things in order here so that we can understand what we are talking about. I understand there were some advance payments that has been made to the two companies in connection with the A-12 program; is that correct?

Mrs. SPECTOR. No.

Mr. HORTON. No?

Mrs. SPECTOR. No, there were never any advance payments made to McDonnell.

Mr. HORTON. How did they get the $1.3 billion?

Mrs. SPECTOR. The $1.3 billion was made in progress payments. When we terminate for default, we are entitled to get back progress payments for which deliveries have not been made, for which items have not been delivered.

All of that money was spent by the companies. It was not an advance payment.

Mr. HORTON. Well, let me understand now. What you are saying is that there were payments that had been made, and when there was the default or when the contract was canceled by Secretary Cheney, then that money was then due, $1.3 billion; is that correct?

Mrs. SPECTOR. Secretary Cheney did not cancel the contract. The Navy canceled the contract, and the amount due back to the Government was $1.3 billion.

Mr. HORTON. All right, the Navy, but the Secretary made the decision, didn't he?

Mrs. SPECTOR. No, he did not. The Navy made the decision.

Mr. HORTON. Well, that is interesting. Is that right, Mr. McCormack?

Mr. MCCORMACK. Mr. Horton, I was not involved in the deliberations relating to the cancellation of A-12. I would like to answer that question for you on the record, but I am not the appropriate person. I know it has been talked about a great deal.

Mr. HORTON. Who is the appropriate person?

Mr. MCCORMACK. The contracting officer?

Mrs. SPECTOR. Yes.

Mr. MCCORMACK. I am advised that it is the contracting officer.

Mr. HORTON. I didn't think we were going to have a problem about who canceled the contract. The contract was canceled, was it not?

Mrs. SPECTOR. The chronology of events was the Secretary of Defense made a decision not to provide extraordinary contractual relief to the contractors, at which point the Navy terminated the contract for default.

The contracting officer of the Navy terminated the contract for default.

Mr. YOCKEY. Congressman Horton, can I interject a point here? We are dealing with a technicality.

Mr. HORTON. I understand that. I am trying to get that on the record.

Mr. YOCKEY. The Secretary of Defense did make the decision that he was not going to allow this contract to be reformed. That left only two options left basically for the Navy, either a termination for convenience or a termination for default.

The contracting officer, in deliberation with everyone else, made that determination for termination for default.

Mr. HORTON. Right. OK.

Mr. YOCKEY. That determination is the sole duty of the contracting officer.

Mr. HORTON. That sets the stage. Now, as a result, there was at that point $1.35 billion owed by these two contractors; is that correct?

Mrs. SPECTOR. Yes.

Mr. YOCKEY. Which was disputed, of course, by the two contractors.

Mr. HORTON. Mrs. Spector, you work for Mr. Yockey, is that right, and you are part of his operation?

Mrs. SPECTOR. That is right, I do.

Yes, I do.

Mr. HORTON. All right. Well, now, that money was owed to the Federal Government, was it not?

Mrs. SPECTOR. We believe it is. The contractors do not believe that it is.

Mr. HORTON. Well, we have an argument about that?

Mrs. SPECTOR. Yes, indeed, we do, absolutely. That is one of the basic——

Mr. HORTON. Is then a lawsuit, has somebody started a lawsuit?

Mrs. SPECTOR. Yes, there is a lawsuit.

Mr. HORTON. What is the status of that?

Mrs. SPECTOR. A complaint on behalf of the contractors was filed in April in the Claims Court.

Mr. HORTON. Both contractors?

Mrs. SPECTOR. Yes, sir. It is a joint venture.

Mr. HORTON. Well, now, there came a time when somebody, either the Department of Defense or the Navy, informed these contractors that there was a claim that $1.3 billion was owed. Is that not right?

Mrs. SPECTOR. That is correct.

Mr. HORTON. How much of the $1.3 billion is owed by McDonnell and how much is owed by General Dynamics?

Mrs. SPECTOR. The joint venture owes the total amount.

Mr. HORTON. They both owe the whole and also whatever part that they split up, is that right?

Mrs. SPECTOR. However, they decide to split it up, the total is what they owe.

Mr. HORTON. So they both owe it?

Mrs. SPECTOR. Yes, sir.

Mr. HORTON. Well, now, was General Dynamics part and parcel of the request for the waiver?

Mrs. SPECTOR. Yes, they were. Waiver, I'm sorry, it is the deferment, yes, they were.

Mr. HORTON. Or the deferment.

Mrs. SPECTOR. Yes, they were.

Mr. HORTON. I am sorry. The word I want to use is deferment. If I say waiver, it means deferment, OK?

Mrs. SPECTOR. OK.

Mr. HORTON. There came a time when somebody requested that. Who requested that deferment?

Mrs. SPECTOR. The two contractors signed the request. I would have to check the names of the individuals who signed.

Mr. HORTON. As I understand it, there are certain restrictions as to when you can and when you cannot defer, is that correct?

Mrs. SPECTOR. Yes.

Mr. HORTON. Now, what was the basis on which you felt you could make a deferment here?

Mrs. SPECTOR. There were two bases. The amount was in dispute. The fact that it was owed at all was in dispute and that was one basis. The other is that the contractors were unable to pay. The weak financial condition was the second basis, so it was both.

Mr. HORTON. Well, now, did you look at the financial ability of General Dynamics?

Mrs. SPECTOR. Not to the extent we did McDonnell, but, yes, we looked at both.

Mr. HORTON. What was General Dynamics?

Mrs. SPECTOR. They could not have afforded to repay the total amount for which they would have been liable had McDonnell——

Mr. HORTON. What is the basis on which you make that statement?

Mrs. SPECTOR. Defense Contract Audit Agency reports that we had.

Mr. HORTON. Do we have copies of all that information?

Mrs. SPECTOR. Yes, I believe you do, yes.

Mr. HORTON. But you looked at that, and you felt that General Dynamics was not able to do that?

Mrs. SPECTOR. That's correct.

Mr. HORTON. And then you also looked at the McDonnell, and you felt they were not able to do that?

Mrs. SPECTOR. That is correct.

Mr. HORTON. Just so get the sequence, there was a request—this letter that is up here from the President of the CEO of McDonnell, dated January 24, that was after the Navy canceled for default the contract; is that correct?

Mrs. SPECTOR. Yes, it is.

Mr. HORTON. And that was also prior to the time that the waiver or the deferment was granted; is that correct?

Mrs. SPECTOR. Yes, it was.

Mr. HORTON. Was that unusual?

Mrs. SPECTOR. The request?

Mr. HORTON. Yes.

Mrs. SPECTOR. Yes.

Mr. HORTON. What reaction did you have to that?

Mrs. SPECTOR. We were generally concerned with the health, the financial health of the company when we received this. We had been concerned for several months about the financial health of the company.

Mr. HORTON. Well, now, what does all this mean, that little statement up there? Is that your handwriting?

Mrs. SPECTOR. Yes, it is.

Mr. HORTON. You are Eleanor?

Mrs. SPECTOR. Yes.

Mr. HORTON. A tax is dated January 31, 1991. Is that prior to the time that the decision was made on the deferment?

Mrs. SPECTOR. Yes, it is prior to the decision. Yes, prior to the decision on the deferment.

Mr. HORTON. What is your understanding as to who makes the deferment? Who made the decision?

Mrs. SPECTOR. The Navy made the decision officially, but it was well understood and well known within the Department. It was certainly approved by the Deputy Secretary, and it was a coordinated Department agreement that this was the right thing to do.

Mr. HORTON. Is it a who or is it a composite?

Mrs. SPECTOR. The official "who" is the Navy. The Assistant Secretary of the Navy for Financial Management.

Mr. HORTON. Who is that?

Mrs. SPECTOR. Mr. McCormack.

Mr. HORTON. He said he didn't.

Mrs. SPECTOR. He said he did. He said the Navy did, I believe is what he said.

Mr. HORTON. Is that what you said?

Mrs. SPECTOR. The official decision is made by him. Obviously it was well-known in the Department. It was approved by the Deputy Secretary.

Mr. HORTON. I am not arguing about that. I am not arguing about anything. I am just trying to get information. All I want to do is find out who made the decision. You said the Navy made it, and he is the man who made the decision.

Mrs. SPECTOR. Officially that is what occurred, but it was well studied within the Department.

Mr. HORTON. He signed the paper?

Mrs. SPECTOR. Yes, he did.

Mr. HORTON. You made recommendations on it, did you not?

Mrs. SPECTOR. I made recommendations to Mr. Yockey, and——

Mr. HORTON. Mr. Yockey, did you make the decision? You made a recommendation?

Mr. YOCKEY. What I did say, as I tried to explain earlier, I made a recommendation, and that recommendation was concurred in by every Secretary: the Secretary of the Air Force, the Secretary of the Navy, the Secretary of the Army, because all of the programs in McDonnell Douglas at the time cut across that board.

Mr. HORTON. Is there a piece of paper that says all that?

Mr. YOCKEY. Yes, sir.

Mr. HORTON. Where is that?

Mr. YOCKEY. That is the one that has been withheld from this committee for the reasons that were cited earlier.

Mr. HORTON. Which reason? Executive privilege?

Mr. YOCKEY. Yes.
Mr. HORTON. That is the one the chairman was referring to?
Mr. YOCKEY. That's correct.
Mr. HORTON. But there is a document like that?
Mr. YOCKEY. What was that question?
Mr. HORTON. There is a document or a piece of paper?
Mr. YOCKEY. It was the document with my recommendation, that's correct.
Mr. HORTON. That is what you are not furnishing to this committee?
Mr. YOCKEY. Yes. That recommendation was concurred in.
Mr. HORTON. What was that recommendation?
Mr. YOCKEY. Say that again.
Mr. HORTON. What was that recommendation?
Mr. YOCKEY. The recommendation was to grant the deferment.
Mr. HORTON. To both these companies?
Mr. YOCKEY. I am sorry, I didn't hear the last question.
Mr. HORTON. To both these companies.
Mr. YOCKEY. Yes. The contract is with a joint venture. The joint venture is a team of McDonnell Douglas and General Dynamics. It is a single entity in the contract. Therefore, the request for the deferment which relates to that contract, is from both those parties who are part of the joint venture.
Mr. HORTON. Just so I understand the procedure, you made the recommendation, and then the various Secretaries made the recommendation.
Mr. YOCKEY. They concurred in my recommendation.
Mr. HORTON. Concurred. Then the Navy made the decision, is that correct?
Mr. YOCKEY. It is back to that technicality we were talking about earlier. The actual implementation of that recommendation was done, of course, by the Navy.
Mr. HORTON. OK. Well, now, what happened, Mrs. Spector, to this request for $1 billion loan that was made by that letter from Mr. O'Donnell, dated January 24 to Mr. Yockey?
Mr. YOCKEY. I didn't receive a request for $1 billion loan from Mr. McDonnell. I received a request to look at advance payments, which I subsequently denied.
Mr. HORTON. And what happened to that?
Mr. YOCKEY. We denied it, and they withdrew their request.
Mr. HORTON. Did you write a letter of denial?
Mr. YOCKEY. I informed Mr. McDonnell of that verbally, and then additionally in a later letter which I sent. I believe your subcommittee has a copy of that letter. I informed him of the dramatic management actions he would have to take before we would entertain providing unusual progress payments against the F-18 and the F-15, restricted to only those two programs, where we would be assured that the work was already accomplished.
In effect, all we would be doing is paying for work that was already owed. We, under no circumstance, agreed to provide McDonnell Douglas with any advance payments in any way, shape, or form.
I am pleased to say, though, that Mr. McDonnell and the McDonnell Corp. did listen to some of the arguments that we made re-

garding what they could do to enhance their own position. They did take those actions, and in fact that is one of the reasons that they are starting to turn around.

Mr. HORTON. In the court action—Mrs. Spector said there is a court action. In the court action, is there a request and has it been granted to prevent the Navy from collecting this money?

Mrs. SPECTOR. May I answer it, sir?

Mr. HORTON. Yes, if you know.

Mrs. SPECTOR. The court action is questioning whether or not the money is owed at all. They don't believe—the contractors do not believe that this is a valid termination for default. They believe it should be a termination for convenience, in which case they would be owed the money.

Mr. HORTON. But the Navy, with all these recommendations and all the other things, I don't want to go through all that again, but the Navy is claiming that there is a $1.3 billion obligation; is that correct?

Mrs. SPECTOR. There is a dispute here. There is a disagreement.

Mr. HORTON. You gave them a deferment. How long is that deferment for?

Mrs. SPECTOR. Deferment is until resolution of an appeal or to be revisted December 1992 for a reevaluation of the financial situation of the two companies.

Mr. HORTON. Is there a criminal investigation into the A-12?

Mrs. SPECTOR. Unrelated to what we have discussed this morning, I believe there is one I don't know going on a different issue.

Mr. HORTON. Do you know that, too, Mr. Yockey?

Mr. YOCKEY. I am not aware of it specifically. I have heard that is true, but I have no knowledge of it specifically.

Mr. HORTON. Mrs. Spector, what is the status of that critical investigation?

Mrs. SPECTOR. I don't know.

Mr. HORTON. Who is doing that?

Mrs. SPECTOR. The Justice Department.

Mr. HORTON. Oh, it is under the Justice Department?

Mrs. SPECTOR. Yes, sir.

Mr. YOCKEY. We are generally not privy to all the actions——

Mr. HORTON. No, I understand that. It has been referred to Justice and Justice is making an investigation; is that correct?

Mrs. SPECTOR. Yes, that is my understanding.

Mr. HORTON. Now, have any deferments been made, either before or after with regard to any other company?

Mrs. SPECTOR. Yes.

Mr. HORTON. Is that normal, you believe?

Mrs. SPECTOR. Yes.

Mr. HORTON. Does that all go through your office?

Mrs. SPECTOR. No.

Mr. HORTON. Well, how are you so authoritative about it?

Mrs. SPECTOR. It normally is done by the military departments themselves. This one came to our office and was reviewed in our office because of the magnitude, the size of the contracts involved, and the size of the companies involved.

We normally do not get involved in deferments.

Mr. HORTON. Well, now, you just said others have been made. What others are you going through now?

Mrs. SPECTOR. I believe we furnished a list to the committee.

Mr. HORTON. But you have a list and we do have it?

Mrs. SPECTOR. Yes, sir. We were asked to accumulate it. We don't normally keep those sorts of records at my level.

Mr. HORTON. Well, now, the General Accounting Office was somewhat concerned about and evidenced at least to us that they didn't think you had good documentation and sufficient information to make this kind of deferment decision.

What is your answer to that?

Mrs. SPECTOR. My answer is, I think they are drawing a fine line between sufficient documentation and good information. I believe the information is available, and we have stacks of it, that would lead anybody reviewing it to believe we made the right decision.

There is not a single document that summarizes all of that information. That is also a true statement. But certainly there is sufficient information and documentation and documents available that would say that the Department of Defense took the only course of action it could have taken at the time.

Mr. HORTON. Thank you, Mr. Chairman.

Mr. CONYERS. The gentleman from Connecticut, Mr. Shays.

Mr. SHAYS. Thank you, Mr. Chairman.

I said in the beginning that the longer I serve on this committee, the more I feel that there is really not a separation between the DOD and the contractors, and I have really been wrestling with what are the key issues and where do we have our disagreements, and even if I accept your arguments, I am still left extraordinarily troubled.

Mrs. Spector, your basis for saying that you followed the regulations for deferment explicitly and so on would almost give the impression that there was some very explicit things that would have had to happen.

There are some points, a description of the debt, the date of the first demand for payment, notice of interest charges, identification. But we are focusing on something that is not stated under the parts that you think govern this situation.

We are also applying basic common sense. I mean, the common sense that we are trying to apply is that we have a $4.8 billion, up to a $4.8 billion program, $4.4 to $4.8 billion.

We see that it was canceled because the contractor simply did not live up to its contract. We had a payment of $2.7 billion.

We feel that we, in a sense, overpaid them for what they delivered to us, which were six design packages, no planes, just some parts, so we spent what we think legitimately should have been spent, about $1.35 billion. But what we got for it is basically nothing.

And the companies think they deserve the additional $1.35 for their $2.7, and what we now have is nothing, except we are going to go to the AX, and we are even letting McDonnell Douglas and General Dynamics apply for the new AX. We think it is going to cost $12 billion.

We don't know, really how that is going to work out. That is what we have on the surface. Then what we have is the first hearing where you came, and you made the implication that there was thorough analysis, and then acknowledged that there was really no documentation.

There were a lot of different information pieces that were provided. You have told us that the information that you have gotten was supplied by McDonnell Douglas and General Dynamics, is that correct?

Mrs. SPECTOR. And other sources.

Mr. SHAYS. Pardon me?

Mrs. SPECTOR. And other sources.

Mr. SHAYS. What are the other sources?

Mrs. SPECTOR. DCAA, Defense Contract Audit——

Mr. SHAYS. Slow down a bit, please. What were the other sources?

Mrs. SPECTOR. Defense Contract Audit Agency, Defense Contract Management Command, Standard & Poors, Moody's.

Mr. SHAYS. Pretty much all supplied by the company, the Standard & Poors and others?

Mrs. SPECTOR. We got it from all the independent sources that are pubicly available that analyze financial data of contractors.

Mr. SHAYS. There are public and private documents, and there is proprietary information which you feel the public doesn't have a right to know, and there is a law that basically protects them. One reason we are getting nowhere is you are defining "proprietary" very strictly, and we can't even comment on your comments about this information. We cannot even talk about data. It is basically taking the fifth, except using a different piece of information.

My problem is this. Bottom line, McDonnell Douglas wanted to get some information, and their financial house in order in a certain kind of way by getting advance payment, so that they could go to stockholders and the investing public and give them the impression that they were doing OK, when they are telling you they are nearly going bankrupt.

And you are party to, in my judgment, a very serious thing; and that is, on one hand, you are saying they are going bankrupt, but we can't let the public know it, but on the other hand, they are going to their investors and saying they are doing just fine. I have a common-sense problem with that. It bothers me, the Government is a part of the coverup, because, in essence, you covered it up.

Whether you think you did it for the right reasons, you have been involved in allowing the investing public to think McDonnell Douglas is doing well, when you know it is not doing well. It is in serious financial problems; they could go bankrupt.

Now, I want to just focus on the other company. Is your testimony that both companies are in serious financial trouble?

Mrs. SPECTOR. No.

Mr. SHAYS. But you gave a deferment to both?

Mrs. SPECTOR. Yes.

Mr. SHAYS. So you are saying that one company is not in financial trouble, but you gave a deferment to both? Why?

Mrs. SPECTOR. The companies were jointly and severally liable. We did not feel either company could repay the total amount, and that if we were to go only to General Dynamics, they could have sued McDonnell Douglas for half of whatever we asked General Dynamics for. Had they done so and had McDonnell Douglas gone under, General Dynamics would have been liable for the full amount.

We felt they could not have repaid the full amount.

Mr. SHAYS. The basis for deferment under your category and your rules, the ones you are following, the regulations you narrowly define, apply, and you choose not to feel that other regulations apply; and that is something that will be debated.

But the basic regulation you feel applies is, "Deferments pending disposition of appeal may be granted to small business concerns and financially weak contractors with a reasonable balance of the need for the Government security laws and undue hardship on the contractor." You either have to be a financially weak contractor or a small business concern.

Why would we give a windfall to a contractor that was financially weak and on what basis do you do it under the regulation?

Mrs. SPECTOR. The responsible official may authorize the deferment pending the resolution of an appeal. There was an appeal here, as well; there was a compounding of both things, the joint and several liability and the pending appeal over whether the amount was actually owed. It was both.

Mr. SHAYS. Isn't it possible that you could have divided and made an agreement that you wouldn't hold either side joint and several?

Mrs. SPECTOR. We did not feel that that was——

Mr. SHAYS. But the problem I have is that you are talking about $1.3 billion, and you chose to give a company that did not have a financial problem approximately $600 million. You made that recommendation. And you tell me you think it is right.

But they didn't need the $600 million. They were not in financial trouble. They are buying other companies now.

Mr. Yockey, you have been shaking your head. I am happy to have you comment.

Mr. YOCKEY. I am delighted to be here, and I would like to respond to those questions.

Mr. SHAYS. Sure. I would love it.

Mr. YOCKEY. We made the basic fundamental business decision based on the facts available to us, and I believe those were very precise facts. And I believe that a lot of the information that we have, made available to us by both those corporations, would fall in the category of insider information. There were published reports, including the McDonnell Douglas 1990 annual report that reported negative cash-flow.

Of the other analysis that was available to us, we had in addition to Mr. McCormack's background in the financial community, we had other people in the Department available to us. We have been working this problem since June of the prior year. We knew it was coming. We saw it. We had DCAA's audit.

I would like to say this. In addition to those briefings—those were extensive briefings, and an awful lot of conversation took place.

Mr. SHAYS. I think it is morally wrong for you all to make a decision and not be able to show us a document, a document that summarizes all the facts. I think it is an outrage that—I am not finished.

I think it is an outrage, an absolute outrage, that you cannot show the American people and us a document that justifies this decision. And, instead—I am not finished. You may speak when I am finished; I am not finished. Then you will have your chance.

I happen to think it is an outrage that you do not have a document that shows this decision, so that we have to send GAO hunting for a lot of documents to see if maybe you considered those documents. I think it is an outrage that we weren't able to see a document.

I think it is pathetic that you would rely on one part of the regulation, when common sense would say that outside sources should also do some checking.

Mr. YOCKEY. You had better describe what documentation, what—we get proposals; we could fill this room with them. We could also do the same thing on the analysis and still come up with the same fundamental conclusion.

How far do you have to go?

If a paraplegic came into this room and said he wanted to enter the Boston Marathon, do I need a medical report to say he can't make it? There is a point in time when you have to say, enough is enough.

Mr. SHAYS. No, you are wrong. You are in charge of acquisition. You are the most important person in this whole process. You are not an underling; you are the man in charge. And you have to provide documentation that can be seen and read and reviewed, not have us hunt for it.

And your analogy of someone who comes in here who obviously can't run a marathon is not acceptable. That is not acceptable.

Mr. YOCKEY. I intend in the fulfillment of my responsibilities to fully comply with the laws of this land. If they require specific documentation, you can rest assure we will provide it. We will put together, if you would wish, all of the analysis that we have done; and we will, in fact, put it in documentation form to support the conclusions.

Mr. SHAYS. It is an outrage to have it after the fact. And you, in your position, should know better. You should. And we shouldn't even have to be dealing with this problem. You should be able to give us, this is the document, and so we can analyze it and make a determination of whether you came to a proper one.

When you made the deferment, did you send a letter to the press; did you notify us?

Mrs. SPECTOR. There was a press release and press conference.

Mr. SHAYS. Are you legally required to tell people?

Mrs. SPECTOR. No.

Mr. SHAYS. So you could come back to us and say, under the regulations, we had no right to even tell you, Members of Congress and the American people?

Mrs. SPECTOR. It is publicly available information. Everything the Department does in terms of contractual——

Mr. SHAYS. Ma'am, please don't tell me everything the Department does is public information, because there are a lot of things that were not public information. Let's get to some of them.

Mrs. SPECTOR. Please, if I may, I wasn't finished.

Mr. SHAYS. I am sorry.

Mrs. SPECTOR. Contractual actions that we take are public information, by and large, with certain few exceptions for security. This was public information——

Mr. SHAYS. And proprietary information and so on.

Mrs. SPECTOR. This was information on which we issued a press release the day after we did it. We had a press conference on it. It was very public information.

Mr. HORTON. Will the gentleman yield? This is on another point, but one that I meant to ask you about.

You indicated that there were really two bases for the deferment. One was the financial condition of the two companies, and the other, you said, was because the claim was in dispute; is that correct?

Mrs. SPECTOR. Yes, sir.

Mr. HORTON. Was that basis made in the recommendations? In other words, was that basis, that second basis that the claim was in dispute, was that set forth in the recommendations as they went to the Navy, and signed off by all the Secretaries?

Mrs. SPECTOR. It was a condition for the deferment. We knew——

Mr. HORTON. Was it enunciated in the document?

Mrs. SPECTOR. It was enunciated in certain documents, yes. It was enunciated that the contractors planned to appeal. We were aware of that. The Navy was aware of it, and we were aware of it.

Mr. HORTON. Is that language or something to that effect in the document which is being withheld because of executive privilege?

Mrs. SPECTOR. My lawyers advise me, yes. I would have to read it, but I am advised, yes.

Mr. HORTON. You have been advised that it is?

Mrs. SPECTOR. Yes.

Mr. HORTON. What is the basis for a deferment, because a claim is in dispute? Is that in the——

Mrs. SPECTOR. Yes, it is in the regulations. It says, "Although the existence of a contractor appeal does not of itself require the Government to suspend or delay collection action, the responsible official shall consider whether deferment of the debt collection is advisable to avoid possible overcollection. The responsible official may authorize a deferment pending the resolution of appeal."

Mr. HORTON. What are you reading from?

Mrs. SPECTOR. Federal Acquisition Regulation 32.613, Deferment of Collection.

Mr. HORTON. Thank you very much.

Mr. SHAYS. Thank you, Mr. Yockey. I would like to ask a question of you in regards to the letter that was sent to you by John McDonnell.

On the second paragraph it says:

> In accordance with the provisions of FAR 32.403(f), McDonnell Douglas requests that an advance payment pool arrangement be established to assist in the financing of key programs for the U.S. Government, specifically, programs proposed for inclusion in the pool are designated pool contracts F-15, F/A-18, Apache helicopter, the Delta rocket production, the Harpoon missile, the C-17, as well as the T-45 and so on. We request the advance payment pool in the amount of $1 billion be established for a period of two years to accomplish this financial objective. A special bank account will be established in the Chase Manhattan Bank, if required.

This letter was withdrawn?

Mr. YOCKEY. Yes. Specifically, we told McDonnell that we would not anticipate—entertain, I should say—any advance payments, and rather, we would look at the possibility of unusual progress payments on specific programs, that were well under way, such as the F-15 and F-18. We made specific reference to those two.

Mr. SHAYS. At the same time they were asking for the deferral of $1.3 billion, which they would share? They were also going in with this request, as well?

Mr. YOCKEY. I don't understand that question.

Mr. SHAYS. At the same time they were seeking a deferral of $1.3 billion, they were also going in for another billion. They weren't shy about doing these kinds of things?

Mr. YOCKEY. We weren't shy in telling them no, either.

Mr. SHAYS. I wonder. I wonder how shy you were.

I would like to ask Mrs. Spector about the letter that you wrote to Herb—the Chief Financial Officer—Lanese. That is the letter right up here.

It says, "Attached are the assumptions we would like you to use in a revised cash-flow analysis. Please have it for us when you come in Thursday. If you have any questions—" Did they come in with a revised cash-flow?

Mrs. SPECTOR. Yes, they did.

Mr. SHAYS. Attached to that was a document, Assumption for Pro Forma Financial Forecast. It says, "I assume Lot 3 negotiations will be completed by the end of February 1991."

You seem to refer very confidently that GAO was satisfied that the deferment was proper. But the GAO found, when Mr. English questioned them, that this was a pretty shocking disclosure to McDonnell and said it could, in fact—it does kind of smell.

The question I want to ask you is, you then say, "Upon completion of Lot 3 negotiations, assume an additional $338 million will be added to the existing Lot 3 Lockheed document to cover termination liability incurred until a signed contract is executed."

Then you say, "Upon completion of Lot 3 negotiations, assume an additional $52 million." And then you go down further and say, "Assume that on June 1st, 1991, an additional $2.1 million will be obligated. As a result of this obligation, an additional $2.1 million." That adds up to about $770 million.

How far have you proceeded along that line?

Mrs. SPECTOR. I think there is a gross misunderstanding of what this document is, an absolute misunderstanding of what this is.

McDonnell Douglas had come in with a cash-flow analysis that we felt was too optimistic. We were concerned with some of their assumptions. One of their assumptions was that on the C-17, as they billed, they would get paid.

What these assumptions tell them is they will not get additional money on the various contracts until certain dates. They were spending money in advance of being paid on these programs. They were advancing the Government money, if you will, and spending money for which they were not being reimbursed. For their cash-flow projection to indicate they would be paid as they billed was too optimistic.

So we were telling them, do not expect additional money on the C-17 until certain dates when you may expect to get additional money.

These were contracts that were not fully funded.

Mr. SHAYS. Let me just go down then very quickly.

The C-17, lot three, February 1991, $338 million, did they receive that?

Mrs. SPECTOR. I do not know whether any of this was received. This was hypothetical. It said do not expect to get reimbursed dollar for dollar of what you spend or even get progress payments on some of what you spend until these dates.

Mr. SHAYS. Your testimony is that they have not received this money, or you do not know?

Mrs. SPECTOR. I do not know.

Mr. SHAYS. Why not?

Mrs. SPECTOR. It is not something we followed through on after we suspended doing their cash-flow analysis for the unusual progress payments. So I do not know whether these were ever fulfilled. They were assumptions.

Mr. SHAYS. I am going to conclude, but I am very puzzled by this. We are talking about $770 million of money, and you cannot tell me whether they received this money or not?

Mrs. SPECTOR. No, sir, I cannot. This is Air Force action. This was Air Force data given to me on when the Air Force planned to provide funding so that progress payments could be paid on these contracts.

Mr. SHAYS. And it is your testimony that this basic document is, therefore, irrelevant?

Mrs. SPECTOR. It is irrelevant to the discussion of whether or not they got unusual payments. It was part of that analysis, but whether or not they ultimately got these amounts, we did not go back and check. Because, we suspended doing our analysis to provide unusual progress payments.

So all this was was a list of assumptions for cash-flow, because the company itself was showing assumptions that we considered to be too optimistic.

Mr. SHAYS. But if, in fact, they received that amount of money, they would have gotten three-quarters of what they were looking for in the $1 billion.

Mrs. SPECTOR. No, sir. This has nothing to do whatsoever with that. This was money to pay them back for money they had spent on the C-17 that we had not reimbursed.

Mr. SHAYS. So basically you are saying you didn't provide sufficient money, so you wanted to speed up the process?

Mrs. SPECTOR. They were entitled to this money.

Mr. SHAYS. I know they are entitled to it. So they don't get the $1 billion, so they get it this way.

Mrs. SPECTOR. That is a misunderstanding. The $1 billion they asked for was advance payments in advance of spending it on all their programs.

Mr. SHAYS. But instead you did this.

Mrs. SPECTOR. We did not do this in any way, shape, or form related to that request for advance payments.

Mr. SHAYS. Yield back.

Mr. CONYERS. I recognize our final member, Mr. Glenn English.

Mr. ENGLISH. Thank you very much, Mr. Chairman. I appreciate that.

Mrs. Spector, I want to read to you a little bit from the 1990 annual report, McDonnell Douglas. And this is on page 45, over in the second column. And it states that "McDonnell Douglas has entered into agreements with two major insurance companies to purchase single-premium annuity contracts on a participating basis to provide certain benefits for approximately 37,000 retired participants and McDonnell Douglas salary and hourly pension plans. The purchase of the annuity contracts constitutes a statement under SFAS number 88. No plan asserts"—excuse me—"No plan assets revert to MDC, and no cash was received by MDC as a result of these transactions."

Does that sound like a gimmick to you?

Mrs. SPECTOR. That is McDonnell Douglas's statement of what they did. I assume it was audited.

Mr. ENGLISH. I didn't ask you that. I asked you, does that sound like a gimmick to you?

Mrs. SPECTOR. If they show earnings on the basis of that, it would be earnings on an adjustment of a pension plan, not on company operations.

Mr. ENGLISH. It would be a gimmick, then?

Mrs. SPECTOR. I don't choose to characterize it that way.

Mr. ENGLISH. How do you choose to characterize it?

Mrs. SPECTOR. As I stated in the prior answer to your question.

Mr. ENGLISH. Have you characterized it as a gimmick in the past?

Mrs. SPECTOR. Sir, the information that I provided in confidence to my supervisors is not information that should be discussed in this open forum on this subject.

Mr. ENGLISH. I guess I have got a problem. We have got the 1990 annual report. When McDonnell Douglas puts it out in their own report for the whole world to see, stockholders or anyone that wants it, that is not proprietary information. They are the ones, and I read you their quote, their words in their report, characterizing this maneuver. I ask you, is that a gimmick?

Mrs. SPECTOR. Sir, may I say something here?

Things I say at this hearing can have a very serious effect on McDonnell Douglas's ability to get financing from the banks, which they are seeking right at this moment, and can have serious impact on some short sellers who are very eager to see the stock go down because of adverse financial news.

I am not eager to harm the company in either of those instances by damaging their ability to get financing or by appeasing some short sellers who are very eager to get bad news.

Now, I am an official of the Department of Defense, and for me to characterize something they are doing appropriately in their financial statement as a "gimmick" is not something appropriate for this hearing; and I do not wish to characterize it that way, nor do I.

Mr. ENGLISH. Well, inspector, I am sorry that you feel that way about it. Certainly, I don't know of anyone on this committee, of course, that wishes McDonnell Douglas any kind of harm. But——

Mrs. SPECTOR. Wish it or not, some of the statements that are being released here at this hearing are causing that harm, whether you wish it or not.

Mr. CONYERS. You don't know that. Look, it is a little difficult for you to tell us, first of all, what this is going to do. We have got as many lawyers or more than you. And the question that the gentleman from Oklahoma is asking about, "gimmick," is your language; he didn't invent it. It is not his characterization, Mrs. Spector; it is yours.

For you to deny it now is a little bit after the fact, and I think it begs the question.

I would ask the gentleman to move on.

Mrs. SPECTOR. Sir, it is information that our lawyers denied being available for release at this hearing, in a public hearing. It is information——

Mr. CONYERS. There is some more information that your lawyers are not eager to give up that we will use due process to get. This is not a matter of my opinion and the Department of Defense as to what materials are available to us. It is a matter of law and procedure. And that is all we are doing.

Mr. ENGLISH. Inspector, I would point out, I read the characterization by McDonnell Douglas that they published for the public.

Mrs. SPECTOR. I gave you my answer.

Mr. ENGLISH. I asked you simply if that was, in fact, in your opinion, a gimmick. I simply wanted a yes-or-no answer.

I think we got our answer, Mrs. Spector, but I think the bottom line, too, I would suggest to you, I can certainly appreciate that I, you, no one in this room wishes McDonnell Douglas ill.

We also have a primary responsibility as officials of the United States Government to the taxpayers. And in this particular situation, there are some very serious questions that have been raised as to whether or not the taxpayer has been ill served.

Now, Mr. Yockey made the point that these were business decisions that were made, and I have got to say that that concerns us somewhat. Were these business decisions being made for business or were these decisions that were made to benefit taxpayers? And that is what we have got some serious questions about. That is what this whole hearing is about.

I would think you would take note of the fact that these concerns and questions that are being raised, not just by one side of the aisle in the Congress, but by both sides, Republicans and Democrats alike, are raising these questions with you folks. And I would hope that you would take it seriously.

Now, I do have some additional questions, and I hope that you will give us a candid, honest answer to them. Now, the issue with regard to the letter that was sent on January 24 by Mr. John McDonnell to Mr. Yockey, as it makes the statement in here, "advance payment pool arrangements." Twice, this statement is made, "advance pool arrangements," and the amount of $1 billion was raised.

Now, according to the General Accounting Office and their characterization, they characterized no difference between what an advance payment pool arrangement was and a loan. From the way they characterized it, from what they do, there is no difference. That is a loan.

Now, the thing that troubles us a good deal is that 7 days later, 7 days after this request for $1 billion loan, we have your personal note to Herb Lanese, signed "Eleanor," in which you were making these requests that they revise the analysis and—or revise the cash-flow analysis and change the assumptions that were made, basing it on the assumptions that you laid out.

Now, that timing troubled us a good deal. Seven days—and that is carrying through a weekend, so basically we are talking about 5 working days later—after this request was made by Mr. McDonnell for $1 billion loan, we have some very favorable assumptions that you forward; and these assumptions were things that evidently haven't come to pass.

I will ask you the question, with regard to the aircraft that were mentioned, the two aircraft, was the T-1 delivered in June?

Mrs. SPECTOR. I don't know.

Mr. ENGLISH. You don't know?

Mrs. SPECTOR. No. I told you——

Mr. ENGLISH. Let me ask you the question. What about the P-2? Was it delivered in December?

Mrs. SPECTOR. I don't know.

Mr. ENGLISH. Now, I guess then the thing I would ask you is, if you don't know now whether or not the assumptions that you were urging be considered would, in fact, come to pass, how could you request that the assumptions be made in the first place?

Mrs. SPECTOR. Sir, these were used as more negative assumptions for a cash-flow analysis than the company itself was making. McDonnell Douglas gave us a cash-flow analysis. We wanted to be sure that that analysis had the latest Government planning information on when things would occur. We think we provided a more pessimistic set of assumptions than the company was using.

We said, use zero claim recovery. We said—these were assumptions. They were not prognostications. They were our best guess at the time of when certain funding would be provided, funding that the company was entitled to.

Mr. ENGLISH. And the way it has turned out, the way it has turned out with regard to the manner in which the contracts were completed, item four that is listed to be completed by the end of February, the timing seems just a bit too close.

Mrs. SPECTOR. Sir, it wasn't completed by February. I know that.

Mr. ENGLISH. It was signed on March 3.

Mrs. SPECTOR. It was not signed. I don't know that it has been signed yet.

Mr. ENGLISH. It was my understanding it was signed on March 3, which turns out, interestingly enough, to be a Sunday.

Mrs. SPECTOR. There may have been additional long-lead-time funding provided, which would have been appropriate, because the contractor was continuing to perform the contract.

Mr. ENGLISH. What was not appropriate, though, was the fact that you were stating in the assumptions being laid out that, in fact, this contract was going to be negotiated by the end of February. That, as I went through—could I complete my point?

As I pointed out to the General Accounting Office, this gives a substantial benefit to the person on the other side of the negotiating table.

Mrs. SPECTOR. No, it does not.

Mr. ENGLISH. Well, I am sorry. GAO seems to agree with me that it did.

Mrs. SPECTOR. GAO appeared to be unfamiliar with the implications of this document. The fact is, it did not give any sort of negotiating advantage to anybody. It was a guess at the time of when additional long-lead-time money would be provided. That guess was predicated on the conclusion of negotiations occurring. It said, we will provide more money when you conclude negotiations.

Meanwhile, they were performing on their own nickel. They were spending their own money up until then, until we provided more money, which was putting them deeper and deeper into a cash-flow problem. So we said, we will provide this money on this date—that is what it said—assuming negotiations are concluded.

That is all it said. It was a list of assumptions. There is no cash pool here. There is no loan. Your understanding of this is not correct.

Mr. ENGLISH. Evidently it is not just my lack of understanding, Mrs. Spector. It is evidently the General Accounting Office and most of the members of this committee.

In fact, the way it appears, you seem to be the only one who has a good understanding of exactly what has happened here. And that seems to be selective, in part—certain areas that you don't want to discuss, certain items you have no information about, such as the T-1 and the P-2, which you are asking other people to make assumptions on.

And the simple fact of the matter is, as Mr. Horton has pointed out, that we have a company that evidently their financial standing has improved substantially. Somebody knows something as far as the stock market is concerned, because their stock is selling at an all-time high.

Something is fishy here, Mrs. Spector. That is what we are trying to get to the bottom on. I have got to say, the lack of candor we have had from you with regard to certain items hasn't helped. That is the way it is.

The reality is, we have a request from McDonnell Douglas for a loan for $1 billion. We have, 7 days later, a note coming from you, which, in fact, makes assumptions which, bottom line, could benefit this company by nearly $750 billion—excuse me, $750 million, which is getting pretty much in the neighborhood with regard to what the original loan was.

We find that the contract was, in fact, very close to the date which you had within your assumptions. So all this, added up, raises some very serious questions as to whether or not you were more concerned about looking after McDonnell Douglas or looking after the taxpayer. And that is the bottom line, Mrs. Spector.

I am sorry if, in fact, you don't like that particular characterization, but that is the way it looks on the surface.

Mrs. SPECTOR. The characterization is wrong.

Mr. ENGLISH. OK. Mr. Chairman, I do have some other questions of Mrs. Spector that I would ask be answered.

You directed—Mrs. Spector, were the assumptions that we have up here on the board, were those assumptions put forth in order for the Department of Defense to try to arrive at a decision of whether or not to make $1 billion loan?

Mrs. SPECTOR. No.

Mr. ENGLISH. Cash-flow statements had nothing to do with it?

Mrs. SPECTOR. We never thought about providing $1 billion loan.

Mr. ENGLISH. With regard to the assumptions that you put forth, tied to the contracts that were eventually negotiated and which, accordingly, McDonnell Douglas signed them on Sunday, March 3, did McDonnell Douglas benefit substantially from that contract, that agreement, from those assumptions?

Mrs. SPECTOR. No.

Mr. ENGLISH. They have not benefited in any way?

Mrs. SPECTOR. They have not benefited from those assumptions in any way.

Mr. ENGLISH. Did they change the cash-flow in any way?

Mrs. SPECTOR. They changed their cash-flow analysis on the C-17 based on those assumptions and on the T-45 based on the assumptions that I gave them. They changed their cash-flow projections that they gave us.

I don't know if their initial ones changed. They were doing it for us, so we could see how it looked. I don't know if their initial cash-flow predictions changed.

Mr. ENGLISH. Did you rely on those changes.

Mrs. SPECTOR. Rely for what? We didn't make any decisions based on them. So, no, we did not rely on them for any decision that was made by the Department.

Mr. ENGLISH. There have been no decisions that have been made based on that cash-flow?

Mrs. SPECTOR. The information that came in related to the revised assumptions was after the deferment. There has not been a decision to provide McDonnell Douglas additional cash-flow since that time.

Mr. ENGLISH. And no decision based on McDonnell Douglas cash-flow?

Mrs. SPECTOR. Not since that time. Not a decision to give them any more. There has been a decision not to provide them any additional money.

Mr. ENGLISH. The question arises, what was the purpose of those assumptions?

Mrs. SPECTOR. We were trying to analyze, to enhance further the analysis that we were doing of cash-flow problems that they might be having.

Mr. ENGLISH. You directed that after the negotiations were concluded, that the McDonnell Douglas company should assume large sums would be added to the long lead count for lots three and four. Was that done?

Mrs. SPECTOR. I don't know.

Mr. ENGLISH. You also directed that a change in assumptions for May and June of more large sums be added to other contracts for the C-17. Have these been done?

Mrs. SPECTOR. I don't know. You will have to ask those questions to the Air Force. This was Air Force contract management that we were dealing with. It was when the Air Force planned to provide increments on an incrementally funded contract.

Mr. ENGLISH. What was the planned source of the funds?

Mrs. SPECTOR. The planned source was the budget for the C-17.

Mr. ENGLISH. Mrs. Spector, the difficulty is that you are asking people—as I pointed out before, you are asking people to make assumptions, make changes, make adjustments about things that you tell us that you have no information about. You don't know whether it has been done. You don't know whether—you know—what was done with the information. No decision has been based on that information.

And that is very hard to believe. That doesn't make any sense.

Mrs. SPECTOR. Sir, I am obviously not making myself clear.

These were assumptions for cash-flow projections, for predictions. They were assumptions we asked the company to make for cash-flow predictions. We were going to use those predictions to see how severe the cash-flow problems were, and we wanted to make sure the latest Government planning was in the cash-flow predictions.

I work for OSD, and I handle hundreds of different actions in a week. The fact was we suspended the detailed analysis that we were doing because we did not provide advance payments, unusual payments or any unique payments to McDonnell Douglas.

These were assumptions. We ultimately decided not to provide additional money. Whether the Air Force carried through on these predictions, I don't know. I didn't go back and check. It is checkable. I can certainly provide you the information point by point by point by point of what was provided and when, if you would like to know that. It was perfectly legitimate. It would withstand any audit by GAO or anybody else. There is nothing unusual or irregular. You are picking on something that is not unusual, is not——

Mr. CONYERS. This is the way you do business?

Mr. YOCKEY. If I may, I can——

Mr. CONYERS. Excuse me, Mrs. Spector. Can I ask him to conclude at his earliest convenience?

Mr. ENGLISH. I have just one final question, Mr. Chairman.

Mrs. Spector, what was the purpose?

Mrs. SPECTOR. The purpose was so we could analyze their cash-flow to determine if they had insufficient bank resources to borrow money to support the cash-flow and whether the United States Government needed to assist the contractor with unusual progress payments on programs that would have been continuing.

Mr. ENGLISH. Which, basically, brings us back to the point, one way or the other, McDonnell Douglas needed, either through a loan or through an outright grant from the Federal Government, nearly a billion dollars. And that is what this is all about.

Mrs. SPECTOR. No, it was not.

Mr. ENGLISH. That is the way it looks.

Mrs. SPECTOR. That is not what this was about.

Mr. ENGLISH. Your last statement, that is what I interpreted it to say. They had to have the money to keep going, and this was the decision of the Department of Defense, and they found a way to funnel it to them.

Mrs. SPECTOR. This money was not funneled to them. This was money we owed them on the C-17. It was money we owed them to perform those contracts. It was not unusual money. It was money they were owed to fund long-lead-time activities, advance activities on the C-17.

All we were saying is, you can plan to receive that money in these months. That is all we were saying. If you—you may have to carry those programs at your own expense until you get that money. That is all this was saying. To please plan for that in your cash-flow, that you may not get repaid on time.

This was a negative for the company, not a positive. It was saying, you will not get money necessarily when you need it on the C-17. Plan to get it at certain times. That is all it was.

We can answer when each of these events occurred. It is auditable. It is legitimate. It was a set of assumptions. That is all it was.

So we could look at their cash-flow. It did not provide them a penny. Zero.

Mr. ENGLISH. Thank you, Mr. Chairman.

Mr. CONYERS. Thank you very much.

For one comment or one question, the gentleman——

Mr. SHAYS. Just very quickly, I want to make the comment to you that we will be going into the C-17 this fall, and there is no doubt that we have serious problems with the program. I think you will acknowledge there are problems with the program, is that not right, Mr. Yockey?

Mr. YOCKEY. Yes.

Mr. SHAYS. So the payment schedules and when you started to pay are clearly open to interpretation.

But I just—Mrs. Spector, you have been trying to wrestle with just an attitude that says, somehow what you say will very tremendously impact on a company. And that is a terrible burden for you to have, and we put you in an unfair situation if, in fact, you carry this incredible amount of influence over the stock market and this company.

But if you do, what that must say is that if you feel that way, then how do you answer this question. If you think the company has done something wrong, you think it has done something wrong. But you are also a player in trying to prop it up, which you are, then how do you decide what the public has a right to know?

Because the bottom line to this, as far as I have seen, is that we have artificially helped this company, and gone out of our way to, and there are stockholders who don't realize it is in the financial problem it is in. So I guess it works both ways. People get hurt on both sides, don't they? If you say one thing, some investors benefit. If you say another, some others.

So isn't it the best thing to just tell the truth? If they are doing a gimmick, it is a gimmick. If it is not, it is not. But don't you feel that whatever it is you should just say the truth?

Mrs. SPECTOR. Yes.

Mr. SHAYS. So if the company has done something wrong, it is your job to keep it quiet?

Mrs. SPECTOR. No.

Mr. SHAYS. And to only have it be internal?

Mrs. SPECTOR. No. I don't believe the company has done anything wrong, Mr. Shays.

Mr. CONYERS. Thank you very much.

Let me just point out that the Under Secretary of Defense under proposed actions was going to adjust unusual payments to provide minimum financing needs for McDonnell Douglas. Correct, Mr. Under Secretary?

Mr. YOCKEY. I don't believe that is a correct statement. Would you repeat it again so I can make sure I understood what you just said?

Mr. CONYERS. Yes. That the Under Secretary of Defense for Acquisition will adjust unusual payments to provide minimum financing needed.

Mr. YOCKEY. We didn't say we would. We said we would look at it.

Mr. CONYERS. No, you said will. I wish it did say that. I would feel a lot better.

Mr. YOCKEY. Where is the quote coming from?

Mr. CONYERS. It came from Mrs. Spector's presentation on January 30.

Mr. YOCKEY. I don't have that in front of me, so I can't answer.

At no time did we ever have in mind that we would do anything. What we did agree to do was to look at it. But I rejected out of hand any advance payments, and the only thing we would look at is to see if there was anything potentially possible under unusual progress payments, under specific programs, that we knew that they could perform under.

If they did go into bankruptcy, the probability is they would continue to perform because those programs were profitable, and we would only pay up to the amount due them for work accomplished, period.

Mr. CONYERS. Mrs. Spector, do you remember this statement?

Mrs. SPECTOR. I recall the statement, sir. This is one of the documents that I would prefer to discuss with you in private. This presentation that I gave. I recall it well. It was a plan at the time to——

Mr. CONYERS. That is all I am asking. If you recall. I don't want to go into detail. I am trying to close down the hearing.

So the answer I interpret to be yes. I think that is what you said.

Now, here, as we close, I just want to point out the contradiction that has been raised by the gentleman from Connecticut repeatedly. We have got in one picture a nearly bankrupt procurement firm, needed vitally for the national security interest, and we have its chief financial officer quoted this week, boasting that his profitability in defense contracts are such that he expects to make $11 billion to $12 billion on defense contracts over the next 5 years.

Now if that doesn't disturb you, it disturbs me. And that is the nature of the problem, and I hope, Mr. Secretary Yockey, that we will look very carefully at the direction we are going on the C-17 contract in terms of funding and the contracting provisions.

That concludes this hearing. I thank you for the time that you have put in, and the subcommittee stands in adjournment.

[Whereupon, at 2:45 p.m., the subcommittee adjourned, to reconvene subject to the call of the Chair.]

APPENDIX

Material Submitted for the Hearing Record

GENERAL DYNAMICS CORPORATION
Pierre Laclede Center
St. Louis, Missouri 63105

314-889-8200

17 May 1991

The Honorable John Conyers, Jr.
Chairman
Legislation and National Security Subcommittee of the
Committee on Government Operations
United States House of Representatives
Washington, DC 20515

Dear Mr. Chairman:

I have been advised that on April 17, 1991, a letter was directed to me requesting answers for the record to certain questions of the Legislation and National Security Subcommittee. For reasons unknown, I have not received that letter. On May 13, 1991, I received the attached copy of that letter. I hope this delay in responding has not inconvenienced the Subcommittee.

My answers to your questions are as follows.

1. You stated in your testimony that a meeting took place on January 16, 1991 to present your case for a deferment to the Department of Defense. How long after that meeting did you receive notice that the deferment had been granted?

Answer: On February 4, 1991, we were notified that the Department of Defense was prepared to discuss specific language of a deferment agreement under which the contractors' request for deferral might be granted. On February 5, 1991, the contractors met with representatives of the Department to discuss the agreement and reached agreement thereon, at which time the Department's officials indicated that they would grant the request for deferral.

2. Were you ever asked to consider some principal reduction, interest payments, or putting up sufficient collateral?

Answer: General Dynamics was not requested to consider any reduction in the principal amount. Such a request is not contemplated by the applicable regulations since the amount owing, if any, is the essence of the dispute which gives rise to the deferment agreement. General Dynamics is responsible to pay interest on whatever portion of the amount is ultimately determined to be due and owing to the United States. With respect to the question of collateral, I believe that is addressed in paragraph 7 of the deferment agreement, wherein the companies are specifically required to "maintain sufficient assets or available credit" to pay the government the full amount of the debt.

(235)

3. Did anyone at the Department of Defense suggest in any way that you should not release the financial documents presented to DOD, to the Subcommittee? If so, who?

Answer: No.

4. To whom did you specifically present your case for deferment, either oral or written, at DOD?

Answer: RADM W. R. Morris, Assistant Commander for Contracts, Naval Air Systems Command, Robert C. McCormack, Assistant Secretary of the Navy, and members of their staffs.

5. Is there a list of the documents presented, either before, during, or after the January 16, 1991 meeting related to the deferment decision? Will you provide that list to the Subcommittee?

Answer: General Dynamics made a single submittal to the Navy. For that reason a listing was not created. That submittal, which occurred on January 16, 1991, consisted of a document entitled <u>Statement of Financial Condition General Dynamics</u>, which included Appendices A through E and four enclosures. The document contained proprietary information of the company, and was marked accordingly. It is understood that this document has been furnished to the Subcommittee by the Department of Defense.

A point which may confuse the subcommittee on examination of the document is that it is identified as "Attachment 2." At the time of its preparation, it was anticipated that the document would be an attachment to the letter of the contractors requesting deferral. The McDonnell Douglas material would have been attachment 1. However, at the time the actual deferral request was prepared, it seemed sufficient to simply refer to the fact that data had been provided by each company to support the request.

I trust that the foregoing responses are sufficient for the needs of the Subcommittee.

Very truly yours,

Donald W. Putnam
Corporate Director of Contracts
and Technical Analysis

DEPARTMENT OF THE NAVY
OFFICE OF THE SECRETARY
WASHINGTON. D C 20350-1000

NOV 28 1990

BEACH REPORT

MEMORANDUM FOR THE SECRETARY OF THE NAVY

Via: Assistant Secretary of the Navy (Research, Development and Acquisition)

Subj: A-12 ADMINISTRATIVE INQUIRY

1. <u>Purpose</u>. This reports the findings, conclusions and recommendations of the administrative inquiry directed by SECNAV memorandum of 9 July 1990.

2. <u>Background</u>. In December 1989, the Secretary of Defense (SECDEF) directed a review of four major aircraft programs, including the A-12 Full Scale Development (FSD) Program. During the course of that review, the Navy and the contractor team (McDonnell Douglas (McAir) and General Dynamics (GDFW)) projected first flight of the A-12 by early 1991, and completion of the FSD program within the current fixed-price incentive contract ceiling. On 26 April 1990, following completion of that review, SECDEF announced his decision to continue the A-12 Program, albeit at a reduced procurement quantity. He indicated that the A-12 would likely fly in early 1991, and did not identify any impediments to completion of the FSD effort within the scope of the current contract.

On 1 June 1990, the contractor team advised the Navy of a significant additional slip in the schedule for first flight, that the FSD effort would overrun the contract ceiling by an amount which the contractor team could not absorb, and that certain performance specifications of the contract could not be met. Following the failure of the contractor team to meet the 17 June 1990 first flight date specified in the contract, the Navy acted unilaterally to establish a new delivery schedule under the contract. The schedule now requires first flight by December 1991.[1]

In late June 1990, SECNAV determined to order an administrative inquiry into the variance between the status of the A-12 program as it was understood during the MAR and that reported subsequently by the contractor team, but deferred the inquiry pending completion of the final phase of the Critical Design Review (CDR) then in progress, after consulting with the Under Secretary of Defense (Acquisition) (USD(A)). On 9 July 1990, following completion of the CDR, SECNAV ordered this administrative inquiry to determine facts and circumstances surrounding the variance between the current status of the A-12 Program and representations made to the Office of the Secretary of Defense (OSD) on behalf of the Department regarding the program during the course of the Major Aircraft Review (MAR). He directed that the inquiry focus upon "the cause of the variance, accountability, and any systemic or other changes or improvements needed to ensure that significant information is developed and made available to appropriate officials in a timely, accurate manner."

Subsequently, at the request of the USD(A), members of the USD(A) staff joined the Navy inquiry support team, and the USD(A) requested that the inquiry also consider OSD staff processes and the MAR process itself to "identify the process root causes that permitted the problem to develop to the extent it did before management of either the contractor or the DoD were aware of the risk let alone the problems."

Accordingly, I established an inquiry support team comprised of representatives from the Office of the Judge Advocate General, Naval Audit Service, Naval Inspector General, the USD(A) staff, the Defense Product Engineering Services Office, and Defense Contract Management Command.2 Clerical support personnel with requisite security clearances were provided by Commander, Naval Legal Service Command, and Commander, Naval Military Personnel Command. Additional clerical support and guidance in security matters was provided by the Assistant for Special Programs to the Under Secretary of the Navy.

In carrying out the direction provided, I have attempted to answer three questions:

-- Did the Navy, OSD or the contractor know of or have reason to anticipate substantial additional cost increase and schedule slip at the time of the Major Aircraft Review?

-- If not, why not?

-- If so, were senior DON and DOD leaders sufficiently apprised in the course of the Review? If not, why not?

In 1984, the Deputy Secretary of Defense (DEPSECDEF) directed the Navy to develop and acquire the A-12 as a replacement for the aging A-6 Intruder, and directed that the A-12 achieve Initial Operational Capability (IOC) not later than 1994. In November 1984, two teams (McAir/GDFW and Northrop/Grumman/Vought) were awarded contracts for concept formulation. Both teams continued into demonstration validation under contracts awarded in June 1986. The two teams competed for the Full Scale Development (FSD) contract, which was awarded to the McAir/GDFW team on 13 January 1988. The fixed-price-incentive contract established a target price of $4.379 billion, a ceiling price of $4.777 billion and a 60/40 share line between target and ceiling, and contained an economic price adjustment clause. Target cost for the contract was $3.981 billion, with a resultant profit to the contractor team of $398 million, or 10 percent of the target cost. Under the FSD contract, the contractors agreed to deliver 8 flight test aircraft and 5 full-scale ground test articles, and first flight of the A-12 was scheduled for June 1990. The contract also contains fixed price options for three production lots, for 8, 16 and 30 aircraft respectively, with not-to-exceed ceiling prices and a requirement for the contractor to provide a not-to-exceed ceiling price for a fourth production lot at the completion of Critical Design Review. The first two production lots are for pilot production, and the third and fourth are designated as low-rate initial production (LRIP). The USD(A) Acquisition Decision Memorandum of 11 January 1988 approving entry into Full Scale Engineering Development also approved pilot production and long lead funding for the first LRIP buy.

For the Government, the A-12 FSD Program is managed by a Program Manager (PM), who has full authority, responsibility and accountability for the program under DON and DOD policy, subject to any limitations imposed by approved program documentation or direction from his superiors. The current PM has served since 30 June 1986.

In performing his duties, the PM is assisted by a small immediate staff, by a larger program management team drawn from the functional disciplines represented within Naval Air Systems Command's (NAVAIR's) matrix organization, and by personnel assigned to the PM or to the cognizant Defense Plant Representative Offices resident in the contractor team facilities in St. Louis (McAir) and Fort Worth (GDFW). For convenience, these latter offices will be referred to as the NAVPRO and AFPRO, respectively, reflecting their status prior to the 1 July 1990 establishment of the Defense Contract Management Command.

Prior to 16 April 1990, the PM reported directly to the Commander, NAVAIR (COMNAVAIR), who served as Program Executive Officer (PEO) for all assigned major programs. As such, COMNAVAIR also had full authority, responsibility and accountability for the A-12 Program, and reported directly for all matters affecting its cost, schedule and performance to the Navy Acquisition Executive (NAE). Since 16 April 1990, the PM has reported to a PEO for Tactical Air Programs established separately from COMNAVAIR (and through the PEO to the NAE) pursuant to DON initial implementation of a requirement of the Defense Management Report. COMNAVAIR remains responsible for the level and quality of matrix support provided to the PM.

The NAE, in turn, reports to the USD(A) in his capacity as the Defense Acquisition Executive. Under DOD policy, the USD(A) exercises program decision authority for the A-12 Program through the Defense Acquisition Board (DAB) at program milestones (0 - concept formulation; I - demonstration/validation; II - full scale engineering development; IIIA - LRIP; IIIB - full-rate production). He may also conduct program reviews directly through the DAB, or indirectly through a DAB Committee, in this case the Conventional Systems Committee, between milestone decisions as events warrant. The Defense Acquisition Executive Summary (DAES), a quarterly report prepared by the PM and forwarded through the PEO and NAE, along with informal contacts and/or briefings, is the principal source of information to the USD(A) and his staff regarding ongoing program developments between milestone or other formal reviews.

3. <u>Summary of Analysis</u>. In order to respond comprehensively to the tasks prescribed by the Secretary of the Navy and the USD(A), it was necessary first to identify and analyze the operation of the principal program management control mechanisms available to the Navy and DOD A-12 program management structure. Accordingly, we examined each of the key program management controls bearing on identification of the cost and schedule difficulties identified in the A-12 program. We then analyzed the MAR process against the information environment created by operation of these controls.

   a. <u>Cost/Schedule Performance Reporting</u>. DOD policy requires contractors to operate internal management systems that meet specified Cost/Schedule Control Systems Criteria (C/SCSC). The principal purpose of these criteria is to provide an adequate basis for responsible decision-making by both contractor management and DoD Components. Contractors' internal management control systems must provide data which indicate work progress; properly relate cost, schedule and technical accomplishment; are valid, timely and auditable; and supply DoD managers with information at a practicable level of summarization.

   Contractor management systems are inspected by DOD and determined to be C/SCSC compliant. Systems are also subject to a review as soon as practical after award of a major contract. The purpose of this review is to verify that the contractor's accepted system complies with the DOD criteria as applied to the particular contract at issue.

DOD and DON policy further require contractors for designated major systems acquisition programs periodically to submit Cost Performance Reports (CPRs). CPRs identify the cost and schedule status of contract performance at the total contract level, by individual Work Breakdown Structure (WBS) elements specified in the contract, and by functional categories that are selected to reflect the way the contractor is organized to perform the work. A narrative problem analysis is required explaining variance at whatever level is specified in the contract. CPRs are normally required on a monthly basis. Under DON policy, they are intended "for use in making and validating management decisions," to provide "(e)arly indicators of contract cost/schedule problems," and to facilitate assessment of "(e)ffects of management actions taken to resolve problems affecting cost/schedule performance."

Utilization of CPR Data By the Contractors

McAir and GDFW have submitted CPRs in the A-12 program quarterly since June 1988, and monthly since February 1989. Both McAir and GDFW have excellent cost and schedule performance reporting systems that have continuously provided the detailed information necessary to make reasonable assessments of contract status as contemplated in DOD policy. As Figure 1 indicates, these systems have identified significant and increasing negative cost and schedule variances throughout the period of contract performance.

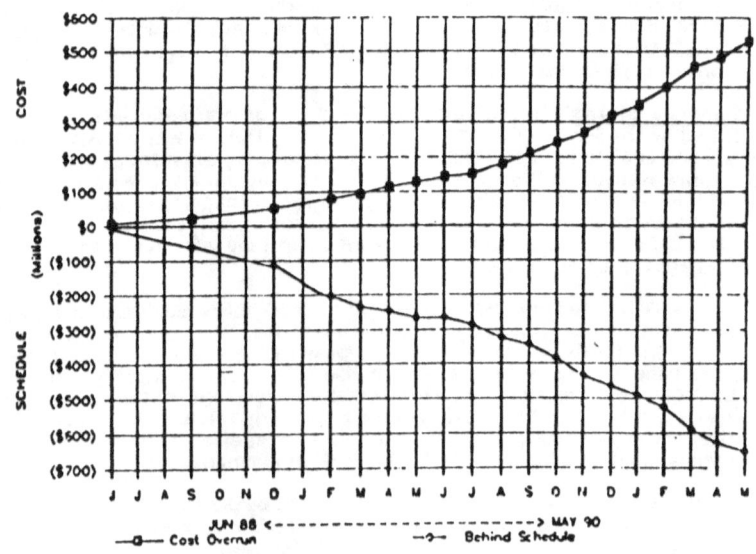

Figure 1

A number of recurring reports circulated within the McAir/GDFW program management organizations contained thorough analyses of cost and schedule variance. However, the McAir/GDFW team failed to utilize the CPR information to identify to the Government the potential schedule and cost implications of the performance problems it encountered. Notwithstanding the consistently negative trend of the cost and schedule performance data, the McAir/GDFW team continually made best case projections of cost at completion based upon overly optimistic recovery plans and schedule assumptions. The evidence indicated that the contractor team perceived significant pressure from upper management throughout the performance of the FSD effort to maximize cash flow. Such pressure would create an incentive to be optimistic, inasmuch as progress payments would be subject to reduction in the event of a contractor or Government estimate of an overrun.

Figure 2 illustrates the estimates at completion submitted by the contractor team.

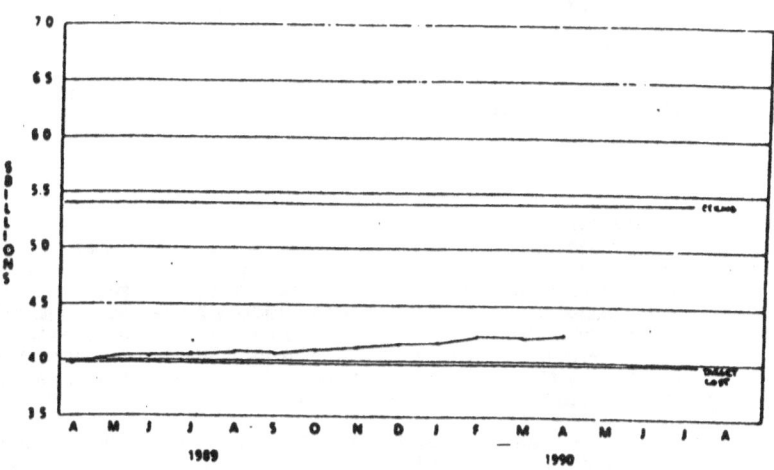

Figure 2

Utilization of CPR Data By the Government

CPR data should be utilized by the Government PM in at least three ways:

-- to analyze contractor design and manufacturing activities, especially the reasonableness of contractor cost and schedule recovery projections.

- to assess the validity of requests by the contractor for progress payments and other payments predicated upon completion of work under the contract.

- to estimate the cost at completion (EAC) of the contract on a quarterly basis in the DAES, and in briefings regarding program status.

Utilization of CPR data in analyzing contractor design and manufacturing activities and assessing the validity of requests for payment under the contract are discussed in Sections 3b and 3c, respectively, below. This section focuses upon the role of CPR data in the development of the PM's EAC and his understanding of current contract status.

Trends in the cost and schedule performance data reported in CPRs can be extrapolated to produce a range of estimates at completion of the contract. Three bases for extrapolation which are commonly used in establishing the range of estimates are:

- the cumulative cost performance index (cum CPI), which represents the actual cost of work performed to date divided by its budgeted cost.

- a more recent period CPI (e.g., 12-month, 6-month, 3-month).

- equal weighting of the CPI and the cumulative Schedule Performance Index (SPI), which represents the budgeted cost of work performed to date divided by the budgeted cost of the work scheduled to be performed.

DOD experience in more than 400 programs since 1977 indicates without exception that the cum CPI does not significantly improve during the period between 15% and 85% of contract performance; in fact, it tends to decline. Accordingly, extrapolation from the cum CPI tends to produce a lower EAC than extrapolations based upon more recent periods of performance or equal weighting of CPI/SPI. Equal weighting of CPI/SPI tends to produce higher estimates, but experience also demonstrates it to be the best predictor of actual performance at completion. However, once a range of estimates is established, the analyst must apply knowledge of the contract, experience and professional judgment to narrow the range of estimates toward the most likely outcome.

Within Naval Air Systems Command (NAVAIR), a Cost Analyst analyzed each A-12 CPR. She provided a written Cost Performance Summary (CPS) to the Program Office and briefed the PM or his Business and Finance Manager (BFM) regarding her findings. The CPS contained a single point EAC based upon the cum CPI, rather than the Cost Analyst's best professional judgment. This comported with the standard practice of her office, but facilitated reliance by the PM upon the single written cum CPI estimate as her best estimate. In fact, the PM testified that he considered the written estimate her best estimate. Her supervisor stated that the practice of providing the cum CPI as the written estimate, rather than the Cost Analyst's best estimate, was intended to afford the PM maximum flexibility in representing his program.

Nevertheless, the evidence establishes that the Cost Analyst also briefed the Program Office regarding other, higher estimates. The Cost Analyst's working papers in March and July 1989 included her assessment that a continuation of recent performance trends would cause completion costs to meet or exceed the contract ceiling. Moreover, in a footnote to her formal CPS for July 1989, she noted that a "weighted CPI" would result in an estimate some $200M above ceiling. Her subsequent briefing notes make repeated references to the difference between the cum CPI and less favorable six-month and three-month indices. The documentary evidence and the testimony of the Cost Analyst and the BFM establish that by July 1989, and certainly after the cost performance index began to deteriorate again in September 1989, the BFM and the PM, either directly or through the BFM, were aware that recent period contractor performance was substantially below the cumulative CPI, and that the cum CPI estimate was the lowest estimate she could provide.

The PM apparently chose to rely upon the cumulative CPI as a ceiling, rather than a floor for his own estimate, notwithstanding the other, higher estimates briefed to the Program Office. In the November 1989 and February 1990 DAES reports, the PM reduced the Cost Analyst's written estimate in making his own EAC, in reliance upon other information which he believed would result in an improvement in the contractor team's cumulative cost performance. Figure 3 indicates the relationship between the range of estimates available during the performance period, the cumulative CPI, and the PM's EACs.

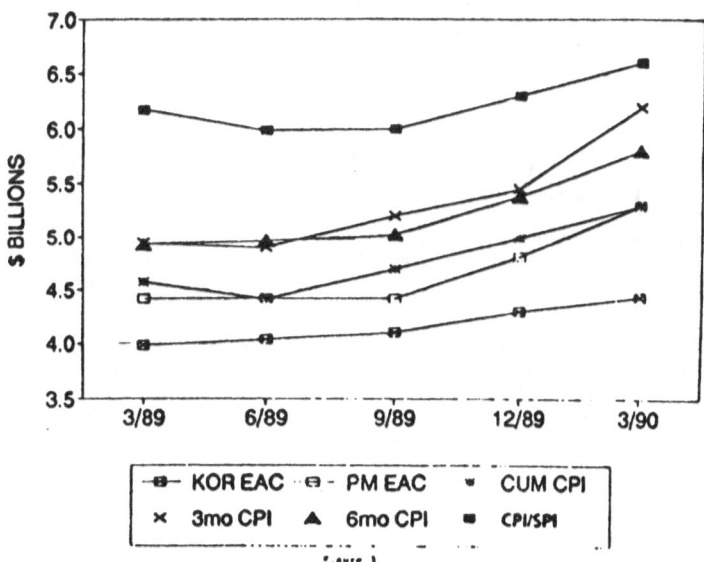

Moreover, it appears that the special access nature of the A-12 Program was allowed to interfere with normal mechanisms for higher-level oversight of contractor cost performance. Specifically, the Contract Performance Management

Reporting and Assessment normally forwarded through the matrix to COMNAVAIR was not prepared because of the limited number of personnel cleared for the program and the lack of cleared spaces. Additionally, the Program Performance Oversight Data Report normally provided to the Navy Secretariat was not prepared because the computer program resided on a mainframe computer in an uncleared, non-government facility. In the absence of formal reporting, information was transmitted verbally only, in couched terms, and with no feedback to confirm that the data had been received or its implications understood. At the OSD level, the OUSD(A) Cost Management staff was not cleared for the A-12 Program until 26 March 1990. Prior to that time, the DAES cost performance information forwarded by the Program Office was not independently analyzed at the OSD level. Consequently, the OSD DAES process did not recognize the significance of unfavorable cost and schedule variances until more than a year after such variances would normally have become DAES meeting issues.

b. <u>Engineering and Production Oversight</u>. Review of CPRs and other data prepared and submitted by the contractor is one means by which the PM fulfills his broader responsibility to measure compliance with program cost, schedule and performance requirements through engineering and production oversight.

PMs are responsible for planning and executing production management and conducting engineering surveillance over contractor operations. They accomplish this by their own assets, assets drawn from the SYSCOM matrix, and the services of the cognizant contract administration office to identify variances from cost and schedule in time to direct remedial action.

In this regard, Federal Acquisition Regulation 42.302(a) establishes standards for production surveillance by Plant Representatives Offices stating that they shall, among other things:

> Perform production support, surveillance, and status reporting, including timely reporting of potential and actual slippages in contract delivery schedules.
>
> Perform engineering surveillance to assess compliance with contractual terms for schedule, cost, and technical performance in the areas of design, development, and production.
>
> Evaluate for adequacy and perform surveillance of contractor engineering efforts and management systems that relate to design, development, production, engineering changes, subcontractors, tests, management of engineering resources, reliability and maintainability, data control systems, configuration management, and independent research and development.

The primary problem encountered during FSD was weight growth due to the thickness of the composite material necessary for the structural strength required to support the stress and loads experienced by carrier-based aircraft. Both contractors have had limited experience in building large composite structures and, in large measure, have had to develop the technology as the program progressed.

The initial schedule proposed by the contractors and established in the contract for the production of the A-12 was highly demanding from the start. In an effort to meet the schedule, both contractors had to compress activities for the design phase, subassembly at each manufacturing site, and for final assembly/ramp site at Tulsa, Oklahoma. The original schedule envisioned four and a half months for assembly of the aircraft sections at St. Louis and Fort Worth and another four and a half months for final assembly and ramp at Tulsa. This nine to ten month period for production of the first aircraft was ambitious. I am advised that most aircraft programs in production take anywhere from twelve to fourteen months from start of assembly to flight operations.

At the time the PM's production oversight team assembled in the summer of 1989, first flight was projected for June 1990. In order to meet this date, the contractors should have had a firm design in hand and already released it to their manufacturing elements. Assembly tooling should have been designed, built, and on the assembly floor by September 1989. Ample parts flow to support initial assembly should also have occurred in this timeframe. Accomplishment of these tasks would have allowed assembly of the airframe sections by the end of January 1990 for shipment to Tulsa for final assembly.

However, as the first CPRs indicate, there was early evidence of trouble affecting the production schedule. The amount of engineering effort required for the design of the airframe and the fact that added design engineering resources (outside engineering design subcontractors) put in place in the summer of 1989 could not maintain the recovery schedule was the first indicator that first flight of June 1990 would slip. By then, the first flight date of June 1990 was likely unattainable due to lack of ample tooling and parts flow.

To meet the fall-back September 1990 first flight date, formally projected by the PM in the November 1989 DAES, design release and initial tooling/fabrication should have occurred no later than late fall 1989. Tooling should have been in place and initial assembly initiated no later than December 1989 for assembly and shipment to Tulsa by the end of April 1990. Similarly, for a December 1990 first flight date, assembly should have been initiated no later than April 1990, and shipment of the completed aircraft sections to Tulsa would have had to take place no later than August 1990.

When these key dates were missed, it should have been evident to the contractors that first flight was sure to slip further in the calendar year. The contractors underestimated the level of effort needed to stabilize aircraft design, as well as the impact this would have on tooling and fabrication. In addition, they overestimated their internal capability and capacity for tool design/fabrication of metal/composite components. At best, these failures resulted from a plain lack of objectivity at the contractor team level, and wholly inadequate oversight by General Dynamics and McDonnell Douglas corporate management.

With the ongoing late release of engineering design drawings, primarily reflecting efforts to overcome weight growth, the next stage of the manufacturing process, tool design and fabrication, was severely impeded. The stop work orders resulting from the limited engineering drawing releases continually delayed production. In addition to the tooling problems, further delays in initial fabrication of the composite, sheet metal, and machined parts pushed back the initial load dates for assembly jigs and fixtures at both contractor facilities. The fact that parts flow was not occurring at a rate significant to sustain loading and assembly operations was another indicator that the program was in trouble and first flight would slip.

At McAir, contract administration services for the A-12 were performed by the NAVPRO. At the NAVPRO, the Program Manager's Representative (PMR) was responsible for coordinating all contract administration functions pertinent to the A-12 program, including the monitoring and coordination of such functions as engineering change proposals, configuration management, and producibility. The PMR is also required to evaluate contractor cost, schedule and technical performance, and analyze variances between planned and actual accomplishment. The PMR relies on a functional matrix within the NAVPRO, as well as assistance from NAVAIR, in the accomplishment of production monitoring and oversight.

On 25 July 1989, the PM and the NAVPRO Commander executed a Memorandum of Agreement (MOA) addressing NAVPRO support of the technical and management requirements of the A-12 Program. The MOA states that the following requirements, among others, will be performed by the NAVPRO:

> Monitor and evaluate contractor's plan for fabrication and assembly of the A-12 aircraft, placing special emphasis on the areas of plant facilities, test equipment or tooling inventory as it may relate to the contractor's ability to avoid conflict with other ongoing production systems (such as the F/A-18, F-15 or AV-8 programs).

> Evaluate the feasibility of the contractor's production plan as it relates to sharing other program assets to the advantage/disadvantage of the government and the A-12 program.

> Keep Navy personnel with valid need to know, continually informed of fabrication and assembly problems that have been identified or resolved.

> Review monthly, the contractor's structural components schedule. Provide the PMA with an analysis of problem areas and proposed workarounds as a part of the NAVPRO monthly program management reports.

At GDFW, the AFPRO was responsible for contract administration. The focal point for the A-12 program was the A-12 Program Director. His responsibility, as outlined in relevant Air Force regulations, is to improve communications and facilitate teamwork between the AFPRO and the Program Office. Among his duties is to develop management systems and indicators providing visibility into the contractor's accomplishment of all contractual requirements and to collect, integrate and analyze program data to provide the buying agency with a total program assessment.

The AFPRO Commanding Officer declined to sign an MOA with the PM regarding A-12 support, because he felt he could not comply with it due to personnel shortages. Additionally, he felt it would be premature to sign the MOA in light of the then-pending creation of the Defense Contract Management Command, the full implications of which were not yet known. The specific impact on the program of not having an MOA is difficult to quantify. However, the level and quality of support did not equal that provided by the NAVPRO.

Notwithstanding the PMs initiation of the MOA with the NAVPRO and AFPRO, production oversight responsibilities and the process through which they would be carried out between the Program Office/NAVAIR matrix and the NAVPRO/AFPRO, did not appear to have been clearly established prior to the outset of the manufacturing process. This is reflected in the failure to establish an acceptable support relationship with the AFPRO, and the consequent need to assign Program Manager's Technical Representatives (Tech Reps) to GDFW one at a time until now there are three. It is also reflected in the fact that as late as the winter of 1989, the Deputy PM-Production was having difficulty getting the NAVPRO and AFPRO to focus their activity reports on program issues rather than measurements having no management utility, such as the raw number of data deliverables received during the reporting period. Finally, it is reflected in the fact that the Program Office failed to follow-up on its direction in October and November 1989 to the PRO organizations to track "on the floor" the contractors' progress in reducing backlog, work in process, and slipped or missed promise dates and the impact of these events on the asserted schedules. The Deputy PM-Production testified that he was only able to assess these issues in March and April 1990, after spending several months developing his own "PERT" chart here in Washington. He should not have had to do so; the NAVPRO and AFPRO should have provided such analysis.[3]

We found no focused utilization of the CPR data by Navy program management beyond the contract summary level analysis and limited analysis of major variances at the detailed functional level provided by the Cost Analyst to the PM and his BFM. Specifically, although the CPRs highlighted weight growth, late drawing releases, and tooling problems continually from as early as June 1988, there is no evidence that either the functional level of detailed data or the detailed Work Breakdown Structure data was provided to or utilized by the Deputy Program Manager-Production, NAVAIR design engineering or production oversight personnel, or engineering or manufacturing oversight personnel at the NAVPRO/AFPRO to facilitate assessment of the contractor team's problems.

Analysis of this information at the detailed level, and integration of it with other data which was developed from time to time, would have strengthened the position of the NAVPRO (and, had it been fully utilized, the AFPRO) in challenging the contractors' optimistic assessments in the analysis provided to the Program Office.

There were shortcomings at the NAVPRO in integrating engineering, industrial, and C/SCSC oversight functions into a "program" perspective. This was particularly evident in their efforts in 1989 to track the number of design drawings released following redesign efforts to reduce the weight of the aircraft. Although they tracked the number and percentage of drawing releases, NAVPRO personnel failed to make any industrial assessment of the increased requirements those more complex drawings would place on tooling. This is a conspicuous example of how review of the detailed CPR data at the NAVPRO level might have focused the NAVPRO staff on the impact the engineering design problems quickly began to have in other functional areas. While the support and information provided by the NAVPRO was sufficient to alert the Program Office and NAVAIR to the problems with the A-12, it does not appear to have furthered the understanding of their impact on cost and schedule, nor did it transcend the information the Program

Office and the NAVAIR matrix were receiving throughout the period directly from the contractor.

The performance of the AFPRO on the A-12 program was ineffective. Despite the size and criticality of the program, the AFPRO dedicated inadequate resources to the program to fulfill its responsibilities under the FAR. Although the AFPRO Commander requested additional resources, he did not choose to reallocate his existing resources when additional personnel were not provided. AFPRO personnel provided little useful oversight or assessments. As a result, the Program Office and NAVAIR found it necessary to place "their own" technical representatives in the plant.

There was a substantial flow of raw data from the contractors to the Program Office and NAVAIR, and the PM made frequent visits to the contractor facilities. With respect to information flow, then, the adverse impact of the shortcomings at the NAVPRO and AFPRO may have been mitigated to some extent. However, is noteworthy that as the PMRs alerted the Deputy PM-Production to their concerns during the fall and winter of 1989-1990, he told them he needed hard data and analysis rather than mere "gut feel." They did not effectively generate such data and analysis, although the contractors appear to have responded fully and in a timely manner to their data requests. Consequently, their contribution to production oversight was insufficient to challenge effectively the contractors' optimistic assertions.

In summary, the Program Manager underestimated the cost implications of adverse engineering and manufacturing process data in his program estimates. Areas which appear to have been underappreciated include:

- the impact of the late release of detailed design drawings on manufacturing, particularly on the contractors' ability to facilitate initial tool design and fabrication of tooling to support assembly operations and piece part fabrication.

- the instability of the design releases to manufacturing.

- the high degree of design change notice activity and the resulting stop work orders to manufacturing, which delayed tool design and fabrication and initial piece part fabrication.

- the impact that the late start on tool design and fabrication, for both assembly and piece part fabrication tooling, would have on the proposed schedules.

- the inability of the contractors' tool shop/outside vendors to support initial fabrication of piece parts necessary to sustain asserted assembly schedules.

Under DOD and DON policy and approved program documentation, the NAVPRO and AFPRO should have been the PM's primary "eyes and ears" on-site in identifying and analyzing the implications of these problems, and the feasibility of the contractor team's response to them. In order to do so, they should have made extensive use of detailed CPR data and a PERT or similar system to assess contractor progress and the likely systemic impact of various sources of delay. As indicated, the NAVPRO and AFPRO did not effectively fulfill this responsibility. The precise impact of deficiencies in NAVPRO/AFPRO support upon the PM's ongoing assessment of program status cannot be stated with precision; however, they plainly did not fulfill the primary and close oversight role contemplated by existing policy, and it is not clear what additional insight they contributed by virtue of their presence in the contractor facilities which the PM did not or could not readily obtain directly from the contractor team. On balance, I believe that the fact that the NAVPRO and AFPRO did not play a primary, aggressive role in engineering and production oversight pursuant to well defined and accepted responsibilities contributed to the PM's underestimation of the cost and schedule implications of the contractor team's performance difficulties.

c. <u>Program Contract and Payment Controls</u>. As previously noted, the A-12 FSD contract is a fixed price incentive contract, and provides for payments upon completion of each of a series of event-based line items. These features of the contract establish a relationship between progress and other payments during the course of contract performance and actual progress toward its completion. Accordingly, we examined the process of contract administration to determine the extent to which that process might have illuminated the contractor team's performance problems, and the extent to which it actually did.

With respect to the A-12 contract, Government progress payment and billing price administration were inadequate to provide visibility into the contractors' performance problems. Contractor requests for progress payments were not properly reviewed to assess their validity, and required analyses supporting critical estimates used to determine contract physical progress were not performed. Adverse information on contractor financial condition and contract performance from the limited reviews that were performed was not effectively utilized in the review of progress payment requests, adjustment of billing prices, and administration of the progress payment liquidation rate. Special procedures established to expedite progress payments to the contractor team diffused Government personnel responsibilities for review and approval of contractor requests. The Government may be due substantial credits to liquidate excess progress payments associated with contractually-accepted work.

Review of Progress Payments

The contractor team is permitted to request progress payments no more frequently than monthly based on eligible costs associated with contract work-in-process. Due to the unique teaming arrangement on this particular contract, the progress payment request process provides that GDFW will submit a combined request for progress payments including the McAir request, and subsequently disburse financing received in accordance with the progress payment request. The administrative contracting officer (ACO) at the AFPRO at GDFW is responsible for approval of the progress payment request. This approval by the ACO should be based on an analysis of contractor cost and schedule progress as well as contractor financial condition. The analysis of cost and schedule progress should be based on actual physical progress on the contract and the Government estimate of the cost to complete the contract. Subsequent to ACO approval, the progress payment request is forwarded to the A-12 Program Office for review, approval and subsequent processing. The Program Office, in conjunction with the procuring contracting officer (PCO), reviews the progress payment request, approves it, and determines how the expenditure is to be spread among the outstanding contractual obligations. This information is then transmitted to the disbursing officer for payment to the contractor.

The ACO can request that the Defense Contract Audit Agency (DCAA) audit contractor progress payments in order to verify the amount claimed in the progress payment request to the contractor's books and records as a basis for approving contract financing through progress payments in accordance with the provisions of the contract. A progress payment audit includes examining on a test basis evidence supporting the amounts and disclosures in the data and records used for progress payment verification in order to obtain reasonable assurance that such data and records are free from material misstatement. In addition, an audit also includes assessing the accounting principles and significant estimates made by the contractor that support the progress payment audits periodically on progress payment requests by these contractors. The ACO can also request or perform analyses of contractor performance based on CPRs submitted by the contractors on a monthly basis as a means for comparison with progress payment requests.

Government oversight of contractor requests for progress payments by the ACOs at GDFW and McAir did not comply with policy guidance, including the Federal Acquisition Regulation (FAR). Specifically, they failed to reconcile physical contract performance with costs incurred and charged to the Government despite the substantial cost and schedule variances being reported in the CPRs. Nor did they take action to compute a loss ratio factor and utilize it to adjust progress payments once available evidence indicated the likelihood that the FSD contract would exceed ceiling.

In addition, the Defense Contract Audit Agency (DCAA) Resident Audit Offices at both contractor locations did not perform essential audit requirements as specified in the DCAA Contract Audit Manual in auditing the contractor Cost/Schedule Control System and specific requests for progress payments on the FSD contract.[4] The combined effect of these control deficiencies was failure to detect significant contract "overprogressing," and initiate prompt corrective action.[5]

Acceptance of Incomplete Line-Items

The Navy accepted three contract line items as complete on 15 December 1989, although contractor team performance was incomplete. Specifically, Critical Design Review (CDR) Phase II was accepted as complete although numerous significant issues were unresolved.[5] Associated testing requirements for CDR Phase II were also accepted as complete although an aircraft mockup meeting contract specifications was not available at the time of CDR Phase II to accomplish required critical testing. In addition, the first of two contractual Program Management Reviews (PMR) was accepted as complete although required drawing release for nine critical systems, subsystems, and structures was significantly below contract requirements (74% v. 100% required). Like the failure properly to administer progress payments, the failure to administer the event-based line items in the contract in a disciplined manner -- especially those pertaining to the CDR Phase II and the PMR -- fostered the illusion that internal program milestones had been successfully passed, when critical elements of the substance of them had, in fact, only been pushed downstream. This stands in sharp contrast to the PM's "Good News" slide at the November 1989 CSC and subsequent briefings that CDR was "nearing completion."

As a result, the contractor team received payments for work not substantially completed at the time of payment. These payments for incomplete work, like the overprogressing discussed above, obviated the visibility into the contractors' performance problems which more disciplined administration of the contract might have provided.

Exercise of the Lot I Production Option

The Navy unilaterally exercised the Lot I production option for 6 aircraft on 31 May 1990 at the not-to-exceed ceiling price of $1.198B. The PM, PEO and AIR-02 sought and obtained the NAE's approval to exercise the option on 21 May 1990. At the time they did so, the PM and PEO were aware of recent information indicating significant cost, schedule and technical risk not previously displayed to senior management.

Shortly after completion of the MAR, as part of the indoctrination of the new PEO, the PM arranged a technical overview for him, which the A-12 Class Desk (Chief Engineer) presented in early April 1990. It had become clear at this point that Phase 3 of the CDR was slipping even further because of large weight increases and significant technical issues such as lagging software development, structural test schedule weaknesses, and antenna problems. The incoming PEO was greatly concerned about these issues and insisted COMNAVAIR be briefed as soon as possible. This briefing took place on 16 April.

The Class Desk identified Weight, Performance and Structural Testing and Integrity as his primary concerns. He noted that NAVAIR's estimate of aircraft weight at IOC would be 7,930 pounds over the specification with resultant adverse impact on operational performance and the current A-12 structural design. He identified resolution with the contractors of minimum acceptable structural test requirements for first flight as a significant issue. He also pointed to other technical issues still outstanding, which were likely to lead to schedule delays affecting first flight and IOC, and likely to jeopardizing successful conclusion of CDR. His "Summary" slide for the brief stated:

> We have significant technical problems that must be resolved before CDR can continue
>
> Development is behind schedule and present first flight and OPEVAL dates are too optimistic
>
> Some technical problems will require significant lead times to fix. This suggests we should reexamine aircraft early procurement rates to protect effectivities

COMNAVAIR directed the PM to develop a "second opinion" overnight and brief him the next day. He also telephoned each of the contractor CEO's to express his concerns and to inquire into their corporate commitment to the program. He received assurances from both that they were committed to the A-12 Program and that they would be personally involved in addressing Navy concerns.

In his brief on 17 April, the PM emphasized the positive aspects of the program, asserting that the technical issues were significant but manageable. He addressed the concerns raised by the Class Desk in the context of proposed solutions to these technical problems. He displayed a chart indicating the risk of completing key milestones as scheduled that showed only the engine problem affecting projected first flight in December 1990. The PM also pointed out the pros and cons of a Navy-directed slip, contending it would open the FSD contract to renegotiation, delay IOC, jeopardize FY90-91 funding, and result in loss of production options. His "Summary" slide stated:

Tech/Performance/Schedule Issues Are of Major Importance - Do Not Warrant Immediate Program Slip

Directed Program Slip Will Be Extremely Expensive - Slip, If Necessary, Should Result From Contractor Action

Directed Program Slip Relieves Contractor of Technical and Contractual Obligations

Acquisition Strategy Review Can Provide Orderly Approach to These Issues

The PM recommended that COMNAVAIR maintain the current program structure and conduct a total acquisition strategy review with the contractors in light of the current situation relative to CDR, schedule, contract specification, contractor costs and cash flow, Lot I option definitization, and prime competition. The PM alluded to the MAR in his brief, noting that its focus had been on the "Changing Threat, Validation of Requirement, and Cost/Affordability" issues. He reminded COMNAVAIR that the USD(A), SECNAV, and the MAR Working Group already had been briefed on 9 March 1990 by the contractors at GDFW on all technical issues (less those relating to the engine), been commended for their candid approach, and that the technical situation was aggravated in only three areas (engine, weight, and antenna). He observed that the MAR seemed more oriented towards re-validating the program requirements rather than probing technical details.

COMNAVAIR concurred with the recommendation of the PM, and an Acquisition Strategy Board was scheduled with the contractors on 25 April.

Meanwhile, on 29 March 1990, during the MAR, the ASD(PA&E) had suggested that the A-12 production options be renegotiated to be event-based rather than schedule-based. Subsequently, the NAE directed the PM and PEO to consider this issue. They, together with AIR-02, initially briefed the NAE on 24 April 1990.

The slides utilized at this briefing did not mention the concerns briefed by the Class Desk the week before, and emphasized the need to adhere to the current contract. Specifically, they noted the favorable performance specifications, their protection through the production options, and the strong warranty provisions. They also emphasized the risk of increased cost through "reopening" the contract, noting that the contractor "has acknowledged going to ceiling" and "some feel he may go above" (without mentioning the NAVAIR Cost Analyst's estimate or the USD(A) Deputy Director for Cost Management's estimate of $1B above ceiling, which had been briefed to the PM on 29 March 1990), and that the contractor was "in (a) severe negative cash flow position." The slides asserted that "technical performance to date meets program objectives" and that the program was "on track to make major milestones (IIIA, IIIB, IOC)," while "first flight delay may drive contractor costs higher." The briefing asserted that it would be "difficult to limit the scope of negotiations" over the options, and that the contractor would likely seek to "recover financially, eliminate spec(ification) difficulties, and neutralize all Government leverage." The Lot I option was portrayed as "just about fait accompli," while it was asserted that the Lot II and III options should be exercised within the current contract and the Lot IV option could be negotiable. In summary, "opening the current contract/option package" would "provide no additional Government leverage" and "jeopardize all favorable aspects of the contract."

No decision was made at this briefing, pending development of an overall Navy strategy regarding event-based contracting. The following day, 25 April 1990, the PM and his principal assistants met with the contractors at St. Louis. As he recounted this meeting--

> I opened the discussion by taking the contractor to task on their credibility, and the way it was impacting overall A-12 program credibility. I highlighted eight specific areas, including aircraft weight, first flight schedule, and FSD costs vs. ceiling. This discussion generated an action item for the contractors to "submit alternatives for rephasing program to realistically accomplish our mission. Approaches will show assumptions, pros/cons and schedule. Due 4 May 1990 to PMA."

On 4 May 1990, the contractors briefed the PM in response to his 25 April tasking. In his written statement, the PM summarized their presentation and his impressions:

> For the first time, they acknowledged the very strong likelihood that they would exceed their ceiling costs on the FSD contract if some major changes in approach were to undertaken. They also presented a first flight date of March 91, which was three months later than their previous estimate, but was consistent with the date the program office has independently determined and had been briefing. This date was also consistent with what (SECDEF) briefed to the MAR on 26 April. The business concerns, however, were the most alarming aspects of our discussions. The contractors advised us that "corporate" had initiated an independent "red team" assessment of the program, focusing on costs and schedule to first flight. Corporate was particularly alarmed at the overall outcome of the MAR (beyond A-12 issues), the declining Defense budget in the out-years, and the impacts of these items on their future business base. My concern was that the A-12 would lose the corporate support necessary in a development effort for adequate resources to successfully execute the program. The contractor's re-phased schedule included the delay of production by one year (roughly matching the first flight delay), and the transfer of APN funds freed up by that delay to augment the R&D funds for the FSD program. I and my staff unanimously rejected the fund transfer approach as a "bailout," and reminded the contractor that the FSD contract was valid, we intended to enforce it, and that they should continue to execute that contract. The contractors also indicated that corporate involvement was such that they fully expected a corporate initiative (letter or visit from the Chairmen) on the A-12 program to (the USD(A)) or (DEPSECDEF) very soon. I advised them that it would not be prudent to bypass the Navy (SECNAV or ASN(RD&A)) in this

process. Having dealt with this contractor program management team for almost four years at the time, I sensed that this was definitely not "posturing" on their behalf, but the onset of a potential crisis.

After this meeting, the PM alerted the PEO, a member of the NAE's staff, and the A-12 Requirements Officer on the staff of the Assistant Chief of Naval Operations (Air Warfare) (OP-05).

The following Monday, 7 May 1990, the PM briefed AIR-02, the PEO and COMNAVAIR regarding this information, and recommended that ASN(RD&A) "and appropriate authority" be promptly briefed regarding the potential corporate approach to senior OSD officials and the cost and schedule projections. However, the PM "was not fully successful in convincing them that (his) concerns were ready to be briefed up the chain." He testified that the PEO responded to his recommendation in substance: "I'm not going to take a problem to (the NAE) without a solution, because if I do, he may give me a solution that I may not like." The PEO testified that although he could not recall having made such a statement, it would not have been out of character for him to have done so, and it was consistent with his reaction to guidance he was receiving during frequent meetings with the NAE regarding another program at this time.

In any event, the PM proceeded to brief the Requirements Officer and the NAE staff member later that afternoon "fully ... on what the contractor presented ... and what (he) perceived as the potential ramifications."

On 10 May 1990, the PM presented a proposed "information only" brief for ASN(RD&A) to AIR-02, the PEO and COMNAVAIR, because he felt that this situation was "so complex and potentially explosive that no easy solution existed, and that it would be better to elevate the issues and concerns while potential solutions were being developed."

This briefing presented a substantially changed picture from that briefed to the NAE two weeks previously on 24 April. After reaffirming the threat and projected A-12 capabilities as the "program drivers" and summarizing key aspects of the current contract, the proposed brief highlighted the following "basic issues."

Cost - Prime Team Will Incur Major Loss In FSED

Schedule - First Flight Has Slipped - Milestones IIIA, IIIB, IOC Will Slip

Technical Performance - Weight Growth Continues - Lot I Specification Issue

The next slide indicated that on 25 April the contractors had acknowledged being "at or over ceiling on FSED," that "first flight (was) still uncertain," and that "weight and related performance (were) unachievable." On 4 May, the contractors had proposed to "slip major milestones, re-structure (the) FSED contract, (and) delay Production Lot II and beyond." The slide noted that "proposed delays have positive engineering and support impacts." The following slide depicted the contractors' proposed rephasing plan.

The following slide assessed "cost" issues as follows:

OSD Analysis: About $1 Billion Over FSED Ceiling

AIR-524 Analysis: Confirms About $1 Billion Over Ceiling

Potential Scenario: Up to $1 Billion Over Our FSED - No Profit
On Lots I, II, III - Net Loss For 620 Aircraft Program

With respect to "Cost Options," the proposed brief indicated that if the current contract were enforced, "contractor default or PL 85-804 (was) possible; claims/litigation (was) likely," although it would be a "weak case"; there might be "further reduced performance, (and) shortcuts," with the potential that "warranties may not be effective," and "future contract mods" would be "expensive." It was noted, alternatively, that "reshaping" the program would require additional research and development funds and Congressional notification, but could be done "within existing FYDP."

With respect to "Schedule" issues, the proposed brief indicated:

First Flight: March 1991?

Concurrency Has Increased

Sea Trials Will Not Support IIIA

OPEVAL Will Not Support IIIB

FY-94 IOC Unlikely

"Schedule Options" were first to enforce the contract as written, rendering the "test program overly compressed," allowing concurrency to "degrade production configuration, and thereby forcing "improper use of warranties." The alternative displayed was to "delay production (of) Lot II and beyond," which would "retain (the) NTE options, restore acceptable concurrency," and provide "incentive for (the) contractor" with "reduced warranty cost."

Finally, with respect to "technical" issues, a slide identified "weight growth" as a "major technical spec deficiency," with impacts on single engine rate of climb, launch/arrest wind over deck, structure, future capabilities, and recurring/life cycle cost. While "pursuing technical solutions to mitigate impact," the slide indicated the "ultimate" possibility of "spec write-down-after flight test."

A summary slide emphasized the need for and capability of the A-12, the financial jeopardy of the contractor team, and the benefits to the Navy of restructuring, and indicated "dialog continuing at program level" with anticipation of "GD/McAir Corporate initiatives."

The PM could not obtain approval from the PEO or COMNAVAIR to present this briefing to the NAE. "Again," he stated, "I was asked to structure the presentation as an issue and recommendations brief, and was given the opportunity to try for a fifth and sixth time the following week."

On 16 May, the PM proposed a two-page talking paper to be used to brief the NAE. The proposed talking points emphasized differences in the "acquisition environment" between 1986 and 1990, summarized the history of the FSD contract, and assessed the cost, schedule and technical issues. The only significant difference from the substance of the 10 May 1990 proposed brief was with respect to cost: the FSD contract would "most likely be over ceiling; to what extent is debatable." Finally, the talking paper assessed three options: enforce the current contract, restructure the program, or exercise the Lot I option and then pursue restructuring within the existing contract.

The PEO directed the talking points be revised to one page. This was done principally by eliminating the discussion of options in favor of a recommendation to exercise the Lot I option and "pursue possible contract mod to reflect schedule realities, incorporate event-based options and emerging requirements." However, at a subsequent meeting between the PM, PEO and COMNAVAIR, it was decided to focus only on the urgency of executing the Lot I option in the upcoming meeting with the NAE, and not to discuss the issues raised by the contractors on 4 May. The PM testified that the PEO directed that he not bring the talking paper, or any other papers or slides regarding the business issues to the meeting with the NAE. He further testified that he believed that to have raised those issues at the meeting would have been contrary to the PEO's desires. In any event, neither he, nor the PEO, nor the NAE staff member raised the issues presented by the contractors with the NAE at the 21 May 1990 meeting in which they secured his approval to exercise the Lot I production option. Nor were these issues brought to the NAE or SECNAV's attention at a subsequent meeting on 30 May where he was briefed regarding total program cost issues arising out of the MAR decision to reduce the procurement quantity. As the PM put it, "(The PEO) was attending that particular meeting and his direction had not changed on the particular issue earlier of potential corporate involvement, so I was not inclined to initiate discussion on that particular topic."

In his testimony, the NAE staff member confirmed the PM's testimony that he had been informed regarding the information received from the contractors and the PM's efforts to provide the NAE a briefing regarding it. He had reviewed the 10 May 1990 slides, but had not seen either version of the 16 May 1990 talking paper. He knew that the PM had been directed not to bring any slides on the issues raised by the contractors to the 21 May 1990 meeting with the NAE. The NAE staff member did not inform the NAE of these matters for three stated reasons: he did not and does not believe they were of sufficient magnitude to warrant alarm at the time; he felt that under the reorganization of the Office of the ASN(RD&A) it was the responsibility of the PEO to develop solutions and bring the matters forward unless the NAE was likely to be "blind-sided" regarding them by higher authority; and he did not wish to jeopardize the willingness of the Program Office or NAVAIR personnel to share information with him in the future. Neither the NAE nor SECNAV learned of the issues raised by the contractors on 4 May nor the information presented in the 16 April Class Desk brief until on or after the contractor presentation to the NAE on 1 June. After receiving the contractor presentation on 1 June, the NAE immediately alerted SECNAV and the USD(A), and DEPSECDEF and SECDEF were informed.

d. <u>Major Aircraft Review</u>. On 19 December 1989, SECDEF directed DEPSECDEF to conduct a review of the Navy's A-12 Aircraft and the Air Force's B-2 Bomber, C-17 Transport Aircraft, and Advanced Tactical Fighter. The primary emphasis in conducting the Major Aircraft Review (MAR) was to determine the impact that recent changes in world events would have on the need for the weapons systems in the future. SECDEF directed that DEPSECDEF report the results of the review by 30 March 1990.

On 19 December 1989, DEPSECDEF designated the Under Secretaries of Defense and the Chairman of the Joint Chiefs of Staff as members of the Major Aircraft Review Steering Group. The USD(A) was designated as Chairman of the MAR Steering Group. Upon being designated as Chairman, the USD(A) issued a memorandum on or about 22 December 1989 to the Steering Group members that summarized their agreement regarding the questions to be answered during the conduct of the MAR. These questions were:

(a) What are the U.S. defense aircraft capability needs for the next 15 years in light of the world's projected political environment and the nation's defense strategy?

(b) How well will those needs be met by our current aircraft?

(c) What are the priorities of the needs not projected to be met by our current aircraft?

(d) What are the alternatives to meeting those needs?

(e) What resources can we afford to devote to meeting those needs?

(f) How effectively do the programs identified in (SECDEF's) and (DEPSECDEF's) memorandums satisfy those needs?

On 4 January 1990, the Acting Deputy Director for Tactical Warfare Programs, OUSD(A), established an A-12 Aircraft Review Working Group to support the MAR Steering Group. The Working Group included representatives from the USD(A) and the Under Secretary of Defense (Policy) (USD(P)) staff and the Joint Staff, as well as the Office of the DOD Comptroller; the DOD Cost Analysis Improvement Group (CAIG); the Director, Operational Test and Evaluation; and the Navy and Air Force. The A-12 Action Officer on the USD(A) staff served as Executive Secretary of the Working Group.

Principal Navy participants were two officials from the ASN(RE&S) staff, OPNAV-50, OPNAV-501, OPNAV-502, and OPNAV-76. Because the number of Navy seats was limited, the A-12 PM's request to participate as a member of the Working Group was denied.

On the basis of DAES reports and previous briefings, the A-12 was widely perceived as having no significant problems and had consequently not been subject to exceptional scrutiny by OSD prior to the MAR. The first OSD-level indication of an A-12 problem came in an October 1989 draft Program Budget Decision (PBD), which recommended elimination of additional FY 90 funds for advance procurement of Lot I, elimination of FY 91 procurement funds, and elimination of FY 91 funding for pre-planned product improvement. These recommendations were based upon cost and schedule concerns arising from, among other research, the DOD Comptroller staff's review of the CPRs and visits to the contractor facilities. On the basis of his review, the DOD Comptroller staff Budget Analyst estimated that the program was two years behind schedule and would likely overrun the FSD contract ceiling by $500M.

Based upon input provided by the Program Office, SECNAV on 2 November wrote the DOD Comptroller expressing strong opposition to the proposed PBD. He expressed particular concern about the cost implications of losing the favorable option prices for Lot II and beyond in the current contract, and the potential adverse impact of the PBD upon achieving IOC.

On 3 November 1989, the USD(A) also wrote the Comptroller to oppose the PBD, but indicated that it raised "a number of issues I want to explore in more depth." A Conventional Systems Committee (CSC) Program Review had been scheduled for December 1989 to review exercise of the Lot I production option. Because of the PBD issues, the USD(A) advanced the CSC meeting to 9 November.

At the CSC, the PM presented a "Good News" slide stating that Critical Design Review was nearing completion, test planning was on schedule, and manufacturing facilities were in place. He stated that even if there was some risk in the first flight date, it could slip to December 1990 or January 1991 and still support the planned IOC. The CSC briefing concluded with the Program Manager's assurance that the program was "on schedule, on cost and on track." The DOD Comptroller representative did not vigorously press the contrary assertions of the draft PBD. Although the Budget Analyst had prepared a set of slides addressing counter arguments to the Navy's 2 November PBD reclama, they were not presented. The Budget Analyst was, however, offered the opportunity to raise the question on the potential over ceiling cost of $500 million. The PM responded by emphasizing that the FSD contract was fixed price incentive and that the government would not be liable for costs above the ceiling price. Additionally, he emphasized that the PBD proposal would breach the existing favorable contract.

A representative from the Office of the Deputy Assistant Secretary of Defense for Production Resources also noted concern about the A-12 schedule. A member of his staff had been scheduled to conduct an A-12 production readiness evaluation from 6 to 10 November in support of the planned December CSC meeting. Because of the short-notice rescheduling of the CSC to 9 November, he telephoned an interim report on 8 November. At the CSC meeting, the representative mentioned that he had received a telephonic report from his production readiness person on the scene that things were not going well. However, since the review was currently ongoing, the information was tentative and he could not press the issue.

Following this meeting, the DOD Comptroller made the decision to withdraw the draft PBD rather than forward the issue to DEPSECDEF for resolution. In an interview, he indicated that he did so after discussing the issue with SECNAV. He indicated that he made the decision because "no one agreed with us," and he thought it was "a close judgment call" on the merits of the issues.

The Production Readiness Specialist completed his written report and provided it on 16 February 1990 to the USD(A) A-12 Action Officer, a Navy Captain, who put it aside and forgot about it. Consequently, the MAR Working Group never saw the report. Among other things, it warned that first flight might slip "well into CY91."

As previously noted, the PM was not a member of the A-12 Working Group. He did provide an overview briefing to the Working Group on 5 January 1990; brief the DOD Cost Analysis Improvement Group on 13 February 1990; and brief those Steering Group and Working Group members who visited GDFW on 9 March 1990.

The PM was directed to limit his 5 January 1990 presentation to the Working Group to 15 minutes or less and to address "total costs and expenditures to date." The PM prepared and presented six slides showing program structure and schedule through the second year beyond Initial Operating Capability; total program flyaway costs; program costs for FY 1984 through January 1990; five year budget projections for FY 1990 through 1994; status of the FSD contract (emphasizing its fixed price nature and the fully funded ceiling price); and an assessment of FSD contract cost performance showing that his estimate to complete FSD was between target and ceiling, there was a schedule variance due to late drawing releases with a recovery plan in effect, and all variances were reported quarterly in the Defense Acquisition Summaries (DAES). The PM testified that when he noted that the contract was funded to ceiling, all interest in FSD cost evaporated.

Sometime in January 1990, a Cost Analyst representing the OSD CAIG visited the Program Office gathering information in support of the CAIG's MAR effort. Because she was interested in the CPRs, among other things, the Program Office made the NAVAIR Cost Analyst available. The Cost Analyst briefed the official Program Office estimate. The OSD CAIG Cost Analyst asked if there were alternative estimates; the NAVAIR Cost Analyst informed her that there were, but discussed only the official Program Office estimate. The OSD CAIG Cost Analyst did not pursue the matter directly, but instructed the Navy Center for Cost Analysis to conduct an assessment of FSD costs based on the CPRs. That assessment concluded that there was some possibility of exceeding ceiling but that there was no problem because the contract was funded to ceiling.

On 13 February 1990, the PM briefed the CAIG, whose chairman was a member of the A-12 Working Group. The presentation consisted of 20 briefing slides that outlined the A-12 Aircraft program cost approach; status of the FSD contract; production cost estimates, methodology and factors; integrated logistics support cost, operating and support cost estimates and summary life cycle costs. The briefing also showed a detailed breakdown of A-12 weight problems.

On 8 and 9 March, most members of the MAR Steering Group, including the USD(A), and several members of the A-12 Working Group, visited McAir and GDFW. The most significant of these visits was 9 March at GDFW where SECNAV joined the group. On the morning of 9 March, the PM briefed the group. The presentation consisted of 16 briefing slides that showed the primary and secondary A-12 missions; IOC; a comparison of the phasing-out of the A-6 Intruder with the phasing-in of the A-12; key A-12 design features and support; wind over deck requirements and status; status of FSD; program structure through FY 1996; program security transition from compartmented to general security status; and total program acquisition costs. According to notes taken by a participant, the PM addressed cost and schedule variances, suggesting costs would go to ceiling; schedule risk; and problems with fabrication of "large ribs". He described the GDFW operation as being of "moderate risk."

Later in the day, the contractor briefed the group. The "top 10" problems were discussed including weight, which was described as the number one problem, and schedule, the number two problem. Most people we interviewed, both Government and industry, recalled significant discussion of both problems. The contractor team briefer projected first flight in December 1990, an additional three-month slip from the date briefed by the Navy PM at the November CSC meeting. The MAR Working Group Chairman recalls being "furious" at the first flight slip from September to December 1990. This was the first he had heard about it and, given the "rosy picture" he felt had been painted during the November CSC meeting, he thought this was a major surprise.

The Navy PM described the December 1990 date as "aggressive but achievable." The GDFW program manager described first flight as having an 80 percent probability of achievement by December 1990; however, the GDFW General Manager, was more cautious in stating only a "50/50" likelihood. The USD(A) characterized the 50/50 likelihood as leaving "no room for major glitches."

The contractors projected completion of the FSD contract within ceiling, and assessed that their major areas of cost risk were inflation and business base. The USD(A) was concerned about the level of risk in the FSD program, and questioned both the contractors and the Navy PM regarding the cost and schedule implications of the stated technical challenges. He asked them to identify not only the "top 10" problems, but "the things that might not be problems yet, but which caused them to lose sleep at night ... the storm clouds on the horizon." Neither the PM nor the contractors indicated any risk of substantial cost growth beyond ceiling, or schedule delay beyond a potential slip of first flight to March 1991. The visiting MAR group was left with the impression that while there were some problems, there were no "show stoppers."

On 14 March, SECDEF and USD(A) visited McAir. The PM gave the same briefing he gave to the MAR group the previous week. The primary difference was that McAir did not make a "top 10" problems presentation. However, according to the PM, he made the same weight problem and "aggressive schedule" presentation.

On 17 and 20 March, pre-briefs were held in preparation for a 28 March briefing to SECDEF. There is evidence that cost and schedule risk was discussed at the 17 March meeting with DEPSECDEF. The USD(A) recalls that composite producibility was a principal concern, and that the CAIG had noted its potential cost impact. He discussed his concern regarding this with DEPSECDEF and SECDEF. He also noted that throughout the MAR, CAIG cost estimates were utilized in all cases where they were higher than the Service estimate, as in this case. At the 20 March pre-brief, a slide was added on program status that showed "moderate to high" technical risk.

On 26 March, at the request of the USD(A) for an independent assessment, the Principal Deputy USD(A) directed the Deputy Director for Cost Management on the OUSD(A) staff to review available FSD cost performance information and provide his view regarding the issue of cost risk. He was granted access to the A-12 program on 26 March. On 27 March he concluded an analysis of A-12 DAES reports and immediately reported the results to his superior. His analysis concluded that the A-12 FSD contract would likely exceed ceiling by $1 billion. He provided those results to the Principal Deputy USD(A) either that day or the next.

On 28 March, the MAR Steering Group began the briefings to SECDEF. The first day of briefs was characterized as spending the bulk of the available time on threat issues. The A-12 was the first of the four aircraft to be briefed but was not finished.

The A-12 portion consisted of 20 briefing charts that provided a range of information on the A-12 Program. These charts described policy and strategy considerations relevant to air superiority and strike requirements through 2005; listed selected third world threat increases in terms of aircraft and missiles; identified a potential strike scenario; listed A-12/ATA force levels and shortfalls; displayed a technical, schedule and cost assessment of the A-12 program, indicating "moderate to high risk," and overall program issues; identified alternatives to the

A-12/ATA; compared the Navy's A-6E and A-12 inventory requirements and costs; and presented the conclusions of the A-12 Aircraft Review Working Group.

The briefing showed that there were three and a half years left in the FSD phase and that the Navy's A-12 aircraft performance requirements were being met except in weight (over by 10 percent), which affects wind speed over deck landing requirements. The briefing also showed that the scheduled first flight had slipped three months to December 1990 and that program concurrency was high. DEPSECDEF asked about further schedule slip risk and the Working Group Chairman responded that there was a reasonable risk. The presentation showed that the CAIG identified a possibility of a 10 percent cost growth beyond the Navy estimate because of uncertainty associated with composite manufacturing. The Working Group did not consider this a "significant disagreement" with the Program Office and NCCA estimates.

The Director, Acquisition Policy and Program Integration on the USD(A) staff stated that his office had completed an initial contract cost assessment the night before and that costs could go a "few hundred million over ceiling." He indicated he would report back later with details. Some participants recall that someone responded that the contract was funded to ceiling so this would not be a problem, but there was no further discussion.

On 29 March, the OUSD(A) Deputy Director for Cost Management briefed the PM, his BFM and the NAVAIR Cost Analyst's second level supervisor concerning his estimate of contractor FSD costs. The PM notified his immediate superiors and the Office of the Assistant Chief of Naval Operations for Air Warfare (OP-05) that he found the presentation "compelling," but it was noted that the Deputy Director for Cost Management had only had access to the program for two days, and did not have detailed knowledge regarding the contract.

On 2 April, representatives of the CAIG met with the Deputy Director for Cost Management and his supervisor to review the basis for his over ceiling estimate. As a result of these discussions, the CAIG Cost Analyst prepared a memo on 3 April 1990 to the Assistant Secretary of Defense (Program Analysis and Evaluation) (ASD(PA&E)), describing the estimate and indicating that the CAIG estimate was within 10 percent of it. She termed the Deputy Director for Cost Management's "preferred estimate ... consistent with our concerns with the date of first (f)light and with materials cost." The largest element of the CAIG's increase was related to the cost of an additional schedule slip, the possibility of which, the memo suggests, had been discussed with the ASD(PA&E) at an earlier date. The memo notes, in that regard, the CAIG's view that "the date for first flight now accepted by the Navy is achievable, but probably optimistic and indicates an additional six months slip would result in virtually identical estimates." The memo concludes: "The A-12 FSD contract is a fixed-price incentive contract, and the Navy has budgeted to its ceiling, so the government's liability is covered." Neither the Deputy Director for Cost Management nor his supervisor was aware of the 3 April memo prior to this inquiry. However, the Deputy Director for Cost Management did de-brief his supervisor on his 2 April meeting and indicated that the CAIG did not disagree with his estimate. It was his opinion that the CAIG found his estimate consistent with theirs, given that they were within 10 percent, and consistent with their MAR position that FSD would most likely reach or exceed ceiling.

On 4 April, the day before the second MAR brief to the SECDEF, the USD(A) was briefed on the projected over ceiling cost for the A-12 contractors. His immediate reaction was to call the CEOs of both companies to get their reaction to this estimate. The Director, Acquisition Policy and Program Integration, the Deputy Director for Cost Management and the Principal Deputy USD(A) counseled him to wait. They noted that the Navy PM had been briefed on 29 March, and the SECDEF had been alerted on 28 March. Furthermore, the Principal Deputy USD(A) had directed the NAE to initiate action to renegotiate the A-12 options to make them event-based. In this context, they cautioned the USD(A) that he should not assume the contractors, and especially the CEOs, were aware of this potential overrun. Raising the issue immediately might jeopardize the possibility of making the contracts event-based. The USD(A) indicated that, if the estimate was accurate, he felt they either knew and withheld the information or there was a serious communication problem within the companies. However, he agreed to wait, indicating that if they did not agree with the estimate they should be willing to revise the contracts." It was also noted by someone that this might be a good way to ascertain their real cost position. He then directed the Principal Deputy USD(A) to proceed with the effort to revise the contract to, as he put it, "bring the issue to a head."

At the 5 April continuation of the 28 March briefing to SECDEF, the Director, Acquisition Policy and Program Integration again mentioned the over ceiling estimate, this time as being $1 Billion. He recalls no specific reaction. Mr. Betti has indicated that "since this was a new estimate and did not appear to be consistent with either the Navy or the CAIG estimates, it was not discussed in detail." At the meeting, SECDEF emphasized the need for the best program cost estimates possible because "we cannot go back to Congress after the MAR with new estimates." This comment resulted in a tasking to the Director, Acquisition Policy and Program Integration to gather together the best estimates of each of the aircraft programs. The 5 April session was continued to 10 April, but no discussions occurred on that date known to be relevant to this inquiry.

As a result of the 5 April briefing, the Director, Acquisition Policy and Program Integration met with the CAIG Chairman and members of his staff on 9 April. Information developed at that meeting resulted in a 12 April memorandum to the USD(A) showing a comparative listing of CAIG versus Service constant dollar estimates. On 13 April, the information was expanded to include then-year dollar estimates. Both memos recommend using CAIG estimates which, for the A-12, are about 10 percent higher in acquisition cost. The memos also include the following statement:

> Another indication of cost risk is the analysis of current contracts that we discussed earlier. The highlights were: A-12. We believe MACAIR and GD could go over ceiling by $1 billion total.

As previously indicated, the USD(A) followed the recommendation that CAIG estimates be used whenever they were higher than the Service estimates.

On 13 April, the USD(A) telephoned the CEO of GD and the President of McDonnell Douglas. He reiterated the concerns he had expressed at the 9 March meeting at GDFW regarding cost and schedule risk, and noted that information developed since that meeting had not allayed his concerns. Mr. Betti does not recall whether he mentioned the $1B over ceiling estimate specifically. The CEO of GD indicated that he still believed that the FSD contract would be completed within ceiling, but that in response to the concerns expressed during the MAR, GD and

McAir had that day initiated an independent corporate "Red Team" assessment of program cost and schedule. He indicated that results would not likely be available until June. In an interview during this inquiry, the CEO stated that at the time of this conversation, he thought there might be some risk of going over ceiling by no more than $100 to $300M, an amount which he considered the contractors could absorb. The President of McDonnell Douglas indicated that McAir would cooperate in the "Red Team" review, but that he did not believe there was a problem.

Following these conversations, on 17 April, the USD(A) sent a memorandum to SECDEF that includes the following:

> The bottom line is that only the A-12/ATA is assessed as having a cost or schedule risk. No specific problem has been identified but they [the contractors] agree with our assessment that the work progress versus the cost incurred indicates a cause for concern. General Dynamics and McDonnell-Douglas are initiating a "corporate team cost to completion" study involving both companies and will advise us of results.
>
> - 1st flight at end of 1990 very tight in spite of recent 6 mo. slip

Meanwhile, in response to a February memorandum from the Principal Deputy USD(A), the NAE had made a preliminary review of the feasibility of renegotiating the Lot I option exercise, and concluded that it should be exercised under the current contract. On 18 April, he met with the Principal Deputy USD(A) to make that recommendation. The Principal Deputy USD(A) would not agree to do so, and the NAE agreed to review the matter further with his staff. The Principal Deputy USD(A) did not indicate that renegotiation of the option could also be a strategy to ascertain the contractors' understanding of the status of the FSD contract. The NAE, who had been confirmed on 12 March 1990, had not participated in the MAR process and was unaware of the variance between the contractors' and PM's position regarding its status and that emerging from the OSD staff. The NAE stated that he thought the issue was "event-based contracting in general, because of the problems emerging in many programs with NTE options," and that the A-12 "was simply the first case on (the USD(A))'s scope."

The Principal Deputy USD(A) told the NAE that the Deputy Director for Cost Management had estimated that the FSD contract would go $1B over ceiling. According to the NAE, the Deputy Director for Cost Management, who was present for the latter part of the meeting, showed him a "CPI slide" indicating his estimate. The Principal Deputy USD(A) indicated that the NAE should obtain a detailed briefing from him, and the NAE agreed. According to the NAE, the $1B over ceiling estimate was no particular surprise, as he was "already of the view that these programs had problems," but he assumed that the contractor team had anticipated a loss during FSD with the expectation of recovering it through production. Nothing was said to indicate to him any connection to the MAR. The NAE reviewed the event-based issue on 24 April and 21 May, and in discussions with the Principal Deputy USD(A) obtained his approval to do so without incorporating event-basing on 28 May. The NAE's office did not obtain the briefing from the Deputy Director for Cost Management on his estimate until after the contractors' presentation on 1 June 1990.

The USD(A) understood the need to make a close examination of FSD costs and schedule issues implicit in SECDEF's direction to conduct a thorough review of the A-12 program during the MAR. He also understood the potential implications for program executability of a substantial overrun of the FSD contract ceiling price, and utilized the meeting with the PM and the contractor team (including the CEOs) on 9 March to make a personal inquiry into these matters. At the meeting, he encouraged them to share potential risks to cost and schedule, in his words "potential storm clouds on the horizon," as well as the risks identified during their briefings.

However, it is apparent that MAR participants at the Working Group level did not share a clear vision of the relationship between cost and schedule risk and the contractor team's ability or willingness to perform within the FSD contract. At the Working Group level, and as it appeared to the Navy and the Program Office, the MAR was understood by participants as primarily a requirements, capabilities and affordability review, not a program review. The CAIG reviewed FSD costs from the standpoint of cost risk to the Government, not risk to contract performance. Because its estimate was only 10% or so higher than the Navy, the CAIG did not view its cost position as in significant disagreement with the Navy. By the same token, since the Deputy Director for Cost Management's estimate was only 10% or so higher than the CAIG's, the CAIG did not view his estimate as in any significant disagreement with its own. Inasmuch as the CAIG did not revise its own estimate upwards -- and I do not mean to imply that it should have -- it did not actively reinforce the Deputy Director for Cost Management's estimate to the senior leadership.

It must also be understood in this regard that the Deputy Director for Cost Management's estimate was developed virtually at the end of the MAR, and stood in substantial contrast to the projections by both the PM and the contractor team that the FSD contract would be completed within ceiling. The USD(A) considered it cause for concern, but evaluated it in light of the position taken by the Navy and the contractors, and in light of the fact that he had directed that the MAR utilize the higher cost estimate developed by the CAIG. In my view, given the position taken by the Navy and the contractors and the late breaking nature of the Deputy Director for Cost Management's estimate, the characterization of program risk as moderate to high and the adoption of the CAIG estimates with respect to FSD cost were reasonable, and the USD(A) took reasonable action to indicate the risk of further cost and schedule growth. Regrettably, the last-minute nature of the Deputy Director for Cost Management's estimate and the more optimistic positions taken by the Navy and the contractors regarding completion of the FSD contract impeded a focused, coordinated assessment of the potential impact of the likely overrun upon the contractor team's willingness and ability to maintain the then-projected schedule, or anything close to it, in light of their deteriorating financial situation.

4. Findings

   a. General Findings

With respect to the central focus of this inquiry, I find:

(1) Did the Navy, OSD or the contractor know of or have reason to anticipate substantial additional cost increase and schedule slip at the time of the MAR?

(A) The contractor program management team should have anticipated substantial additional cost increase beyond the ceiling of the FSD contract at the time of the MAR. Their projections of completion at or within ceiling were unrealistic and not supported by the facts available to them. The contractor team should also have anticipated greater schedule risk than was briefed during the MAR.

(B) The PM erred in judgment by failing to anticipate substantial additional cost increase beyond the ceiling of the FSD contract at the time of the MAR. His projections of completion at or within ceiling were unreasonably optimistic and not supported by the facts available to him. The PM also erred by failing to anticipate greater risk to schedule than was briefed at the MAR; however, the dramatic schedule slippage announced by the contractors on 1 June 1990 may have been, in part, a consequence of business decisions following the MAR. The PM did not have reason to anticipate this source of additional schedule risk at the time of the MAR.

(C) Based upon information made available to them through Navy channels prior to and during the course of the MAR, neither the NAE nor the Secretary of the Navy knew or had reason to anticipate substantial additional cost increases or schedule slips.

(D) At the outset of the MAR, members of the OSD Comptroller staff believed, based upon views expressed in the draft PBD developed in August 1989, that the FSD contract would be completed $500M or more above ceiling, and that production would be delayed one to two years. Moreover, officials in the Defense Product Engineering Services Office believed there was a substantial risk of further schedule slippage to first flight. However, the MAR Working Group did not focus on the cost and schedule status of the FSD contract, and thus did not integrate the data supporting these views, as well the implications of the negative cost and schedule performance reflected in the DAES, into a critical perspective on FSD contract performance.

(2) If the Navy, OSD or the contractor should have anticipated substantial additional cost increase and schedule slip at the time of the MAR but did not, why not?

(A) The PM erred in judgment by underestimating the implications of adverse cost performance and manufacturing data in his program estimates in the DAES and program status briefings.

(B) COMNAVAIR, as the accountable PEO until 16 April 1990 and Head of the cognizant Contracting Activity, failed to provide adequate oversight to ensure the disciplined administration of the FSD contract, and that program estimates fairly reflective of cost and schedule risk were provided to the NAE and higher authority.

(C) Higher level officials within the Department of the Navy and OSD relied, in large measure, upon the representations of the PM and the contractor team regarding cost, schedule and technical risk. A Navy oversight mechanism, the ASN cost performance report, was not prepared and forwarded in the A-12 program due to security concerns. Had it been prepared and forwarded, it might have focused attention upon the FSD contract status.

(D) A critical OSD oversight mechanism, OSD staff review of contractor CPR data, would have focused attention upon the FSD contract status, but was not employed until March 1990 in the A-12 program due to security concerns.

(3) If so, were senior DOD and DON leaders sufficiently apprised in the course of the Review? If not, why not?

(A) In late March and early April, after the completion of the MAR but prior to the SECDEF's testimony announcing his decisions, a USD(A) staff estimate that the FSD contract would be completed $1B over ceiling was briefed specifically to the PM, the USD(A) and the Deputy USD(A). This estimate was mentioned by the Director, Acquisition Policy and Program Integration, Office of the USD(A), in the presence of SECDEF, DEPSECDEF, USD(A), other principal OSD officials and staff participating in the MAR review, and SECNAV. It was called to the attention of the NAE in late April, shortly before the Secretary of Defense's MAR testimony, but the NAE was newly appointed, had not participated in the MAR and did not recognize its significance in that context. It was not briefed specifically to SECNAV until June 1990.

(B) Moreover, current program status was, at best, a secondary focus of the Working Group efforts supporting the MAR. Their efforts primarily focused upon threats, requirements, alternatives, and total program affordability. Information regarding current program status was primarily derived from the PM during his briefs to the MAR and CAIG, and from him and the contractors during the MAR Steering Group's 9 March 1990 visit to GDFW. Although principal officials, chiefly the USD(A), questioned the contractors regarding elements of risk, no comprehensive, coordinated OSD assessment of current program status and FSD cost or schedule risk was made. This heightened the reliance placed upon the PM's position and the contractors' representations.

b. Additional Findings

Although not central to the focus of my inquiry, I make the following findings regarding significant matters which arose during its course and are reflected in the evidence of record:

(1) The PEO for Tactical Programs failed to fulfill his responsibility fully to inform the NAE of relevant matters pertaining to cost, schedule and technical performance of the FSD contract in connection with the decision to exercise the Lot I production option, and prior to the contractor team's presentation to the NAE on 1 June 1990.

(2) As senior officer present in the discussions on 7, 10 and on or about 16 May 1990, and Head of the cognizant Contracting Activity, COMNAVAIR failed to fulfill his responsibility to counsel the PEO to inform the NAE of relevant matters pertaining to cost and schedule performance of the FSD contract in connection with the Lot I production option.

(3) An NAE staff member erred in judgment by failing to apprise the NAE of relevant matters pertaining to cost, schedule and technical performance of the FSD contract prior to the decision to exercise the Lot I production option, or prior to the contractor team's presentation to the NAE on 1 June 1990.

5. Recommendations.

a. I recommend that you endorse the following recommendations to the USD(A) for consideration and action:

(1) Review this report personally with the Secretaries of the Military Departments and the Service Acquisition Executives to express your concerns, share reactions and develop consensus views on the best means to ensure that your needs as senior leaders are met by the system. This review should focus on, among other things, how to develop positive incentives for PMs and PEOs to display realistically the full range of cost, schedule and technical risk in development programs.

(2) Direct the team presently revising DoD Directive 5000.1 to draft for inclusion therein

(A) a clear and direct policy statement of the PM's responsibility to provide realistic assessments of the range of program status and risk in all briefings and presentations to higher authorities, to actively manage contract performance rather than merely monitor it, and to make accurate, independent assessments of contractor performance.

(B) a requirement that the comments to Section 7 of the currently proposed DAES revision display a range of EACs, the best professional judgment of the servicing cost analysis organization as to the EAC, and an explanation for a best estimate lower than the cumulative CPI.

(C) a requirement that the PM justify his EAC in the Section 7 comments if lower than the cumulative CPI.

(D) a requirement that the PM display in his narrative comments in Section 7 his top 5 challenges in rank order, indicating his best case, worst case and best estimate regarding their impact on cost, schedule and performance, together with a description of actions he is taking to achieve his best estimate.

(E) a requirement that the PEO and SAE personally review the DAES submission and provide their personal assessment of any changes reported in the relative level of risk associated with the program, the significance of the problems reported by the PM, the PM's proposed action plans, the level of risk associated with them, and other significant changes to the program or issues from their respective vantage points. They should be understood to be accountable for the factual predicate for their comments.

(3) Develop, with the SAEs, a pool of the best functional experts from throughout OSD and the Military Departments, to be formed into special review teams representing OSD and the Department concerned to conduct special reviews as the USD(A), in coordination with the SAE concerned, may deem appropriate to address issues arising in the DAES review process.

(4) Direct DCMC to take appropriate administrative and/or disciplinary action with respect to deficient performance by the ACOs at DPRO-St.Louis and DPRO-Fort Worth, and review, in coordination with the supported Military Department and DCAA, the process for administration of progress payments to ensure adherence to policy and appropriate visibility to program management.

(5) Review the operation of OSD-level oversight mechanisms for all ACAT I special access programs, and resolve any shortfalls in oversight due to security requirements.

(6) Direct your staff to develop, with DCMC and the Military Departments, a requirement for detailed planning of contract performance oversight including CPR or related analysis and manufacturing oversight, as a condition of Milestone II approval. The plan should include completed agreements between the Program Office and the supporting DPRO clearly specifying responsibilities and agreed resources.

(7) Refer pertinent information developed during the inquiry to the Comptroller of the Department of Defense, with the request that he take appropriate administrative and/or disciplinary action with respect to deficient performance by the DCAA Resident Auditors in St. Louis and Fort Worth, and any other actions necessary to enforce accountability and ensure effective contract audit support by the DCAA.

(8) Direct that DCMC review with DCAA and the Military Departments policies and procedures to ensure that there is effective audit followup and unresolved issues are brought to the attention of the Program Manager.

(9) Direct that DSMC, with DCMC and OASD(P&L), develop a case study of lessons learned from this report.

(10) Develop a focal point within the USD(A) staff to assess the financial health of major defense contractors on an ongoing basis and provide assessments to USD(A) and the Military Departments in connection with program and acquisition decision-making.

(11) Assess accountability, if any, among personnel under the supervision of the USD(A) for matters evidenced by this report.

b. I recommend that you take appropriate administrative and/or disciplinary action with respect to the General Findings of this inquiry pertaining to the PM, the General and Additional Findings pertaining to COMNAVAIR, and the Additional Finding pertaining to the PEO.

Subject to the recommendation of the ASN(RD&A), I further recommend that you:

(1) Reconstitute the A-12 Program Manager as a Direct Reporting Program Manager.

(2) Direct that ASN(RD&A), in coordination with the Chief of Naval Operations (OP-08), review the operation of program management controls in all special access acquisition programs, and make any needed improvements.

c. Subject to any guidance you may provide, I recommend that the ASN(RD&A) take the following action:

(1) Prepare a policy memorandum for all Program Executive Officers and Major Program Managers emphasizing the following matters:

(A) The responsibility and accountability of each PM and PEO for realistic risk assessment and reporting of significant adverse developments to higher authority.

(B) That a fixed price contract funded to ceiling is no guarantee of performance, and does not diminish the PM's responsibility to manage the contract.

(C) That reliance on contractor representations is no excuse for failure to develop accurate, independent assessments of contractor performance.

(2) Establish a strong focal point within OASN(RD&A) for oversight of cost performance measurement in the SYSCOMs, with emphasis on ensuring that SYSCOM analysts are independent, calculate a range of estimates, and provide their best professional estimate to supported PMs; fostering utilization of CPR detail level analysis by functional specialists; and involving PMs in establishing and defining their data needs in requests for proposal.

(3) Implement the substance of recommendations a(2)(B) through (E) above immediately within the Department of the Navy within the current DAES Formats 6, 11 and 12, pending issuance of the new DoDD 5000.1.

(4) Identify functional experts from throughout the DON for an ASN(RD&A) special review team, to be detailed for special reviews of problems identified through the DAES report and other special reviews, and to participate in such efforts with OSD if recommendation a(3) above is adopted.

(5) Review the process for review and approval of progress payments within the DON to ensure consistency with DoD policy and DCAA audit policy.

(6) Review the implementation of the Defense Management Report within NAVAIR, to ensure that supported PEOs and their major PMs have decision authority commensurate with their full responsibility and accountability for cost, schedule and performance of their assigned programs.

(7) Take appropriate administrative and/or disciplinary action with respect to the Additional Finding pertaining to the NAE staff member.

6. Conclusion.

The sum and substance of the conclusions and general findings of this inquiry is that existing control mechanisms, properly operated, would have been sufficient to identify the nature and extent of the problems in this contract, but that they were not properly operated. That is true enough, and forms the basis for several of the foregoing recommendations which are intended to make those mechanisms work better.

However, I believe it is not a sufficient response to the problems revealed by this inquiry simply to enforce accountability and strengthen a few existing procedures. The A-12 Program has been treated as the Navy's number one aviation priority in fact as well as rhetoric. The PM is an Aviation Engineering Duty Officer, with three advanced degrees and a career path which would be a model in any of the new Service Acquisition Corps. He has been on-station for more than four years, and was assigned with the understanding that he would remain through first flight. He was afforded the luxury of personally selecting key members of his immediate staff. His program has enjoyed strong Congressional support and full-funding from its inception, at least within the ceiling of the fixed-price contract. No Congressional or OSD direction, let alone micromanagement, has been identified as perturbing the FSD program or impeding his ability to make decisions. Neither did he identify any direction or demands from the OPNAV staff which impeded his ability to manage his program. In short, the PM in this case is the archetype of the well-trained, highly motivated professional, fully empowered to fulfill his responsibility and be accountable for cost, schedule and performance of his program, that we are seeking to develop under the acquisition corps plans and matrix management approach reflected in the Defense Management Report. Nonetheless, it should be plain that neither he, nor the similarly well-qualified and dedicated officers in his chain of supervision, met the needs of senior civilian leaders within the DON and DOD for an accurate assessment of the program's status and risk.

This inquiry raised the question of whether the program management structure reasonably anticipated and met the needs perceived by senior civilian decision makers for information. Unquestionably, it failed that test. However, I am concerned, based upon my observations during the course of this inquiry, that our Program Managers and Program Executive Officers/SYSCOM Commanders and their key advisers are not sufficiently focused upon that objective. They are primarily focused upon their programs, and too often treat their superiors in the acquisition chain -- and perhaps the military service chain as well -- as gatekeepers from whom they obtain necessary decisions and approvals, and whom they enlist to do battle "at the political level" with bigger gatekeepers. They do not perceive in the fullest sense that the NAE or the Secretary of the Navy, let alone the USD(A) or the Secretary or Deputy Secretary of Defense, has any direct responsibility or accountability for what they do.

From the human standpoint, this is not difficult to understand. NAEs, Secretaries of the Navy and higher officials come and go relatively frequently, and are selected by a process significantly different from the disciplined system of rating and selection that produces senior military leaders. The contrast between the selection process, tenure and, all too frequently, the experience and qualifications of civilian leaders and that of their military (and career civilian) subordinates, at least as perceived by the subordinates, is to some extent incompatible with a healthy focus upon the institutional needs and desires of the appointed civilian superior.

At the same time, the senior civilian leaders hold the key to the resources necessary to execute the programs. For this reason, as well as for many others, program-focused managers do not have positive incentives to display the full range of risk in their programs to officials who might respond by cutting their resources. In this case, the PM noted repeatedly and forcefully that he had always kept his superiors informed of the major technical challenges in the program and that he insisted at all times upon candor in any discussion of program issues. The record supports him in that regard. He emphasized that the contractors had been commended for the candor of their presentation during the MAR visit to Fort Worth, and that is correct. He emphasized that he discussed his rating of cost and schedule as "Green" in the narrative portion of the DAES, even though some advised him not to, because he had wanted to highlight those issues for the chain of command. It is true that he discussed those issues although there was no requirement that he do so.

Nonetheless, when one compares the information he received regarding the program with the information he transmitted up the chain of command, it is plain that the possibilities were always cast in a positive, optimistic, light. The PM focused on the fact that the Critical Design Review had been started a month early, not on the fact that it had to be split in three parts to meet the contractors' cash flow needs, and that the last phase had to be delayed six months behind the original schedule because of technical issues. The PM focused on the contractors' future plans for recovery, not the implications of their lengthening record of actual performance. In discussing his estimates in the DAES reports, he indicated why things would get better or, when things clearly were not getting better, he emphasized the protection afforded by the fixed-price contract. Even as his projections increased toward ceiling in February 1990, he chose to base them upon continued performance at the cumulative CPI, without reference to the substantially less favorable record of the preceding six months. His comments in the DAES regarding cost and schedule tended to preempt concern and provide reassurance, and never focused on the indications he had of even greater risk. Whatever his intentions, such actions simply are not the same thing as highlighting risk in a system which depends upon information being pushed up from the bottom. Nor is it sufficient to the needs of superiors that the Program Office always responded candidly to every inquiry received.

The PEO's response -- and COMNAVAIR's acquiescence in it -- to the PM's desire to brief the NAE regarding the contractors' 4 May 1990 presentation is similarly instructive. It was not focused on anticipating and meeting the NAE's needs; rather, it was focused on obtaining the desired decision. COMNAVAIR's failure to bring the adverse information from the 16 April Class Desk update forward -- as he had indicated he would do -- is an additional indicator. On both occasions these leaders considered whether to bring news of adverse developments forward, but decided not to do so.

There is no reason to believe that the factors which made these officials choose to respond the way they did are unique to this Military Department. Indeed, experience suggests that they are not. Unless means can be found to solve this abiding cultural problem, the failures evidenced in this report can be anticipated to occur again in the same or a similar form. The MAR Working Group Chairman expressed one perspective in saying, "I take some responsibility. We should've looked harder. I trust people too damn much." However, although oversight and review mechanisms should have worked better in this case -- and should be made to work better in the future -- I believe that the fundamental problem, and the critical path to effective implementation of the Defense Management Report, is to create appropriate incentives to enable senior leaders to rely upon responsible, accountable line managers for realistic perspectives on the cost, schedule and technical status of their programs. Only by doing so can we increase efficiency and accountability while reducing the burdens imposed by undue regulation and stifling supervision.

Chester Paul Beach, Jr.
Inquiry Officer

FOOTNOTES

1 The contractor team has not filed a certified claim. However, on 12 November 1990 the contractor team did submit a memorandum in support of its position that the FSD contract should be restructured, asserting entitlement to additional payments. The memorandum is presently under evaluation.

2 Two members of the inquiry support team had some involvement in the matters under review. Each fully and candidly disclosed his involvement to me before joining the team, and each provided expert technical assistance with respect to, respectively, cost and schedule performance analysis and production oversight issues. Notwithstanding their superb assistance -- and that of the other team members -- I bear sole responsibility for the analysis, findings and recommendations contained in this report.

3 The A-12 Acquisition Plan provided that "(a) PERT, or similar internal contractor system capable of monitoring program status to at least the third level of the work breakdown structure, will be utilized throughout the (A-12) program to focus management attention on potential problem areas." The McAir system (Automated Integrated Scheduling System (AS)) and the GDFW system (referred to as "P-2") are not compatible, which impedes the free flow of information between the contractors. Data generated by P-2 is periodically downloaded into AS, but AS data cannot be downloaded into P-2. The NAVPRO had direct access to AS from two terminals in its own spaces until 25 September 1989, when access was withdrawn by McAir, osetensibly because the system was not functioning properly. Direct access was restored on 13 February 1990. During this "blackout" period, McAir did provide all information from the system requested by the NAVPRO. P-2 was not as useful as AS, and AFPRO personnel never had direct access to it. As at McAir, however, GDFW did provide all information from P-2 requested by the AFPRO. On balance, the lack of utility of these systems inconvenienced the NAVPRO and AFPRO, but did not preclude fulfillment of their responsibilities. It is nonetheless troubling that these systems, cited in the Acquisition Plan as a factor supporting the acceptability of the risk inhering in the highly demanding manufacturing and assembly schedule, did not fulfill that promise.

4 Progress payment audits are one of a number of audit services and activities accomplished by these audit offices, which are under the direction of a Resident Auditor. Audits of progress payments are generally made on the request of the contracting officer; however, DCAA auditors can initiate an audit whenever they have a valid reason to consider an audit necessary to protect the interests of the Government.

5 Following our trip to the contractor facilities 23-27 July 1990, both the Defense Contract Management Command and the Defense Contract Audit Agency initiated action to determine more precisely the contractor team's physical progress, the amount of excess progress payments, the amount of additional progress payment liquidation required, if any, and whether the contractor progress payment requests were accurate at the time of submission. DCAA audit reports were issued on 7 and 14 September 1990, respectively, regarding the McAir and GDFW portions of progress payment request number 31, covering the period through 12 July 1990. Progress payments have since been reduced to recapture the overprogressing identified in these reports, and a loss ratio has been applied to reflect the present overceiling estimates at completion. These remedial actions are sufficient, in my view, to protect the Government's financial interests with respect to the deficiencies in the administration of progress payments indentified by the inquiry.

6 The Acquisition Plan provided that the CDR would be completed in a single phase by May 1989. However, by January 1989 it was apparent that date could not be met. Program officials decided to split the CDR into three phases, with the first to be conducted in May 1989, and the last to be completed by December 1989. The line-item payment associated with completion of the CDR was divided into payments for completion of each phase. CDR was not actually completed until June 1990.

OFFICE OF THE UNDER SECRETARY OF DEFENSE
WASHINGTON, DC 20301

ACQUISITION
DP/CPF

AUG 1 2 1991

Honorable John Conyers, Jr.
Chairman, Subcommittee on Legislation and
  National Security
Committee on Government Operations
House of Representatives
Washington, DC 20515

Dear Mr. Chairman:

    I am submitting this letter to correct three errors I found while reviewing my testimony of July 24, 1991, before the Legislation and National Security Subcommittee of the Committee on Government Operations.

    In response to your inquiry concerning whether we knew that the Internal Revenue Service (IRS) had a lien on the stock of McDonnell Douglas Helicopter Company, I replied that we were not aware of the existence of the lien (hearing transcript pages 101 through 103, lines 2365 through 2402). I had forgotten that McDonnell informed us on January 26, 1991, that McDonnell Douglas Helicopter Company stock was given to the IRS as collateral. A copy of the company disclosure on this subject was provided to the Subcommittee on April 25, 1991, by the General Counsel of the Department of Defense. The point I was making remains the same. There was adequate evidence to conclude that McDonnell Douglas could not pay the debt without this information.

    In response to your question regarding who caused a change from the cash requirement information submitted by McDonnell Douglas on a chart dated January 11, 1991, and my charts of January 31, 1991, I replied that I had the information, which was provided to me by McDonnell, verified by DCAA (hearing transcript page 106, line 2501). In fact I verified the information with the Administrative Contracting Officer (ACO) rather than DCAA. I later referred again to verification by DCAA; I should have referred to the ACO (hearing transcript page 107, line 2512).

    In response to Congressman Horton's question regarding the status of the lawsuit by General Dynamics and McDonnell Douglas, I said the suit had been filed in April in the Claims Court. In fact it was filed on June 7, 1991.

I request this letter be inserted in the record of the hearing.

Sincerely,

Eleanor R. Spector
Director, Defense Procurement

cc:
Honorable Frank Horton
Ranking Republican

**OFFICE OF THE ASSISTANT SECRETARY OF DEFENSE
FOR PRODUCTION AND LOGISTICS**

Date: 1/31/91

Memo For: Herb Lanese

Attached are the assumptions. We would like you to use in a revised cash flow analysis. Please have it for us when you come in Thursday. Call if you have any questions.
Thanks so much —
Eleanor

C-17

ASSUMPTIONS FOR PRO-FORMA FINANCIAL FORECAST:

1. Use $7.115 billion for the EAC for FSED, Lot I, and Lot II.

2. Assume two aircraft will be delivered during CFY91:
   - T1 in June
   - P2 in December

3. Assume no equitable adjustments for claims will occur in CFY91. Do not assume any adjustment in the outyears for uncertified claims. Do not include in the outyears an adjustment above your legal counsel's best estimate of recovery on previously certified claims.

4. Assume Lot III negotiations will be completed by the end of February 1991.

   - Upon completion of Lot III negotiations, assume an additional $338 million will be added to the existing Lot III Long Lead document to cover termination liability incurred until the signed contract is executed.

   - Upon completion of Lot III negotiations, assume an additional $52 million will be added to the existing Lot IV Long Lead document.

5. In May 1991, when the Lot III contract is executed, assume the remaining amount between the negotiated target price and what has been previously obligated as long lead will be added.

6. Assume that on June 1, 1991, an additional $200 million will be obligated against the FY91 funding profile for R&D. As a result of this obligation of an additional $200 million in FY91, the FY92 funding requirement will be reduced by an equal amount.

7. In June 1991, assume an additional $180 million will be obligated to the Lot IV Long Lead document.

T-45
Assume 0 claim recovery on T-45

www.ingramcontent.com/pod-product-compliance
Lightning Source LLC
Chambersburg PA
CBHW032019230426
43671CB00005B/140